Synchronic English Linguistics

Textbooks in English Language and Linguistics (TELL)

Edited by Magnus Huber and Joybrato Mukherjee

Volume 4

PETER LANG

Frankfurt am Main · Berlin · Bern · Bruxelles · New York · Oxford · Wien

Alexander Bergs

Synchronic English Linguistics

PETER LANG
Internationaler Verlag der Wissenschaften

Bibliographic Information published by the Deutsche Nationalbibliothek
The Deutsche Nationalbibliothek lists this publication in the Deutsche Nationalbibliografie; detailed bibliographic data is available in the internet at http://dnb.d-nb.de.

Cover Design:
© Olaf Gloeckler, Atelier Platen, Friedberg

ISSN 1862-510X
ISBN 978-3-631-56175-1

© Peter Lang GmbH
Internationaler Verlag der Wissenschaften
Frankfurt am Main 2012
All rights reserved.

www.peterlang.de

Preface

Nine out of ten colleagues I talk to are unhappy about the textbook(s) that they use for their introduction to English Language and Linguistics classes: too brief, too comprehensive, too much general linguistics, too much theory, wrong syntactic theory, too little language use, too outdated, too selective, too chatty, too matter-of-fact, too expensive, too this, too that. I certainly belong to those 90% of people who are moaning and groaning about the situation. And out of those 90% about half of the people swear that one day they'll just write their own textbook and that would be the end of it. Most of them never find the time or never have the chance to actually do it. So when the editors of this series asked me if I wanted to contribute an "Introduction to Synchronic English Linguistics" I was completely thrilled. The suffering was about to come to an end. Now would I have the chance and the official time to do it (as a regular project now)! It turned out to be the most difficult and trying time of my academic life. What you see in front of you is the product.

While I was writing this book a few things became very clear to me: writing textbooks is one of the hardest exercises I have gone through. This particular text type is highly demanding, and whatever I was mindlessly complaining about before, I can now only salute all the colleagues who have gone through this before – and who, I am sure, did a much better job in many respects. The second thing that I realized was that a textbook is never finished (and the editors of this series and the publisher can testify to that, after years of continuous - and mostly also gentle – badgering to finish this book). With textbooks, there is always something else to say or something more. So I am sure readers will find this book highly selective in some areas, too brief in some sections, too comprehensive in others, with too much theory here, too little theory there, too chatty, too matter-of-fact, and certainly with the wrong syntactic framework. Looking back, I will gladly accept moaning, groaning, and complaining, and maybe even join in…

Writing a book is like having a baby. It takes forever (at least that's what it feels like), and there is lots of pain involved. But, fortunately, we don't have to go through this alone and there is a wonderful crew of people who help us through. First and foremost, of course, my family, Tanja, Josephine and Julius, who bravely endured all the moods of a grumpy author and were always full of encouragement. I can only promise them that this will be the last textbook for quite a while. Second, heartfelt thanks to colleagues who read drafts and offered comments and criticism. Lena Heine read most of the book, Thomas Hoffmann critically checked the chapter on Construction Grammar and offered invaluable advice (the poor soul has only just begun to write his own textbook on

Construction Grammar...). Without them, this book would be much worse. Third, there is the great team of student assistants at the Institute of English and American Studies in Osnabrück, who helped not only with the typical but important gopher jobs, but who also provided some truly helpful comments and questions from their perspective. In particular, however, I would like to thank the real midwife of this project, Meike Pentrel at the Institute in Osnabrück, without whom this book would not exist. She read every word on every page, and had the most critical, inspiring and important comments, questions, and remarks any author could wish for. By now I think she knows this book better than me (and here's my promise to her that this will be the last one for quite a while... till she writes her own, I guess).

Needless to say, however, all remaining blunders are mine alone; and I am also the one to blame that this, eventually, has not turned into the textbook to end all textbooks.

Osnabrück, Fall 2011

Table of Contents

1. Introduction

1.1 What is language?

What we usually call "language" is a remarkable phenomenon. We spend a good deal of our day talking to each other, or at least we think so. Some popular studies such as Brizendine (2006) suggest that the average woman uses ca. 20,000 words every day, men only ca. 7,000. If we assume that we pronounce about 200 words per minute, this would mean that women talk for about 100 minutes every day, men for only 35. So, apart from this – perhaps for some rather unsurprising – gender difference, it seems as if our actual talk time is much lower than one would expect. Still worse, more reliable studies based on sound empirical data (e.g. Rayson et al. 1997; Mehl 2007) show that the actual time we spend talking is even lower (Rayson et al. arrive at about 9 minutes per day on average; Mehl finds about 16,000 words, i.e. 80 minutes per day). On the other hand, they also find that there is no real difference between male and female speakers. So, eventually, the myth that women talk too much is not more than that, a popular myth. The interesting point is that during our, say, 80 minutes of daily talk we hardly ever think about the fact that we are talking ("I now have to use a subject, then look for a corresponding verb, whoops, I need a preposition here...") and there are almost no problems in our communication. For example, there are surprisingly few misunderstandings and actual ambiguities. How does that work? What are the underlying principles that essentially guide us without intentional thinking through our conversations and help us to see when to talk, when to be quiet, when to start and when to stop, among so many other things?

And there is even more 'magic' involved in language. **Language** is genetic in humans in so far as practically all children learn their first, native language before the age of five, and most of them will never acquire a second language with the same ease, speed, and eventual degree of proficiency. However, in contrast to most other species, humans are not genetically pre-programmed to learn any specific language. Children who grow up in an English-speaking environment acquire English as their native language. If the same children had grown up in Timbuktu, in West Africa, they could have acquired Koyra Chiini, a dialect of Songhia. The fact that humans are not pre-programmed for any specific language may be partly due to the amazing fact that all of the **more than 6,000 languages of the world** share a number of features: apparently, all languages have consonants and vowels, all languages have something like nouns and verbs, all languages have means of expressing negatives and interrogatives. Some features are surprisingly common: Dryer (2005), for example, investigates where languages put their subject, verb, and object with regard to each other in indicative sentences. Looking at a sample of more than 1,000 languages, he comes to the following results:

SOV SVO VSO VOS OVS OSV TOTAL
497 435 85   26   9   4   1,056

Apparently, in most languages we either find **subject-object-verb** (Japanese) or **subject-verb-object** (English). All the other orderings are clearly less preferred, with OSV being almost non-existent. Statistically, this distribution is very remarkable, but it gets even weirder: a language which puts its verbs before its objects (like English, German, French etc.) is very likely to have prepositions in front of nouns (like English, German, French etc.), and not after them (so called postpositions). And the same applies vice versa: when a language has verbs following objects, it often also has postpositions, i.e. prepositions following nouns. And a few more elements, such as adjectives and nouns, or nouns and genitive markers, can also be expected to behave that way. These facts are also part of the great miraculous thing we call 'language' (but at least some of the latter facts can be explained by linguists on the basis of general cognitive principles…).

These are only some of the stunning and spellbinding properties that make human language so special. And yet, in our daily lives we hardly ever think about these properties.

1.2 Where is language?

That language is a **cognitive capacity of humans** is beyond doubt. The question that we need to ask is where that cognitive capacity is actually located. Is there any 'language center' in the brain, like there is an area which is responsible for vision? Unfortunately, the answer is anything but simple. As early as the nineteenth century, doctors began to look for the place of language in the brain. Two of the most famous studies were conducted by the French physician Paul Broca (1824-1880) and the German psychiatrist Carl Wernicke (1848-1905). Both Broca and Wernicke discovered certain areas in the brain which appeared to be responsible for motor, i.e. **productive language skills** (Broca) and sensory, i.e. **perceptive language skills** (Wernicke). Figure 1.1 shows where these areas are located in the brain.

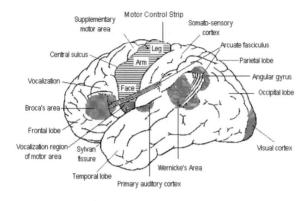

Figure 1.1: Broca's and Wernicke's area, taken from
http://www.ling.upenn.edu/courses/Fall_2001/ling001/brain_func2.gif

Brocas's area is roughly two centimeters in diameter, just above your left hand temple. Wernicke is about the same size, but above and slightly behind your left ear. Damage to these areas, e.g. through disease or accident, leads to very specific language impairments, so-called aphasias. Examples (1) and (2) (both taken from http://pages.slc.edu/~ebj/IM_97/Lecture10/L10.html), illustrate those effects:

(1) B.L.: Wife is dry dishes. Water down! Oh boy! Okay Awright. Okay ...Cookie is down...fall, and girl, okay, girl...boy...um...
Examiner: What is the boy doing?
B.L.: Cookie is...um...catch
Examiner: Who is getting the cookies?
B.L.: Girl, girl
Examiner: Who is about to fall down?
B.L.: Boy...fall down!

(2) H.W.: First of all this is falling down, just about, and is gonna fall down and they're both getting something to eat...but the trouble is this is gonna let go and they're both gonna fall down...but already then...I can't see well enough but I believe that either she or will have some food that's not good for you and she's to get some for her too...and that you get it and you shouldn't get it there because they shouldn't

go up there and get it unless you tell them that they could have it. And so this is falling down and for sure there's one they're going to have for food and, and didn't come out right, the uh, the stuff that's uh, good for, it's not good for you but it, but you love it, um mum mum (smacks lips)...and that so they've...see that, I can't see whether it's in there or not.

Examiner: Yes, that's not real clear. What do you think she's doing?

H.W.:   But, oh, I know. She's waiting for this!

Examiner: No, I meant right here with her hand, right where you can't figure out what she's doing with that hand.

H.W.:   Oh, I think she's saying I want two or three, I want one, I think, I think so, and so, so she's gonna get this one for sure it's gonna fall down there or whatever, she's gonna get that one and, and there, he's gonna get one himself or more, it all depends with this when they fall down...and when it falls down there's no problem, all they got to do is fix it and go right back up and get some more.

Quite obviously, the speaker in (1) is not really capable of expressing his/her thoughts and shows dramatic non-fluency in speech production, whereas the speaker in (2) talks a lot and fluently, but does not really succeed in communicating successfully. (1) is a typical example of Broca as a non-fluent aphasia; Wernicke in (2) is an example of a fluent aphasia. Note that both areas are located in the left hemisphere of the brain, which also led to the lateralization hypothesis. This hypothesis says, in a nutshell, that the two brain hemispheres do different jobs. **The left hemisphere is responsible for 'analytic' computing operations and language, while the right hemisphere takes care of art, emotions, and creativity.** However, a number of recent studies have convincingly shown that this picture is over-simplistic. First, it was shown that patients with a corpus callosotomy, i.e. an operation in which the two brain halves had to be separated at the corpus callosum, the bridge that connects the two halves, showed linguistic abilities in both hemispheres. Second, recent studies on brain plasticity were able to show that functions in the brain can move and develop throughout your lifetime. If some regions are damaged and functions are impaired, these can be recovered by using other areas. Finally, studies using functional Magnetic Resonance Imaging demonstrated that **the processing of language actually requires all parts of the brain to be active, left and right** (see Figure 1.2 and 1.3 below). In other words, there is not one single language center, not even a single hemisphere that is solely responsible for language. Language is processed in multiple centers spread across the two hemispheres.

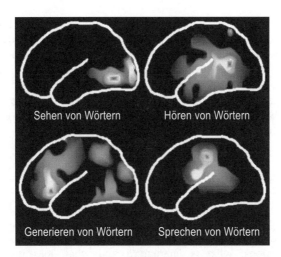

Figure 1.2: Active brain areas during language processing (taken from http://brain.exp.univie.ac.at/16_vorlesung_ss05/bilder.htm; Reproduction with kind permission of Werner Gruber, University of Vienna).

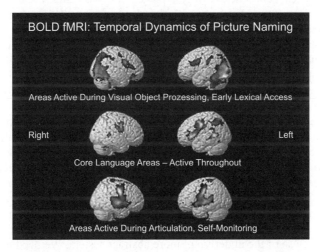

Figure 1.3: Active brain areas during language processing (taken from S. Kemeny, J. Xu, G. Park, L. Hosey & A.R. Braun (2006): Temporal Dissociation of Early Lexical Access and Articulation Using a Delayed Naming Task – An fMRI Study. Cereb Cortex, 16(4): 587-595. Reproduction with kind permission of the NIDCD (National Institute on Deafness and Other Communication Disorders)/NIH).

So, obviously, language is a very mysterious and multi-facetted thing. Neither do we know exactly how much of our life is governed by language, nor do we know exactly where in our head it is. What we do know is that language plays a central role in our existence, and though we could probably survive without it, many aspects of being human depend on or at least go back to having language as a way of communicating our thoughts and feelings. **Linguistics is the scientific discipline that deals with this core aspect of human existence**. How it does that is the topic for the next sections.

1.3 What is linguistics?

Linguistics as a scientific discipline that has its roots both in the **humanities** and in **science** looks at the problems and miracles just mentioned. In brief, it can be defined as the scientific study of language. This definition, of course, raises two important questions: what is language? And what does it mean to study something scientifically? The latter will be discussed later on in this chapter, the former needs to be addressed, at least briefly, right here and now.

The term "language" can and has been understood in many different and sometimes even contradictory ways. In general, we can say that language at least comprises some **abstract semiotic (sign) system**. This could perhaps be compared to traffic rules like the ones you can find in the traffic code. The study of this more or less abstract system is called the study of **language structure**. But then there is another thing we could study when we look at traffic, and that is how people actually use the rules in their traffic code, i.e. how they actually drive. Although every driver should have passed the test required for a driver's license, nobody is perfect and therefore nobody can stick to all the rules all the time. Sometimes we drive more slowly or faster than we should, forget to turn on the lights, maybe miss a stop sign, and so on. But not just violations of the traffic code, but the act of driving itself could also be studied: how do people manage to drive at all, sometimes while thinking about completely different things or calling somebody on their cell phones? This compares, very roughly, to what is called **language use**. This approach basically looks at how the abstract semiotic system called language is put into use in daily communication and how 'external' factors such as age, gender, social class or style may influence the use of the underlying, more abstract system. We need to be careful with the traffic analogy, though. Traffic rules and how we use them somehow seem to compare to linguistic systems and how they are used, but there is also a major difference between the two. Traffic rules are essentially **prescriptive rules**, consciously and purposefully designed by human agents. Linguistic rules and systems in the way they are understood by most linguists are not prescriptive at all, nor were they intentionally designed by human agents.

Rather, the rules and regularities that we seek to discover in language are simply there. They have evolved historically and they can sometimes be changed by outside influences – such as contact between speakers of different languages – but they do not have the same status as man-made traffic rules. This also means that – in contrast to traffic rules, which can be studied simply in code books – linguistic rules and systems cannot always be studied from prescriptive grammar books like the ones we use at school. Grammar books are designed to help pupils learn a language and to be aware of what is seen as good and bad by a language community. But they do not always accurately reflect what we actually find in the linguistic system as such. So, for example, many grammar books at school will tell you that the object relative pronoun in English is *whom* as in *The man whom we saw was lying*. As a matter of fact, however, *whom* is being used less and less frequently by speakers and is quickly being replaced in many contexts by *that* or zero: *the man that / Ø we saw*.... So the 'code book' and what people really do can differ from each other and in fact often do so. Many linguists are more interested in what people actually do, since this is what gives us most insights into the human mind and how language really works inside the individual and the linguistic community. **Linguistics is, after all, a descriptive scientific discipline, which means that linguists try to describe what is there, and not how it should be**. We do not try to develop code books, in other words. You may even want to compare this to biology. When a lion eats a poor little baby rabbit, biologists would not comment on the lion doing something good or bad. The lion feeds on meat, and this is what the biologist seeks to describe. When speakers end their sentences with prepositions (which, according to many prescriptivists, should be avoided), this is what they do, and it is not our job as linguists to tell them that this is good or bad. End of story.

Let us come back for a moment to the two perspectives mentioned above: structure and use. These complement each other: while language use cannot be studied successfully without solid background knowledge of language structure, the investigation of language structure without any link to language use often appears to be a somewhat bloodless and sterile exercise, not unlike mathematics. Later on in this chapter we will see that besides looking at language from a structure and a use perspective, there are numerous other possible divisions which also play a role in defining linguistics and its different branches.

1.4 What is language, again?

We have just described language as an abstract semiotic system which is put to use by speakers in daily communication (and also in special contexts, of course, such as liturgy, manuals, the court and operating room, the lecture hall, and the pub). The first thing that needs to be clarified straightaway is that language need not be spoken. Language can appear in numerous different shapes: spoken, written on paper, written in order to be read out aloud, dictated, electronically on the computer and on mobile phones, and last but not least also signed, for instance by people with acoustic impairments. All these forms of language are equally good and equally interesting – even though some traditions in linguistics show preferences for one form or the other. In the following, when we talk of speakers, we usually use this as an overall term to include speakers, writers, e-mailers, twitterers etc., i.e. language users generally.

Virtually all linguistic studies today share a number of basic assumptions concerning the nature of language. Language is usually regarded as a system of symbolic signs. What does this mean? In **semiotics**, the study of signs, we distinguish between three different types of signs: **icon**, **index**, and **symbol**. **Icons** actually resemble picture-like the thing they stand for. One example would be an airplane sign as an icon for an airport, or the wastebasket on your computer's desktop – which looks like the trashcan near your real desk! **Indexes** are usually in a causal relationship to what they stand for, but they do not resemble the entity they stand for. Smoke is caused by fire and in some sense it means that there must be fire. However, smoke does not resemble fire in any way. Similarly, fever and a general feeling of being sick, combined with itchy red bumps about 5-10 millimeters in diameter that show up all over one's body and which quickly fill with transparent fluid, are an index for chicken pox in a patient. Note that none of the symptoms resembles chicken pox, or the varicella zoster virus, but they are caused by it. **Symbols**, finally, are completely arbitrary, i.e. they do not resemble what they stand for and they are not in any relationship to the thing they stand for. Rather, it is simply the sign-users who agree that they want to use a particular sign for a particular meaning. For example, most road signs are symbols. Just consider the sign for "give way": a white triangle with a red rim. There is nothing about triangles, or the colors red and white that is naturally related to "give way" as a meaning. We simply agree that this sign means "give way". This means that people in our community consciously need to learn this meaning. You cannot guess it. And this is another difference between icon, index, and symbol. Since iconic signs resemble what they stand for, and there is some relationship between an indexical sign and what it stands for, we can usually guess what these types of signs mean. Symbols, however, are not easily decipherable as they depend on culture-specific conventions.

As I have already mentioned, language is usually seen as a **symbolic system**. This means that the elements of that system are symbolic, i.e. arbitrary and conventional. That they are arbitrary is fairly obvious: what we call an *apple* in English, we call *Apfel* in German, *pommes* in French, *tofaa* or *tunda la kizungu kama pera* in Swahili and so on. Apparently, there is nothing that automatically links the concept of "apple" with the words that are used for this concept – which is why we have to learn new vocabulary when we learn a language. Note that even **onomatopoetic words** (words which supposedly resemble the thing they stand for, at least soundwise) are not universal currency: roosters cry "Kikeriki" in German, "cockadoodledo" in English, "cocorico" in French, كوكوكوكو "kukukuuku" in Egyptian Arabic etc. Even the representation of laughter is not universal. In a non-representative study, speakers with an Asian background (Korea and Japan) reported that they would associate the US Santa Claus kind of laughter ("hohoho!") with female, shy laughter, whereas the Western-style witchy kind of laughter ("hihihi!") is neutral or even positive for them, like giggling. Also compare Spanish "ujú ja ja ja ja ja jaaaaaa" or „ñaca-ñaca" which reflects roughly the same as the evil "muahaha" in English. In brief, we can conclude that there is little to no evidence in favor of iconicity here. However, this is not the whole story. One the one hand, one might object that iconicity does not necessarily mean that there is only one representation. In fact, there may be several different iconic representations of one and the same thing, just like there may be more than one picture of, say, an apple.

On the other hand, when we go beyond the level of single, simple words we find some interesting phenomena which also speak against the total arbitrariness of linguistic signs. It is, for example, quite interesting to see that plural formation in virtually all languages around the world means that words get longer: *apple-apples, door-doors, house-houses* etc. Of course, there are exceptions, and some words only change their vowel (*mouse-mice*) or even stay the same (*sheep-sheep*). But these are clearly exceptions. The basic pattern in all languages of the world is clear: plural forms are longer than singular forms. This, one might say, reflects reality in an iconic way. A "more" in reality calls for a "more" in morphology. Interestingly, the same can also be found with abstract complexity. With more complex tense, aspect, mood configurations, like the pluperfect passive subjunctive, for example, we usually also find more morphological or syntactic material as with the simple present active indicative tense: compare *he gives her a pen* (five words, one inflectional marker, -s) and *she would have been given a pen by him* (nine words, three of which are auxiliaries). Some researchers have claimed that we can extend the concept of iconicity even further and that it can also be seen, for example, in sentences such as *John looked up the word in the dictionary in his room* where the verb *look up* is in a closer relationship with its object *the word* and also with the location of the search (adverbial 1), *in the dictionary,* than with the general spatial orientation (adverbial 2), *in this room.* This, arguably, is reflected in the word order and relative proximity of verb, object, adverbial 1 and adverbial 2. The closer the conceptual relationship, the closer the linguistic elements. Also, on the textual-syntactic level we seem to follow the order of the outside world when we tell stories about it, thus mirroring external events with our language: Julius Caesar's famous dictum *veni, vidi, vici* ('I came, I saw, I conquered') strictly speaking says the same as any other order of the three elements, and yet the ordering that Caesar uses tells us that first he came, then he saw, then he conquered – though this is never made explicit here. So there is indeed some support for the idea that there are some iconic elements in language. Note, however, that there is still an ongoing dispute among linguists and philosophers about the nature of language and the role of symbolic and iconic relations (cf., for example, Haspelmath http://www.eva.mpg.de/lingua/staff/haspelmath/pdf/IconicityMarkedness.pdf).

Givón (1985: 34-37) therefore suggests that there might actually be a balance between **symbolic (arbitrary)** and **iconic (motivated) principles** in grammar: some parts of language are symbolic, especially when they are further grammaticalized, i.e. embedded in a language's grammar, whereas some others are (still) more iconic and thus reflect experience. For Givón, this is not an either-or but rather a more-or-less type of question.

1.5 The organization of language

Language is a complex semiotic system. Just like any other kind of system (no matter whether it is public transport, a computer network, your library, or maybe even your cafeteria), it contains various elements as its inventory and rules that link these elements in some way. None of the elements can be independent, or stand alone, i.e. they all must somehow work together. You can see this very easily already when you look at words and what they mean. Can you define the meaning of "cat" without using any other words? Can you talk about the meaning of "off" without mentioning "on"? "Off" means "not on". Is "bachelor" comprehensible without the concept of marriage? Probably not. Ferdinand de Saussure, one of the founding fathers of modern linguistics, therefore characterized language as "une système où tout se tient" – "a system in which everything holds together" (de Saussure [1916] 1995: 104-108).

But what does the inventory of language look like? Language is organized on a number of different levels, as we will see below, but most of the elements on these levels can be characterized as symbolic signs. This means that they have a meaning or function side (de Saussure called this "the signified" or "the image") and a form side (or "the signifier" or "the image acoustique" in Saussurean terms). Figure 1.4 below shows the textbook example "apple". As we have discussed before, there is some reason to believe that the relationship between signifier and signified is to a great deal arbitrary (*an apple, ein Apfel, une pomme, elma*). The **signifier** form/side is the sound sequence [æpl] or the string of letters <apple>, the **signified** meaning/side is the **concept** or mental image of an apple. What exactly is inside that meaning component is still, after more than 2,000 years a matter of debate. Plato talked about "ideas" that we have, de Saussure about "the signified" or mental image, the 1960s psychologist Eleanor Rosch about the prototype or best of exemplar. This is probably not the right place to discuss this issue further. Suffice it to say that it is anything but clear what we actually associate with a given form.

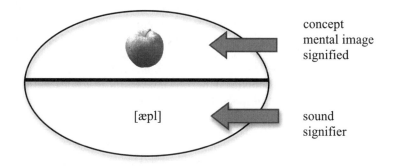

Figure1.4: 'Apple' as a Saussurean sign.

That we do not associate anything at all is rather unlikely, as the infamous exclamation "Don't think of an elephant!" so beautifully shows. When you hear a word, you know you have to process it. Can you ignore a conversation that you are accidentally overhearing in your mother tongue? Probably not. So, it makes perfect sense that we assume some kind of internal mental representation that is connected to the phonetic form. In the case of Figure 1.4 above, this may be any type of *malus,* i.e. a Red Delicious, a green Granny Smith, or a Pink Lady, or whatever your culture and language community sees as the epitome of an apple. Only think what somebody would bring if you just told them "Can you bring me an apple?" But what exactly that **mental representation** looks like is a matter for further research.

As a semiotic system, language is organized on a number of different levels. Speakers are usually familiar with this as they know that sentences are comprised of words (so two different levels: sentences and words), words are comprised of word-parts, and the word parts consist of sounds or letters. This is also recognized by linguistics, of course, which is usually subdivided into several sub-disciplines:

- **Phonetics / Phonology** (which deal with sounds and sound systems)
- **Morphology** (which looks at words and their structure)
- **Syntax** (which studies sentences)
- **Semantics** (the abstract meaning of words and sentences)
- **Pragmatics** (speaker intention and meaning in context)

This subdivision is also reflected in the structure of the current book, although, for organizational purposes, semantics and pragmatics are grouped together into one single chapter on meaning in language.

One interesting fact about language and its general structure is that all of these levels are necessary for successful communication and they interact with each other in very complex ways. At the same time, it also shows **duality of patterning**, i.e. the smaller parts of language, such as sounds, do not have any meaning in themselves but gain meaning in combination with each other. And since human languages only have limited inventories of sounds available (as we will see in the chapter on phonetics and phonology), these sounds are usually very flexible and recombinable in order to generate new higher level elements. Only look at the four sounds or letters "s","i","t","p". They obviously do not mean anything in isolation, but they can be combined into at least four meaningful words: "Tips","stip","pits","spit". These of course have meaning in and by themselves. Hockett, in an early article discussing the features of human language, called this principle "duality of patterning" (Hockett 1960).

In a more recent study, Jackendoff offers a very concise and schematic outline of how language and its different levels are actually organized. This is presented, in a simplified form, in Figure 1.5 below. It shows the different levels of representation for the (simple) sentence: *The little star's beside a big star.* You need not worry about the technical details and strange technical vocabulary at this point. Figure 1.5 is only intended to show you what the different levels look like and how each of them naturally leads to a new higher level. However, once you have finished reading this book you should be able to understand and decipher the figure in much greater detail and depth.

Phonological structure

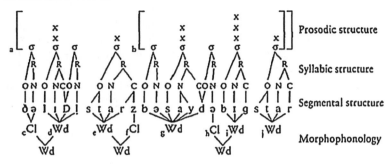

Syntactic structure

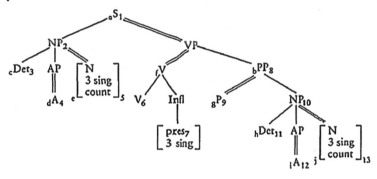

Semantic/conceptual structure

Spatial structure

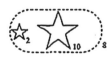

Figure 1.5: The different levels of representation and analysis for "The little star's beside a big star" (taken from Foundations of Language: Brain, Meaning, Grammar Evolution by Ray Jackendoff 2002: 6. By permission of Oxford University Press).

1.6 Methods in linguistics

So far, we have discussed the nature of language and linguistics in quite some detail. The question that remains, though, is how we can study language. What are the methods which are available to us to obtain and analyze linguistic data?

There are a number of ways of getting data for our analyses. First, there is so-called introspection, i.e. looking inside yourself. We are all competent speakers of our native languages and so our perspective on those sentences should count for something. In other words, we do not need complex empirical test to show that sentence (3) below is grammatical or acceptable, whereas (4) is certainly not a good sentence of English.

(3)   Tom plays with Kate, Kate plays with Jane.
(4)   With plays Kate Tom Lotte plays Jane with.

So, speakers have a fairly good feeling about what is permissible or even acceptable in their native languages. Early generative grammar in the 1960s and 1970s in particular often made use of this methodology. Of course, at first sight introspection as a method appears to be very subjective and not really scientifically reliable. However, especially with regard to major patterns and gleaming problems, it also offers very quick and uncomplicated results. Problems mostly arise with marginal deviations and rare phenomena. So, for example, if you test the acceptability of (5a) versus (5b) with a group of 38 native speakers and ask them for a rating of these sentences between 1 (absolutely unacceptable) and 5 (highly acceptable), the following results emerge:

(5a)   *Funny you should mention him. In fact, I was just talking to him.*
(5b)   *Oh, Marc is doing fine. I've actually just talked to him.*

Apparently, not all the people have the same feelings when it comes to assessing grammaticality and acceptability. 84% of the informants thought that (5a) is more or less fine, while only 68% though that (5b) is good. And vice versa. 7% thought that (5a) is bad, while an amazing 32% believed that (5b) is not acceptable (this study is discussed in Bergs, Pfaff & Hoffmann 2012). Note that, grammatically speaking, there is hardly any difference between (5a) and (5b): the former shows a (strictly speaking impermissible) progressive construction, while the latter shows a (strictly speaking required) present perfect construction. Now if there is only one single researcher trusting his or her own intuitions here, there is of course a great danger of missing important points and, naturally, getting things wrong.

This is one of the reasons why we have developed several other methods that help us to arrive at more intersubjectively valid data. One of them we have just seen: the questionnaire (and other empirical data gathering methods, such as the interview, or tests in the lab). The advantage clearly is that the data gathered that way is more reliable. However, these methods also need time and they can only test those issues that we deliberately include in the tests. Occasionally some interesting phenomena can reveal itself in these methods, but usually only the issues implied in the test designs show up. So, if you know what you want to check for, if you have some time, and if you have enough people willing to undergo testing, this is a great approach. Note, however, that test design can be fairly complicated. You cannot simply ask people straightaway what they think. As soon as people know what the test is about they unconsciously begin obsessing about the problem and do not show unbiased reactions anymore. A good test thus works with enough detractors so as to throw people off the track and to get as natural results as possible.

Another massively popular set of procedures comes under the label of **Corpus Linguistics**. A **corpus** (lit. 'body') in linguistics is usually defined as a structured, finite electronic collection of texts and textual material. The first modern corpora were developed about 50 years ago, in the 1960s. The Brown Corpus, for example, is an electronic collection of about 1,000,000 words in 500 word samples of 2,000 words each from 15 different genres, ranging from political press reports to humoristic essays. Brown is thus fairly representative of the written genres of its target variety, American English. The interesting thing is that a complementary project was run in Europe, the Lancaster-Oslo-Bergen Corpus, which is designed exactly along the same lines, but is representative of British English. It thus became possible to contrast these two major varieties on the basis of two parallel one million corpora, which allowed the empirical, quantitative study of the relevant structures. This means that not only presence or absence of certain phenomena in the different varieties could be diagnosed, but also the frequency of use and any differences in collocations. In the 1990s scholars in Freiburg picked up on the idea again and developed two more corpora in the same way: the Freiburg-Brown Corpus (FROWN) and the Freiburg LOB Corpus (FLOB). These also contain 1,000,000 words each and are designed almost exactly like Brown and LOB, and they represent American and British English from the 1980s and 1990s. Analyzing Brown and LOB, FROWN and FLOB thus makes it possible to look at the two major varieties in contrast and across time, i.e. in the 1960s and the 1990s. For example, you might wonder about the use of *need (to)* as a modal or semi-modal verb, as in (6) and (7).

(6)   you needn't come (modal, cf. *you may not come*)
(7)   you don't need to come (semi-modal)

If you search for these structures in LOB and FLOB, Brown and FROWN, you get the results presented in Table 1.1 below. Two things become clear from the results in Table 1.1. On the one hand, *need* is generally more common in British English. On the other hand, the use of *need* as semi-modal also becomes much more popular over time and is used much more often in both 1990s corpora than in the 1960s (irrespective of whether we are looking at British or American English), whereas the use as modal is declining. All these observations about varietal differences and developments over time would not have been possible without modern electronic corpora.

Table 1.1: Modal and semi-modal need in LOB; FLOB; Brown; FROWN.

	LOB	**FLOB**	**Brown**	**FROWN**
Need as modal	76	44	36	31
Need as semi-modal	56	200	71	141
Total	132	244	107	172

Other major corpora apart from the ones just mentioned include the British National Corpus (BNC), the International Corpus of English (ICE, with several varieties as sub-corpora, e.g., ICE-GB, ICE-India...), the Corpus of Contemporary American English (COCA) and Corpus of Historical American English (COHA), the Michigan Corpus of Academic Spoken English (MICASE), the Helsinki Corpus (Historical English from late Middle English to Early Modern English) and the Corpus of Early English Correspondence. There are several more corpora, but listing them all would certainly go beyond the scope of this introduction. An excellent introduction to Corpus Linguistics can be found in Mukherjee (2009), however.

All in all, the main trend in corpus design was and is to develop ever larger corpora. The BNC has 100 million words, 10% of which are from spoken varieties, COCA and COHA have about 400 million words each. The average printed page has about 400 words on it. This means that the COCA for instance would fill about 1,000,000 printed pages, i.e. 3,500 average books of about 300 pages. It is easy to see that without the help of computers such an amount of data would not be accessible or manageable for scholars. A comprehensive overview of available corpora can be found in Mukherjee (2009).

When you are planning to work with corpora yourself, there are a few methodological issues that you need to keep in mind:

1) You need to know and clearly define what you are looking for.
Let's stick with the example of *need* as discussed above. If you just search for the word NEED in the FROWN corpus, you get 463 hits. Why do we not get the same result as above, i.e. 172 hits? Simply because searching for NEED also returns examples such as (8), where *need* is a noun, not a verb.

(8) is deemed to match the information **need**, all other documents fail to match
   (FROWN, FBJ33)

At the same time, we miss all the interesting other verb forms such as *needs* and *needed* because we only searched for the bare form *need*. This goes to show that, before you start, you need to be clear about what it is you are looking for, so that eventually you get the right results. However, some items are not easy to find or define, so that some manual post-editing of the results might be necessary, no matter how time consuming this may be (imagine having to go manually through the 62,307 hits for the article *the* in FROWN!).
    Some corpora are tagged, i.e. they already have grammatical classifications for their words, i.e. parts-of-speech tagging (POS or POST). This of course, makes searches much easier. With an untagged corpus you have to manually filter out nominal *need,* with a tagged corpus you can simply search for *need* tagged as a verb. Note, however, that tagging is never perfect. The best parsers (automatic taggers) today reach up to about 96% accuracy. 4% errors is not much, but in 100 million words this still amounts to 4 million words gone wrong.

2) You need to decide which corpora you would like to use and what the corpus material actually represents.
If you are interested in a phenomenon of spoken English, you need to use the spoken English section of the BNC and exclude the written part. Otherwise, your results would be drastically skewed. Again, using the example of *need*: 54,586 hits in the whole BNC (= 545.86 per one million words), but only 8,943 hits in the spoken part. The written part only (with 90 million words) therefore contains 54,643 hits, i.e. 507,144 per million. The spoken part only has 10 million words in total, so that we arrive at 894.3 per million for this section. Which leads us to the conclusion that *need* is clearly more frequent in spoken than in written English. (Also note, by the way, how this ties in nicely with what we have discovered about *need* in FROWN. Here we found 463 hits per 1 million words, compared to 507 in the written BNC. Again, this confirms the

initial idea that American English on the whole uses *need* a little bit less than British English).

3) You need to be very careful with the figures and results that you get.

Not all corpora have one million words exactly, so it is important to normalize your frequencies to one million words (i.e. to express them as x instances per one million words, for example), so that they become easily and clearly comparable. If you skip this step, you are comparing apples and pears. Also, before you jump to conclusions on the basis of your frequencies alone, always think about the statistical significance of your results. So, at first sight, it might seem that certain frequencies are telling, but in fact, they are not. A very simple test to check for that is the chi-square test (http://in-silico.net/statistics/chi2test/2x2). Look at the following table. It contains information on the sex of students who took a final written test in linguistics, and how many of them passed the test.

Table 1.2: Sex and success rate correlation.

	Passed	Failed	Total
Male	36	14	50
Female	30	25	55
Total	66	39	105

More than 60% of the males passed the test, whereas almost 50% of the females failed. So, were the males more successful? At first sight, we might think so. The chi-square test essentially checks how the observed frequencies relate to expected frequencies, i.e. the frequencies that we get if the results were pure chance. These can be calculated by taking the total of the column, multiplied by the total of the row, and divided by the total of the whole table, e.g. (50)*(66)/(105)=(31). These are shown in Table 1.3:

Table 1.3: Expected frequencies.

	Passed	Failed	Total
Male	31	19	50
Female	35	20	55
Total	66	39	105

Chi-square then calculates how likely the difference between observed and expected frequencies is. Usually, a 5% degree of chance is accepted as random. Anything below that is regarded as unlikely, hence significant. For the case in Table 1.2 we find that the probability of the observed distribution is .09 (9%) with a so-called Yates correction, or .06 (6%) without (with degrees of freedom, df=1). In other words, the results are more likely to be caused by chance than by actual factors. So, being male or female did not significantly matter in passing or failing the test, despite what our initial impressions were. There is a whole lot more about significance and statistics when it comes to corpus linguistics, but this is certainly not the place to go into details (see Gries 2008; Gries 2010; Rietveld & Vanhout 2005). All we need to do here is to make you aware that simply looking at frequencies may give you a first impression and some intuitions, but certainly not scientifically valid results.

4) Make sure you don't forget about qualitative analyses.
Looking into corpora and frequencies, doing statistics and empirical analyses is great and very rewarding – but it is nothing but basic ground work if it isn't coupled with explanatory hypotheses and explanations. So, once you find out that there is a significant increase in the use of semi-modal *need*, and a decrease in the use of the modal *need*, the real question is: why? If you do not face that question and come up with some ideas at least, all you have is a fancy (but eventually very simple) description of facts. Compare this to physics: we know the apple falls down from the tree, we can calculate how fast it will fall. But eventually, we want to know *why* it falls.

1.7 What is science?

This is a question that I announced at the outset of this chapter, and it is a tough one. As I said in the beginning, linguistics is sitting right between the natural sciences on the one hand, and the humanities on the other. This in turn means that both the methods and explanatory principles from the natural sciences and the humanities play a role. Probably the central issue is the question of empiricism and hermeneutics. What is the essential difference between history and chemistry? In history you look back at historical events and try to understand why they have happened. Historians usually would not claim that their work leads to fundamental laws that always apply and help us to predict future events. In chemistry, you run experiments and try to develop laws which are as general as possible, which help us to predict what will happen in a given situation in the future. If that particular prediction is not met, something must be wrong with our theory so that it needs to be amended. The first type of thinking is often referred to as **hermeneutics**, or interpretation theory, which wants to arrive at an interpretation i.e. understanding (not explanation!) why things happened the way they did. But of course there is no natural necessity for that, i.e. things could have happened differently. The key point here is to develop plausible stories that help us to understand the world.

In the natural sciences, we are rather dealing with the so-called Hempel-Oppenheim schema or, deductive-nomological explanation: Therefore there is a natural law (let's call it gravity) that makes things fall down, rather than up, or stay in position. Every time I drop an apple, the apple falls down. Every time the apple falls down, my hypothesis of a law is confirmed. Every time something stays in place or "falls up" I need to reconsider my law. What scholars do here is, they have a law or rule and then test this against reality by making predictions about what should happen if the law were true. Every time the prediction is met, the law is confirmed, every time it is not met, the law needs amending. Another way of developing scientific discoveries is to work inductively. Here you take a number of instances and try to find the pattern, i.e. they induce the law from the observed instances. So, before the law of gravity was discovered and Newton first observed the fall of the apple, he had been working inductively, i.e. he derived at the law or rule after observing a number of instances.

A third way of reasoning, next to deduction and induction, which is very important in linguistics, is **abduction** (or 'guessing', as its inventor Charles Sanders Peirce called it). Abduction means that we posit plausible explanations (laws) which can account for the phenomena we observe (even single instances). In other words, we guess what the probable cause of a given phenomenon could have been. Note that there is of course no strict necessity for any of the causes we assume; the given phenomenon could have been caused by other equally plausible things. In contrast to that, **deduction** forms a strict logical rule that leads us from *a* to *b*: "All languages have nouns and verbs. English is a language. Therefore, English has nouns and verbs". **Induction** works the other way round and usually leads to less strong and strict rules: "All languages we know have nouns and verbs. Therefore languages generally require nouns and verbs". (Needless to say, there are many problems connected with that sort of reasoning). Abduction finally would say something like: "Japanese speakers cannot distinguish between the sound *l* and *r*. This speaker has trouble distinguishing between the English words *lip* and *rip*. Therefore, I assume that this speaker is Japanese". Of course, abduction is not as powerful as deduction, since it only offers possible explanations based on plausibility (the speaker in the example could also have a speech impediment, or be from Korea, which would also explain the problem). But it is certainly stronger and more helpful than induction. We might also add that abduction does not only play a role in linguistic explanations and arguments. Scholars in historical linguistics (most notably Andersen 1973; for some interesting criticism, see Deutscher 2002) have claimed that speakers actually use abduction when they (re-)construct their native language in first language acquisition on the basis of adult language input. The idea, in a nutshell, is that children build their grammatical rules in such a way that they can explain and account for the input they receive. However, this does not mean that their grammar must be the same as that of their parents; it only needs to do (roughly) the same job. If it differs in some details, we observe language change.

1.8 Summary and outlook

This chapter has presented some really big issues: what is language? What is science? How can we study language at all? Most of you will feel pretty overwhelmed now. Don't panic. Think about these things. Most of them are actually quite plausible common-sense ideas. If you, after having thought about them for some time, find these things mysterious, you can either turn to some other introduction to the topic (very recommendable for the beginner is Yule 2010) or simply read on. The next chapters will introduce you to the different linguistics levels that were shown in Jackendoff's diagram. And I am sure many things will begin to make sense.

1.9 Exercises

1. What do all of the more than 6,000 languages of the world have in common?

2. What is linguistics and what are its major subfields?

3. Which of the following statements is correct?
   a) Grammar is a set of rules that tell us how to use a language.
   b) Grammar is a set of rules that describe how a language works.
   c) Grammar is a description of certain aspects of a language.
   d) The question of what is 'good' grammar is decided by the government.
   e) Grammar is made up by ordinary non-specialist people.
   f) People in universities decide what 'good' grammar is.
   g) Grammar has to be learnt by children before they can speak properly.
   h) Grammar is caught not taught.

4. As you have learned, language is regarded as a system of symbolic signs. Name the differences between the three types of signs and give an example for each type.

5. What are the technical terms for the functional side versus the formal side of a word? Who coined this concept?

6. Corpus linguistics: Prove that the word *petrol* is a rather British word compared to the word *gas* which is used more often in American English.

7. Again Corpus linguistics: Show with the help of different corpora that the word *stealer* actually exists in the English language, but that the word *thief* is used more commonly. Discuss, using examples, whether the two actually mean the same thing or not.

2 Phonetics and phonology

2.1 Introduction

Language is, fundamentally, spoken. In human evolution, our ancestors probably first began to speak, more than 50,000 years ago, and only much later developed writing, about 3,000-4,000 years ago. Young children today first learn to speak, roughly between the ages of 0 and 5, and only later learn to write, usually from age 5 or 6 onwards. This is not to say that spoken language is better than any other form (signed, written, electronic), but that it is the natural, inbuilt way for humans to use language, other things being equal.

2.1.1 Describing pronunciation

Describing and analyzing pronunciation in all its details is quite difficult. On the one hand, it is rather obvious that spoken language does not come in easy and clean-cut units. There are no sounds per se, or even words, phrases or sentences in natural spoken language (as discussed, e.g., in Miller & Weinert 1998). Rather, there is only one more or less **continuous stream of sound**, as illustrated in Figure 2.1 below. Here you can see a so-called spectrogram of the line *I love phonetics*. Spectrograms visualize the energy of the frequency content of a signal over time. This energy is essentially what we usually associate with pressure. If the surrounding air pressure is kept constant, you would perceive the pronunciation of sounds as the increase and decrease of pressure over time. This development is then plotted as a graph as in Figure 2.1, for example. The horizontal axis represents time, the vertical axis frequency. The amplitude of a given sound can either be represented as intensity of the dots or through other means, such as colors or different levels of grey.

One very simple and useful tool for students is the software Praat (available free of charge at http://www.fon.hum.uva.nl/praat/). This allows you to generate and analyze your own spectrogram in quite some detail. An example of this is given in Figure 2.1 below.

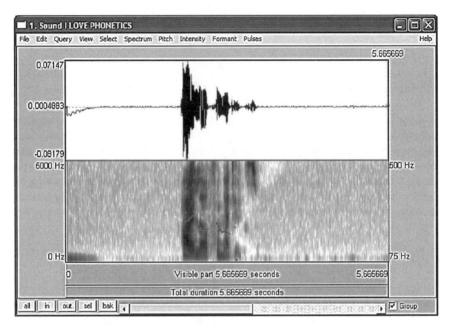

Figure 2.1: Spectrogram of 'I love phonetics'.

Experienced phoneticians can read spectrograms like that in Figure 2.1 as if they were written language, despite the fact that there is nothing in this continuous stream of sound that clearly has any clear connection to the letters, or the 'citation sounds' ('a', 'b', 'c' when you recite the alphabet). It is one task of linguists (and also of children when they acquire language!) to find out where the word, phrase, and sentence boundaries actually are in that continuous stream of sound. And this is already the first point that makes the scientific study of sounds so interesting, but also a bit tricky.

2.1.2 The phonetic alphabet

The second problem that linguists are faced with when they want to describe and analyze pronunciation is the fact that **spoken language is not directly represented in regular orthography**. There are cases where the same letters represent different sounds, as <i>, for example, in *intense* and *ivory*, or <th> in *that* and *thanks*. Sometimes different letters represent roughly the same sound, as, for example, <ue> and <ou> in *blue* and *you*. Sometimes, there are letters which are perfectly silent: you can't hear a <k> in *knight* or a <gh> in *thought*.

Or the letters are pronounced in totally unpredictable ways, as, again, <gh> in *tough*. Matters become even more complicated when we look at words like *event*. The first <e> represents a different sound than the second one. This shows that the relationship between pronunciation and spelling is rather inconsistent and based on convention, a fact which becomes even clearer when we look at languages that have different sounds than English, but use the same spelling system. One example is the variety of possible pronunciations of the letter <o>: just compare English *pony* with the German *Tor* or the Swedish *rot* (which is pronounced like the German 'u' or the English 'oo'). This list can easily be extended. In many South African languages, like Xhosa, we find so-called click sounds (which sound a bit like the horse-calling sounds in English which are produced by putting your tongue against your palate or between the cheek and teeth, creating a tiny vacuum there, and then releasing it with a 'click'). What letter should be used for that? Apparently, the 'xh', which is used in the language name 'Xhosa' [ǁʰosa], does not help, as many people wrongly pronounce the language as 'Kosa' [kɔsa] or 'Sosa' [sɔsa], and not with the appropriate click sound.

   In sum, it should be clear by now that regular orthography usually won't do in a description of spoken language. This is one of the reasons why so-called **phonetic alphabets** were developed, i.e. special characters and writing conventions that help us to describe and characterize sounds as efficiently and precisely as possible. One of the most important phonetic alphabets is that of the *International Phonetics Association*, short IPA. This is reproduced in Table 2.1 below. Almost all known human speech sounds, both consonants and vowels are listed here according to the way in which they are produced by speakers (this will be the topic for the next section). Moreover, you find some **diacritics**, i.e. symbols which give additional information about things like breathing, intonation, length, voicing, etc., but these are mostly restricted to highly specialized research and will therefore only be discussed and used in the following when necessary.

Table 2.1: Full Chart of the International Phonetic Alphabet. Reprinted with permission of the International Phonetic Association. Copyright 2005 by International Phonetic Association.

THE INTERNATIONAL PHONETIC ALPHABET (revised to 2005)

CONSONANTS (PULMONIC) © 2005 IPA

	Bilabial	Labiodental	Dental	Alveolar	Postalveolar	Retroflex	Palatal	Velar	Uvular	Pharyngeal	Glottal
Plosive	p b			t d		ʈ ɖ	c ɟ	k g	q ɢ		ʔ
Nasal	m	ɱ		n		ɳ	ɲ	ŋ	N		
Trill	B			r					R		
Tap or Flap		ⱱ		ɾ		ɽ					
Fricative	ɸ β	f v	θ ð	s z	ʃ ʒ	ʂ ʐ	ç ʝ	x ɣ	χ ʁ	ħ ʕ	h ɦ
Lateral fricative				ɬ ɮ							
Approximant		ʋ		ɹ		ɻ	j	ɰ			
Lateral approximant				l		ɭ	ʎ	L			

Where symbols appear in pairs, the one to the right represents a voiced consonant. Shaded areas denote articulations judged impossible.

CONSONANTS (NON-PULMONIC)

Clicks	Voiced implosives	Ejectives
ʘ Bilabial	ɓ Bilabial	' Examples:
ǀ Dental	ɗ Dental/alveolar	p' Bilabial
! (Post)alveolar	ʄ Palatal	t' Dental/alveolar
ǂ Palatoalveolar	ɠ Velar	k' Velar
ǁ Alveolar lateral	ʛ Uvular	s' Alveolar fricative

OTHER SYMBOLS

ʍ Voiceless labial-velar fricative
w Voiced labial-velar approximant
ɥ Voiced labial-palatal approximant
ʜ Voiceless epiglottal fricative
ʢ Voiced epiglottal fricative
ʡ Epiglottal plosive

ɕ ʑ Alveolo-palatal fricatives
ɺ Voiced alveolar lateral flap
ɧ Simultaneous ʃ and x

Affricates and double articulations can be represented by two symbols joined by a tie bar if necessary. k͡p t͡s

VOWELS

	Front	Central	Back
Close	i y	ɨ ʉ	ɯ u
	I Y		ʊ
Close-mid	e ø	ɘ ɵ	ɤ o
		ə	
Open-mid	ɛ œ	ɜ ɞ	ʌ ɔ
	æ	ɐ	
Open	a ɶ		ɑ ɒ

Where symbols appear in pairs, the one to the right represents a rounded vowel.

SUPRASEGMENTALS

ˈ Primary stress
ˌ Secondary stress ˌfoʊnəˈtɪʃən
ː Long eː
ˑ Half-long eˑ
˘ Extra-short ĕ
| Minor (foot) group
‖ Major (intonation) group
. Syllable break ɹi.ækt
‿ Linking (absence of a break)

DIACRITICS Diacritics may be placed above a symbol with a descender, e.g. ŋ̊

̥ Voiceless	n̥ d̥	̤ Breathy voiced	b̤ a̤	̪ Dental	t̪ d̪		
̬ Voiced	s̬ t̬	̰ Creaky voiced	b̰ a̰	̺ Apical	t̺ d̺		
ʰ Aspirated	tʰ dʰ	̼ Linguolabial	t̼ d̼	̻ Laminal	t̻ d̻		
̹ More rounded	ɔ̹	ʷ Labialized	tʷ dʷ	̃ Nasalized	ẽ		
̜ Less rounded	ɔ̜	ʲ Palatalized	tʲ dʲ	ⁿ Nasal release	dⁿ		
̟ Advanced	u̟	ˠ Velarized	tˠ dˠ	ˡ Lateral release	dˡ		
̠ Retracted	e̠	ˤ Pharyngealized	tˤ dˤ	̚ No audible release	d̚		
̈ Centralized	ë	̴ Velarized or pharyngealized ɫ					
̽ Mid-centralized	x̽	̝ Raised	e̝	(ɹ̝ = voiced alveolar fricative)			
̩ Syllabic	n̩	̞ Lowered	e̞	(β̞ = voiced bilabial approximant)			
̯ Non-syllabic	e̯	̘ Advanced Tongue Root	e̘				
˞ Rhoticity	ɚ a˞	̙ Retracted Tongue Root	e̙				

TONES AND WORD ACCENTS

LEVEL		CONTOUR	
e̋ or ˥	Extra high	ě or ˩˥	Rising
é ˦	High	ê ˥˩	Falling
ē ˧	Mid	e᷄ ˦˥	High rising
è ˨	Low	e᷅ ˩˨	Low rising
ȅ ˩	Extra low	e᷈ ˧˦˨	Rising-falling
↓ Downstep		↗ Global rise	
↑ Upstep		↘ Global fall	

2.1.3 Phonetics versus phonology

In linguistics we have two disciplines that deal with sounds as such, and this is already reflected in the heading of this chapter: phonetics and phonology. **Phonetics is the study of sounds as such**, independent of any given language and of any analysis of their particular function. In other words, phonetics is a very concrete and direct way of dealing with sounds, and it is bordering on disciplines such as physics and physiology. **Phonology, in contrast, looks at the sound system of a given language and what the function of a given sound in a given language is or can be**. Phonetics is usually divided into three different parts: acoustic, auditory, and articulatory. Phonology commonly has two branches: segmental phonology, dealing with individual sounds, or segments, and suprasegmental phonology, which deals with all issues that go beyond the single sound, e.g. syllables, rhythm, intonation, and stress.

The sound system of any given language only uses a small subset of all possible sounds humans can produce and receive in order to create differences in meaning, i.e. contrasts. This subset is usually not the same for two given languages. Even when you compare two languages which are apparently very similar, like German and English, you will find a number of sounds that are specific for one or the other (German: über [ybə], *ach* [ax], *ich* [iç]; English: *this* [ðis], *wet* [wɛt], *mad* [mad]). Note that in the case of *mad* matters are a bit more complicated. Both German and English do have a sound [d], but German – in contrast to English – does not use it in word final position. So German *Rat* und *Rad* essentially sound the same, English *mat* and *mad* don't. Another example comes from Japanese. Here, we usually have syllables which consist just of a consonant (C) followed by a vowel (V), so CV. English is much more complex with words like *streams* [striːmz] which is CCCVCC, or *Christmas* [krisməs], which is CCVC CVC (note that we do not count the orthographic letters, but the actual sounds, so *ea* is counted only once, as [iː], *ch* as [k]). When the word *Christmas* was borrowed into Japanese, it had to be changed to fit the Japanese CV syllable type. Hence, today, we have a word in Japanese like *kurisumasu* (CV CV CV CV CV) for *Christmas*. Again, we can see that the two languages apparently have different systems in which they organize their particular sound inventories.

Obviously, the two perspectives of phonetics and phonology have a lot in common and deal with very similar issues; however, there are also some crucial differences between the two, especially when it comes to methods and aims. Since phonetics is usually seen as the basis for phonology, we will begin with this point of view.

2.2 Phonetics

What happens when we speak, actually? The most fundamental thing that we need for speaking is air. For most languages and for most sounds it suffices to say that this air starts on its way in our lungs and that we breathe out while we speak (with so-called egressive sounds). Note, however, that not all languages and sounds do that. In Owerri Ibo (a language spoken in Nigeria), Vietnamese, and in the Khoisan language family in southern Africa some sounds (for example the clicks mentioned before) are produced with the opposite direction of the airstream, i.e. with air coming in. These are called ingressive sounds. Since all sounds of English are **egressive**, with air being breathed out, we will restrict ourselves to this group in the following discussion. Once the air has left the lungs, it passes through your larynx, which contains your glottis and your vocal cords. For some sounds (the so-called voiced sounds like [v] in *van*) the vocal cords are tensed and begin to vibrate, for others (like [f] in *fan*) they don't. The air then moves further up into your pharynx, your oral and your nasal cavity. From there, depending on which sound you want to produce, it leaves your body either through the nose or the mouth (or both) and can be perceived by the hearer(s). But this can't be all. Obviously, we can produce many different sounds, so we need a few mechanisms that do something with the airstream to produce this variety.

2.2.1 Consonants and vowels

Even if you are not familiar with the American TV game show *Wheel of Fortune*, you are probably quite well aware of the fact that there are consonants and vowels. But why do we make that distinction? Is there a fundamental phonetic difference between the two categories? Is there any systematic reason why you can easily sing vowel sounds like *a, e, i, o, u* in isolation but you can't sing *b, t, g*, for example? In some sense there is. Noises, or what we call sounds, are produced by 'letting the air vibrate'. So you should not hear any specific language like sounds if you breathe normally. We need something else for that, something that creates these special vibrations. **In the case of consonants, this happens through a partial or total obstruction of the airstream**. Instead of letting the air flow freely, we create turbulence of some sort by hindering the airstream from flowing freely. With vowels, the airstream does flow freely, but through shaping our oral cavity in different ways (by raising or lowering different parts of our tongue) we create different shapes for the tube in which the air resonates. Lowering the tongue and opening the mouth usually leads to 'bigger' vowel sounds with a lower frequency (as in *father*), whereas raising it gives you 'smaller' vowel sounds with a higher frequency (*feel, fool*). We will come back to this later on. The main difference between consonants and vowels thus seems to be the obstruction of the airstream. With consonants, we find a partial or total obstruction of the airstream, with vowels, we don't. The distinction between the two is actually a very important one, and will be taken up again in later discussions of phonological issues.

Since vowels and consonants seem to be fundamentally different types of sounds (at least as far as their production is concerned), we also need different tools for describing them.

2.2.2 Consonants

With consonants we can ask three simple questions about their

- **Place of articulation**: where is the obstruction of the airstream created?
- **Manner of articulation**: what kind of obstruction is it?
- **Voicing**: do the vocal cords vibrate when the sound is produced?

This sounds very complicated at first, but it is actually quite simple. Try to pronounce the following words very slowly and carefully, and feel what your tongue and the other parts of your mouth are doing when you pronounce the first consonant: *cut, yes, ship, tea, thanks, feel, bit*. If you have the impression that you somehow start at the back of the mouth with the initial [k] in *cut* and then gradually move forward until you reach initial [b] in *bit*, you are absolutely right. With every word you have changed the **place of articulation** to a place more at the front of the mouth. Now try these two simple words: *bit, fit*, or *tea, sea*. This time you should feel that somehow you stop the airflow with the first word, and release it suddenly, like an explosion (hence you can't make the sound longer), whereas the first sound in the second word somehow takes time and there is a continuous stream of air (so that you could say [f] and [s] for a while). This has to do with different **manners of articulation**, not just different places (in fact, [t] and [s] are even produced in the same place, but with different manners, as we will see below). **Voicing** is what you experience when you pronounce word pairs like *sit, zit*. Only with the second word you should be able to feel some sort of sonorous vibration in your throat. This is because the vocal cords are in action when you produce [z], but not when you pronounce [s]. In the following, we will discuss each of the three features (place, manner, voicing) in some more detail, before we look at the vowels.

When we talk about the place of articulation, we need a few terms from physiology in order to be able to describe where we are in the mouth or throat. These are illustrated in Figure 2.2.

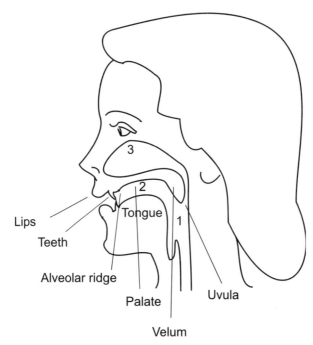

Figure 2.2: The vocal tract. The three cavities and the articulators of the articulatory system (1 = pharyngeal cavity; 2 = oral cavity; 3 = nasal cavity) (Gut 2009: 24; Reproduction with kind permission of Ulrike Gut and Peter Lang Verlag).

So, an obstruction can be created by using your lips, your tongue, your teeth, and the larynx, i.e. the glottis, or some combination of these articulators. Some of the active (moveable) **articulators** (like the tongue, or the lower lip) usually, but not always, come into contact with the passive (immovable) articulators, such as the roof of your mouth or the upper lip. We thus get the major **places of articulation**:

   bilabial (with both lips): *bit, pit, man*
   labio-dental (with lips and teeth): *feel, veal*
   interdental (tongue between the teeth): *this, thanks*
   alveolar (tongue touches roof of the mouth right behind the teeth): *tent, dent*
   palatal (tongue touches the hard palate): *yes, shuttle*
   velar (tongue touches the roof at very back of the mouth): *cut, gut*
   glottal (obstruction is created by the glottis): *hat*

The second point to consider when we talk about the pronunciation of consonants is the **manner of articulation**, or how the sound is produced. There are many different ways in which you can create turbulence in the air stream that leaves your lungs. The most obvious thing to do is to create friction. This happens with the so-called **fricative sounds**, which are produced by a continuous stream of air passing through some partial obstruction. Examples include *fat, vat, sun, zap, shun*, and many more. On the other hand, you can also create a total block of the airstream and seal off the oral cavity altogether. When the air is then suddenly released, you get the effect of a so-called **plosive**, or stop. Examples include: *bat, pat* (which are both produced with a total block created by both lips) but also *cut* and *gut*, where the total obstruction is produced with the back of your tongue and the roof of your mouth at the very back, the velum. Note that, by definition, [m] and [n] and [ŋ] are also stops, since we have a complete closure of the oral cavity (the air flows only through the nose). However, there is obviously no sudden release of the air in this case. The three of them essentially only differ in their place of articulation: [m] is a bilabial *stop*, [n] is palato-alveolar, [ŋ] is velar.

There are at least two more manners of articulation. The initial sounds in *yacht* [jɒt] and *wet* [wɛt], for example, are so-called **approximants**, i.e. the articulators do not touch in any way and thus do not cause any real turbulence of the airstream. The results are sounds which can be classified as consonants, for a number of reasons, but which are very vowel-like in their production. The same applies to the lateral approximant [l], as in *later* [leɪtə], where the air is only blocked in the middle of the mouth, and is free to flow around the outer edges. Yet another group of consonants combines two articulatory features into one. The so-called **affricates** consist of an initial stop [t] or [d], plus a following fricative [ʃ] or [ʒ]: *church* [tʃɜːtʃ] and *jungle* [dʒʌŋg(ə)l] are two examples.

As mentioned above, there is a third feature that we need to consider when we look at the pronunciation of consonants: **voicing**. Inside your larynx are your vocal cords. At rest they are separated from each other and do not vibrate in any significant way when air flows through the larynx. This is what you get when you breathe normally. But you can also tense your vocal cords, and bring them closer together. In that case, they begin to vibrate and make noise (like in many wind instruments). You can hear and feel the difference quite easily when you softly put a hand on your throat (where your larynx sits) and pronounce the two sounds: [v] and [f], or [s] and [z]. With [v] and [z] you should really feel some vibration in your throat, while [f] and [s] cause no such sensation. With [v, z] we have what is called voicing, i.e. the vocal cords are tensed and vibrate, whereas [f, s] are voiceless and produced without using the vocal cords. Note that many sounds in English have the same place and manner of articulation, and only differ in their voicing. Some examples include: [pɪt] – [bɪt], [gɒd] – [kɒd], [bɪt] – [bɪd], [fan] – [van].

2.2.3 Vowels

Vowels need a completely different system to be described accurately. Since there is no partial or total obstruction of the airstream, it makes no sense to talk about place or manner of articulation as such. Also, all English vowels are, by definition, voiced, so that this category is also useless. Instead, let us begin with some experiment. Try to say the following sentence (stress and lengthen all the boldface vowels, try to feel what your tongue and mouth in general are doing): *Eat cool, fat* father [iːt kʰuːɫ fat fɑːðˤɹ]. First of all, it is usually way more difficult to feel and describe the differences here. But of course there must be some, since all four sounds somehow sound differently. How do we shape the tube, our mouth, to create these differences? With the [iː] in *eat* we seem to have a very narrow tube which leads to high frequency sounds; when you contrast this directly with [uː] in *cool*, the tongue seems to move to the back of the mouth. *Fat* and *father* on the other hand are both produced with your mouth fairly wide open, but somehow, the vowel [ɑː] in *father* has the tongue really at the bottom of the mouth, whereas in [a] the tongue is slightly raised and somehow tenser in general. Apparently, the dimensions or factors that we need in order to describe vowels have something to do with the tongue. Most studies now recognize the following **phonetic features for vowels**:

- **Height** of the tongue in the mouth
- **Frontness / backness** of the tongue
- **Tenseness**
- **Length**
- **Lip rounding**

In order to describe vowels properly, we need to see the oral cavity as some sort of abstract space, usually described either as a trapezium or as a triangle. This, roughly, maps onto your sagittal head (as in Figure 2.2 above), so that the left hand side is the front, with your mouth, and the right hand side the back of your mouth. Top and bottom are as usual.

Position of the tongue
By moving the tongue, you can narrow the oral cavity, and hence the acoustic tube, to varying degrees. This narrowing is sometimes referred to as 'closing', and this is what you feel when you compare [ɑː] and [uː], for example. We can thus talk about 'high vowels' and 'low vowels' or 'close vowels' and 'open vowels', and mean the same thing. Vowels such as [i] and [u] are called high or close, since here the tongue is in its highest position. In contrast [ɑ] is a low or

open vowel, as the tongue is at the bottom of the mouth and the oral cavity is wide open. You can always think about your doctor. If your doctor wants to look inside your throat, you will be asked to say [ɑ], not [i].

With the different parts of your tongue (basically front, middle, back) you can narrow the oral cavity either at the front, the middle, or the back of the mouth. This is essentially what gives you different vowels like [i] and [u]. If you don't do anything at all, you end up with a kind of unmarked, unspectacular everyday sound like schwa [ə], which is the sound people like to make when they need time to think or when they are not sure what to say. So, just like we find vowels which are high and low, and in between, we also find vowels which are front and back, and in between.

Tenseness and Length
Another feature that we need to look at is tenseness. This is way more complicated than either height or frontness. You can perhaps feel the difference between tense and lax vowels when you produce word pairs like *beat* [bi:t] and *bit* [bɪt] or *cool* [ku:l] and *could* [kʊd]. With the first word of these pairs your muscles somehow tense, you need to put in more muscular effort than with the second word of these pairs. In some approaches, however, you may find the claim that the difference is between long and short vowels. Long vowels are marked by the diacritic colon [:]. And at first sight, this is quite right. One of the two vowels in the pairs of words we just discussed has a colon, and is long, the other one does not. But then it is also a different phonetic symbol for each of the vowels, so these are also different sounds. This means, eventually, that in English you usually do not find long-short pairs of one and the same vowel; these will usually also differ in their tense-lax qualities. Nevertheless, there is some remarkable overlap. Tense vowels in English are mostly long, while most lax vowels are short. An actual phonetic difference can be heard when you compare the words [bɪd] and [bɪt], [bʌs] and [bʌz], [si:t] and [si:d], [lɒk] and [lɒg]. Technically speaking, there is always the same vowel, and in the transcription we do not see any difference in vowel quality. However, detailed phonetic studies have shown (and many people claim to have heard!) that vowels preceding voiced consonants are produced and perceived as longer than their counterparts with preceding voiceless consonants (see, e.g., Chen 1970; Hogan & Rozsypal 1980; Kluender, Diel & Wright 1988).

Lip rounding
The last feature that we need to discuss is lip rounding. Vowels like [u] are produced with a pursing of the lips, like a kissing gesture, while [i] has no rounding, pursing gesture, but rather uses a smiling, lip-spreading expression. Note that in English, almost all back vowels are rounded [u, ʊ, o, ɔ, ɒ] – the only exceptions may be [ɑ] as in *spa* and [ʌ] in *plus* – while all front vowels are

unrounded [i, ɪ, e, ɛ, a]. In German we have both rounded and unrounded front vowels: [i] as in *Bit* versus [y] as in *Bütt,* [e] as in *nee* versus [ø] as in *nö.* This is not so much a problem for phonetics, where we simply try to describe the vowels as accurately as possible, but rather for phonology, where we want to find the most economical description. So we will return to this question later on.

Cardinal Vowels
It should have become clear that the description of vowels is more complicated than that of consonants. Their articulatory features are much more fuzzy, hard to grasp, and debatable. This is one of the reasons why already in the nineteenth century phoneticians (notably Alexander Melville Bell and Alexander Ellis) began to think about reliable systems of describing vowel sounds. Their efforts culminated in the development of the **Cardinal Vowel System** by Daniel Jones in the early twentieth century. The Cardinal Vowel System contains eight primary and eight secondary vowels, which are completely artificial and which represent clearly defined points of articulation in the oral cavity. The set of primary vowels contains front unrounded and back rounded vowels; the set of secondary vowels exactly the opposite, i.e. front rounded and back unrounded vowels. The oral cavity (when seen as on the sagittal plane) roughly resembles a trapezium. The Cardinal Vowel Chart for the primary vowels is given in Figure 2.3.

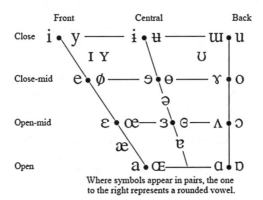

Where symbols appear in pairs, the one
to the right represents a rounded vowel.

Figure 2.3: The Cardinal Vowel Chart (primary vowels). (Courtesy of International Phonetic Association. Copyright 2005 by International Phonetic Association).

Diphthongs
Finally, there is a third group of sounds which technically belongs to the group of vowel sounds, but actually deserves a separate treatment because of its importance. These are the so-called diphthongs. **Diphthongs are two vowel sounds combined into one.** Examples from English include the **four closing diphthongs** [ai] in *five*, [au] in *house*, [eɪ] in *drain*, [oʊ] in *stone*, and the **two centering diphthongs** [uə] as in *shure*, [iə] as in *beer*. Closing means that the diphthong ends in a high/close vowel, centering means that it ends in a center vowel. Note that the latter two can only be heard in English English. General American English has simple vowels (so called monophthongs) plus the consonant [r] in these cases. In diphthongs, the articulation begins with one particular vowel and then moves smoothly into another one in one single articulatory gesture. Note that in English English we even find clusters of three sounds, sometimes referred to as triphthongs, as in *fire* [faɪə].

2.3 Phonology

So far, we have only discussed articulatory phonetics, i.e. the way sounds in general are produced. Phonology, in contrast, is concerned with the sound system of a particular language, in this case English. Phonology seeks to identify, analyze and describe those sounds in a language which are useful and needed in differentiating meaning. One trivial example is [bɪt] and [pɪt]. Here, the two initial sounds [b] and [p] are the essential elements that distinguish between those two words. All the rest is exactly the same. The same principle would apply to [bɪt] and [bi:t], by the way. Here, only the quality of the vowel makes the difference between *bit* and *beat*. We call sounds that help us to distinguish meaning **phonemes** and the test that we just applied (i.e. contrasting two words which only differ in one single sound) the **minimal pair test**. Note that phonemes – in contrast to sounds in phonetics – are not real entities. They are **abstract units** in the linguistic system. You can't see them, you can't hear them. In order to distinguish between sounds in general and abstract phonemes we put phonemes in slant brackets, i.e. /b/ and /p/. The minimal pair test applies to all kinds of sounds, i.e. consonants and vowels, including diphthongs. However, sometimes we can also discover sounds which do not create contrasts between words. Listen carefully to what you are doing when you pronounce the words *kit-cat-cut*. Perhaps you feel that with each word your tongue moves a little further back when you pronounce the first sound. So, despite the fact that all three words begin with a 'k sound', this 'k sound' seems to be different. In phonetics, we would have to say that the [k] in *kit* is a fronted [k], i.e. the place of articulation is a little bit further at the front than with an unmarked [k]. This is shown by a diacritic sign in the transcription: [k̟]. In contrast to this, the [k] in *cut* is retracted, i.e. the place of articulation is a little bit further back in the throat. Again, we have a diacritic marker for this: [k̠]. The [k] in *cat* is neutral and can remain unmarked. Why is that so? The pronunciation of [k] is phonetically influenced by the following sound, fronting it makes it easier to pronounce the following front vowel [i], retracting it makes it easier to pronounce the following low, half-back vowel [ʌ]. The low front vowel [æ] does not need any special [k]. So, eventually, you are not free to choose which [k] you want to use, but there are more or less strict phonological rules that guide you. Does that mean that the 'three *k*s' [k̟], [k̠], and [k], are phonemes of English? When we try to find minimal pairs for them, we have to realize that there are no words in English where the different pronunciations of [k] actually make a difference. These three sounds do not distinguish meaning. What distinguishes meaning is the general consonant sound [k], as in [kɪt] versus [bɪt]. The three different *k* sounds also do not contrast with each other. Where one occurs, e.g. before front vowels, the others cannot occur. We call this particular phenomenon **complementary distribution.** In sum, this means that we find one abstract unit, the phoneme /k/, which has at least three different concrete realizations, depending on the phonetic contexts in which /k/ is actually used. These concrete realizations are called **allophones.** It is important to stress that this is nothing special or extraordinary. Phonemes as abstract units with allophones as their different concrete realizations illustrate the basic mechanism how language works. We generally need to distinguish between the linguistic system (or structure) and its abstract units, and what speakers do with this system and its units, how all this is put into practice. Another well-known textbook example involves the [l] sound. Compare the pronunciation of *lip* and *pill*. In the first case, your tongue should feel somehow neutral, i.e. relaxed and flat when you pronounce the 'l sound'. We call this a 'clear l', [l]. In the latter case, with *pill*, your tongue tightens up a little bit and is actually raised both at the front and at the back. We call this a 'dark l', [ɫ]. And again, just like with /k/, there are clear rules when you use which of the two 'l-sounds'. [l] appears only in the first part of a word or syllable, [ɫ] only at the end. The two never contrast, no word is distinguished by them. This means that [l] and [ɫ] are in complementary distribution, where one occurs, the other one does not occur. Still, if you deliberately pronounce *lip* with a dark [ɫ] and *pill* with an [l], it may sound somewhat odd, but does not create a new word with a different meaning. This shows that they both belong as allophones, concrete realizations, to the abstract phoneme /l/, as can be shown by the minimal pair test: *lip* versus *tip*, *pill* versus *pick*. So, one criterion for allophones is complementary, i.e. non-contrastive, distribution. But this would also mean, strictly speaking, that non-aspirated [t] and [h] should be allophones, since they are in complementary distribution: non-aspirated [t] only shows up in non-initial position ([stɔp], [swiːt]), [h] only in initial position, as in [haus]. However, this does not really make sense. We want to be able to say that certain allophones 'belong' to a given phoneme, while others don't. Allophones as concrete realizations always need to be realizations of something. In order to be able to say which allophones belong together and which phonemes they eventually belong to, we need a second criterion for allophones: **phonetic similarity**. Thus, we can say that aspirated [tʰ] and non-aspirated [t] are allophones of /t/, since they are phonetically similar and in complementary distribution. The same applies to the three allophones of /k/, [k̟], [k̠], and [k] and clear and dark /l/: [l] and [ɫ].

The phoneme can be defined as the smallest meaning distinguishing unit in a language. This means that phonemes help us to differentiate between the different words – such as *cat* /kat/ and *mat* /mat/ – but that the phonemes themselves do not have any meaning like words do. While /k/ and /m/ distinguish between the words, we cannot say what they really mean – only what they do. As has been said before, the way to discover the phonemes of a given language is to perform the minimal pair test in which two words differ (ideally) in only one single sound. This sound, then, must be a phoneme. Some phonemes, however, do not behave the way they should. For example, the two sounds [ʃ] and [ʒ] hardly ever show up in a real minimal pair. The closest we can get is *mission* [mɪʃən] versus *vision* [vɪʒən]. Strictly speaking, these would not qualify as a minimal pair as they differ in two sounds, [m/v] and [ʃ/ʒ]. Nevertheless, as it is clear that the two sounds in question must be phonemes, but only lack the perfect minimal pair, we have to work with this makeshift solution. Similarly, some phonemes do not contrast with each other because they are not available in all positions in the word. [h] and [ŋ], for example, can be shown to be phonemes: *house* [haʊs] versus *mouse* [maʊs], *sin* [sɪn] versus *sing* [sɪŋ]. However, /h/ only shows up word-initially, /ŋ/ only word-finally, i.e. the two never contrast, as good phonemes should do. We call this **defective distribution**.

When we perform a complete analysis of English, we end up with about 26 consonant phonemes, eleven vowel phonemes and eight diphthong phonemes. These are only rough figures, though, since the actual number depends on the variety of English you are looking at.

Phonemes are usually characterized as the smallest meaning distinguishing units. In that sense, they are a little bit like atoms in physics. Atoms can also be characterized as the smallest building blocks of matter and were regarded as indivisible up until about 1900. However, the British physicist J.J. Thompson discovered in the late nineteenth century that there are certain special phenomena that seem to indicate that there must be smaller parts inside the atom, and that these smaller parts can be split off. In 1968, Chomsky and Halle developed a comprehensive theory of phonological (i.e. distinctive) features, basing their work on previous studies by Jakobson, among others. The central idea is that phonemes are actually composed of a number of unique sets of distinctive features. These features are based on both articulation and perception and enriched by theory internal factors. Supposedly, the list of features is universal and capable of capturing all phonemes of all languages as **unique feature lists**. The representation of these is – unsurprisingly – very similar to the description of phonetic features as mentioned above. However, one should be careful not to confuse the two. While phonetic features are actual, physical features that describe real, audible sounds, **phonological or distinctive features are rather abstract and capture theory internal factors and phenomena**, which can never be actually uttered or heard. Phonology in that sense is very abstract and mostly deals with the ideal underlying sound system that forms the basis for what we really say or hear.

There is not enough room in such a brief introduction to describe all features in greater detail or to give a full picture of the theory and its implications. However, we can try to discuss one example in more detail, also in order to illustrate what the difference is between phonetic and phonological features.

In the section on phonetics, we have said that the fundamental distinction between consonants and vowels is the partial or total obstruction of the airstream that we see with the former, but not with the latter. Hence, we describe consonants rather in terms of their place and manner of articulation, plus voicing, and vowels rather by their particular tongue position, tenseness, or lip rounding. The question for phonology now is whether this classification actually holds for the abstract underlying system. One problem that we encounter, for example, is the classification of so-called approximants, i.e. glides such as /j, w/ and liquids such as /r, l/. Phonetically speaking, they are very close to vowels, and yet we see them as consonants, partly because they, for instance, can form the onset or coda of a syllable, but not its peak (cf. section 2.4 below). However, in some words, they do seem to function like a vowel in that they provide a normal peak for a syllable. Only consider the *bottle* and *father*. These are clearly **bisyllabic**, i.e. made up of two syllables (try and tap their rhythm!). However, detailed phonetic studies have shown that the second syllable does not contain any schwas (as could be expected when we look at the spelling). This would mean that we have a syllable without a vowel (or better: a peak) – which is, of course, not permissible in English. In order to explain this and to characterize the major groups of sounds, Chomsky and Halle developed four different distinctive features:

[+/-] consonant: the sounds function as consonants
[+/-] sonorant: the sound has a low frequency periodic energy, like vowels
[+/-] continuant: the airstream is partially or fully interrupted
[+/-] syllabic: the sound functions as the defining 'peak' of a syllable

As you can see, some of these features are more based on the phonetic aspects of sounds (such as [sonorant] or [continuant]), others belong to suprasegmental phonology (such as [syllabic]), while yet other are more abstract and theoretical (such as [consonant]). Needless to say, the whole list of features is much longer and more complex, and other studies have developed yet other sets of distinctive features. The important point to remember is what the difference between phonetic and phonological features is, and why the latter are interesting for phonological theory and abstraction. For example, and coming back to our question of consonants and vowels, when we now consider some of the major groups of sounds and relate them to the features just described, we can arrive at the following picture:

Table 2.2: Phonological feature chart (simplified)

	Syllabic	Consonant	Sonorant	Continuant
Vowels /a/	+	-	+	+
Oral stops /t/	-	+	-	-
Affricates /tʃ/	-	+	-	-
Nasal stops /m/	-	+	+	-
Fricatives /f/	-	+	-	+
Semi-vowels /j/	-	-	+	+

It seems like we can distinguish between those six major groups of sounds on the basis of only four distinctive features. Note that doing the same on the basis of phonetic features would require many more features, a lot of which would be redundant (e.g. there is no need to say that vowels or stops are [-fricative]). So this is a much more elegant and economical way of capturing the groups and their differences here. However, if you pay close attention, you will notice that two groups in the tableau have the same feature list: oral stops and affricates are both [-syll, +cons, -son, -cont]. How can we distinguish between the two? One feature that has been introduced for that purpose is [delrel] 'delayed release'. Affricates show a longer aspiration phase (and delayed onset of voicing) than oral stops. This feature can help us to distinguish between the two classes. Note, however, that it is entirely irrelevant for the rest (and can hence be marked as [0] for these groups). The tableau eventually looks as follows:

Table 2.3: Phonological feature chart (expanded)

	Syll	Cons	Son	Cont	Delrel
Vowels /a/	+	-	+	+	0
Oral stops /t/	-	+	-	-	-
Affricates /tʃ/	-	+	-	-	+
Nasal stops /m/	-	+	+	-	0
Fricatives /f/	-	+	-	+	0
Semi-vowels /j/	-	-	+	+	0

With distinctive features and a tableau like the one just developed we can nicely capture and distinguish not only between consonants and vowels, but also between various other subcategories, such as semi-vowels or nasal stops. But how do we deal with the syllable problem in *bottle* and *father*? This problem is usually solved by saying that certain sounds in very specific environments can change their features. I.e. in words such as *bottle* and *father* the normally [-syl] semi-vowels have the ability to change this features. The following section will look into some more details here.

2.4 Suprasegmental phonology

So far, we have only discussed phonological problems and phenomena on the level of the individual segments, i.e. phonemes and allophones. We now move on and look at the bigger elements in the sound system, such as syllables, stress, and intonation. Here, more than one element is affected and the items may interact with each other. This is phonology beyond the single segments, hence, suprasegmental phonology.

2.4.1 Syllables

Many people have a very intuitive understanding of **syllables** and if you ask them to count syllables in a given word, such as *expensive*, they will mostly find the right answer (three, in this case, *ex.pen.sive* we mark a syllable boundary by inserting a period (.)). But how do we arrive at this result? From a phonological point of view, the central element of each syllable is the vowel, or vowel-like sound. We call this the **peak** or **nucleus**. Every syllable needs one peak, and this is the necessary and sufficient condition for syllables. The peak can be expanded by what we call the **onset** (segments preceding the peak) and the **coda** (segments following the peak). As peak and coda together give us the impression of rhymes, we group them together as a unit unsurprisingly called **rhyme**. What do the extensions of the peak in English look like? The following figure summarizes the available patterns:

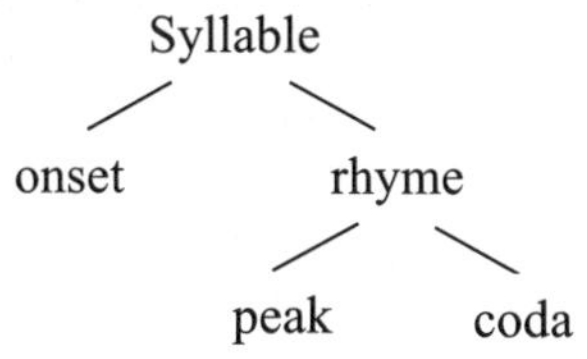

Syllable
├ onset
└ rhyme
  ├ peak
  └ coda

	onset	peak	coda
I		aɪ	
tea	t	i:	
brew	br	u:	
stray	str	eɪ	
up		ʌ	p
east		i:	st
ants		a	nts
unction		ʌ	ŋ(k)ʃn
keep	k	i:	p
sleep	sl	i:	p
strip	str	ɪ	p
tips	t	ɪ	ps
dumps	d	ʌ	mps
sixths	s	ɪ	ksəs
sleeps	sl	i:	ps
streets	str	i:	ts
slumps	sl	ʌ	mps
strengths	str	e	ŋəs

Figure 2.4: Available syllable patterns of English.

As we can see, there are between zero and three consonants in the onset, and between zero and four consonants in the peak (though four is practically non-existent). Note that this is something we do not find in all languages. Languages can differ drastically in the types of syllables they allow. One of the most common syllable types in the languages of the world is simply CV, consonant plus vowel. Japanese has almost exclusively CV syllables. This means that phonologically complex words borrowed from English have to be restructured. Examples include: *stress > su.tu.re.su, trou.ble > to.ra.bu.ru, christ.mas > ka.ri.su.ma.su.*

However, as just mentioned, in terms of sheer numbers, all combinations are attested in English. In present-day English we need to distinguish between light and heavy syllables. Every segment in the syllable is assigned a certain number of **morae** (mora: an entity indicating the 'weight' of a syllable). A long vowel or a diphthong receives two morae, consonants receive one (for reasons of simplicity, onsets are usually ignored in this approach). We then define syllables with monomoraic rhyme (i.e. rhymes with only one mora) as light, those with bimoraic rhyme (i.e. rhymes with two or more morae) as heavy. This can now be represented as follows (where the Greek sign <μ> 'mju' stands for a mora, and <σ> 'sigma' for the syllable).

spinster

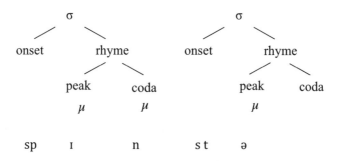

Figure 2.5: Syllabic structure of 'spinster'.

In *spinster*, the first syllable is bimoraic (peak and coda are filled), and thus heavy, the second syllable is monomoraic, with only one short vowel in the peak, and thus light. *Tea*, in contrast, only has one syllable, and this is heavy with a long vowel in the peak.

tea

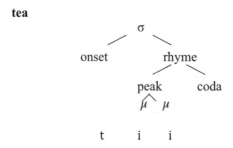

Figure 2.6: Syllabic structure of 'tea'.

2.4.2 Phonotactics

Among other things, heavy versus light syllables play a role in stress assignment in English. Words with three or more syllables usually receive stress on the penultimate syllable when this syllable is heavy (*en'tailment, de'tergent*). If the penultimate syllable is light, stress the antepenultimate syllable: ('*activate* ['æktɪveɪt], *re'vitalize* [re:'vaɪtəlaiz]). We will come back to that below.

The issues mentioned above first and foremost relate to quantity. When it comes to the quality, i.e. type of consonants that can be combined, we also find some interesting, complex restrictions. These are called **phonotactic constraints**. For reasons of space, we cannot go through all of them in detail here, but just point to some general patterns. For example, when we find three consonants in the onset, the first one has to be /s/, as in *string, spring, screen, spleen,* the second one a voiceless plosive, and the third one a liquid, i.e. /l, r/ or semi-vowel /w/ as in *squeak* /skwi:k/ or *square* /skwɛ:/. Similarly, as has been mentioned before, /h/ can only appear at the beginning of a syllable, /ŋ/ at the end. Whorf summarizes the constraints in English syllable structures in an extremely succinct diagram (Figure 2.7 below). But why can't we say *zmrzlina* in English? It's a perfectly good word in Czech, meaning "ice-cream". All languages are subject to language specific phonotactic constraints, some of which are more or less arbitrary (German allows /ps/ and /kn/ clusters word initially, present-day English doesn't. Compare German /psyço/ versus English

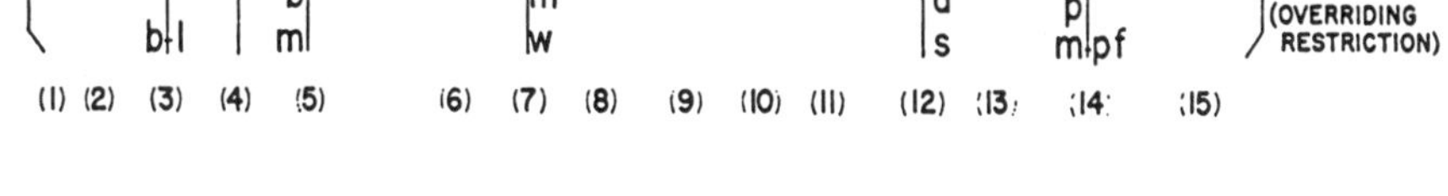

Figure 2.7: Structural formula of the monosyllabic word in English (standard mid-western American). The formula can be simplified by special symbols for certain groups of letters, but this simplification would make it harder to explain. The simplest possible formula for a monosyllabic word is C+V, and some languages actually conform to this. Polynesian has the next most simple formula, O, C+V. Contrast this with the intricacy of English word structure, as shown above (Whorf 1956: 223; Reproduction with kind permission of The MIT Press).

/saɪko/, German /kniː/ versus English /niː/), while others lead to interesting generalizations. One of these generalizations is the sonority sequencing principle. The central idea is that the sounds in a syllable should be ordered according to their sonority value. **Sonority** can be roughly defined as the "noise" that a certain sound makes. Universally, we can find the following hierarchy, from less sonorous to more sonorous:

plosives < fricatives < nasals < liquids < glides/vowels.

Within these categories, however, we can find language-specific constraints and cross-linguistic variation. Within the syllable, we predict rising sonority values in the onset, the peak as the sonority climax, and then falling sonority values in the coda. So, *plump* should be alright, as it begins with a plosive /p/, followed by a liquid /l/, followed by the peak vowel /ʌ/, which in turn is followed by the nasal /m/ and finally again /p/. The result is the predicted Bell curve pattern (Figure 2.8 below). The sonority hierarchy can give us a good, first idea why elements in the syllable are arranged in certain ways. However, the sonority sequencing principle also has its shortcomings. On the one hand, it appears to be underpredicting, i.e. it does not rule out certain combinations which are rarely, if ever, attested, such as /tl/ and /dl/ onsets, or the missing /kn-/ and /ps-/ onset clusters in English. On the other hand, it is also overpredicting in that it rules combinations which are attested, particularly consonant clusters with /s/, both in the onset and coda. *Stops* does not have a bell curve pattern, but rather a hat (see Figure 2.9). Nevertheless, as a first approximation and valuable guide, the sonority sequencing principle is still very useful.

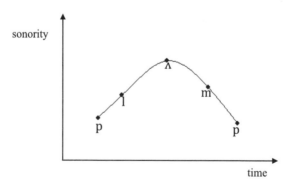

Figure 2.8: Sonority diagram of 'plump'.

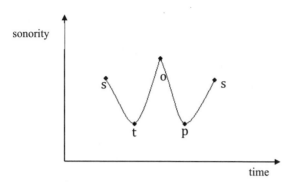

Figure 2.9: Sonority diagram of 'stops'.

2.4.3 Identifying syllables

English syllables offer some more interesting problems, though. Consider the words: *bottle, trouble, father, button.* How many syllables do they have? You may be undecided here like most people. Some claim that there can only be one as there may be only one audible vowel in these words [bɒtɫ], [trʌbɫ], [faːðɹ], [bʌtn]. Others claim that there are two syllables and that these are 'tappable', i.e. you can tap these with your fingers: *bo.tl, trou.ble, fa.ther, bu.ton.* The latter claim is justified by introducing the concept of syllabic consonants. It is interesting to see that the problem only occurs in words that end in the liquids or nasals /l, r/ and /m, n/. These are also classified as sonorants, i.e. sounds with a particular kind of noise, high up on the sonority hierarchy, and therefore not unlike vowels. Which means that they are very vowel like and one might think that this is why they can – like vowels – form the peak of the second syllable in the words just discussed. Syllabic consonants are marked by a diacritic sign in the IPA: [bɒtɫ], [trʌbɫ], [faːðɹ], [bʌtn̩].

How do we identify syllables from a linguistic point of view? Tapping is a good start but we should also aim at making our knowledge explicit. Two principles are important when we syllabify. First, we need to consider the sonority sequencing hierarchy. In the ideal case, syllables should exhibit the bell curve like pattern discussed before, with a low start, rise, the vowel as peak, and then gradual decrease until we reach a final low again (though certain exceptions to this rule can be found). The second principle is called **'maximize onset'** and says that, probably for processing reasons, onsets in syllables should be as big as possible. So, when we have a choice how we want to syllabify (e.g., *na.ture* versus *nat.ure, de.mand* versus *dem.and, re.stric.ted* versus *res.tric.ted* versus *rest.ric.ted, ba.sta* versus *bas.ta* etc.), we aim for a maximal onset: *na.ture, de.mand, re.stric.ted, ba.sta*). Note that, despite the maximize onset constraint, the usual language specific phonotactic constraints still hold. English does not allow for [kt] onset clusters, therefore *re.stri.cted* is not possible (an asterisk * indicates that the following word or phrase is incorrect). Spanish does not have [st] in onsets, therefore, in Spanish we need to syllabify *bas.ta*, not *ba.sta* (as in English).

One final feature of syllables can be observed in words like *spinster* or *hammer*. In theory, one should simply syllabify *spin.ster, ha.mmer*. But this is not what we find. Many people would be rather undecided on where the medial consonants should go: *spin.ster* or *spins.ter, ha.mmer* or *ham.mer*? This might have to do with another principle of English phonology, namely, that stressed syllables want to be big, with long vowels and preferably many consonants in the coda. The solution to this problem is quite easy: /s/ and /m/ are treated as **ambisyllabic** elements, i.e. they simultaneously belong to the coda of the first syllable and the onset of the second. This is illustrated in Figure 2.10 below.

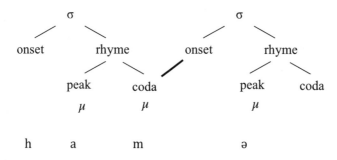

Figure 2.10: Ambisyllabicity in 'hammer'.

2.4.4 Stress

One important phenomenon in suprasegmental phonology is **stress**, both on the word and on the phrase level. Stress can be defined as relative force or loudness (and hence prominence) of elements. This means that stress is not a simple, binary concept, but relative and gradient. Elements do not simply 'have stress', they are stressed more or less in relation to other elements. Within words, we usually mark primary and secondary stress as ['] (primary) and [ˌ] (secondary): [ɪkˌspɛrɪˈmɛntl] *experimental*. As has been said before, there is a strong tendency for stressed syllables to be complex (with long vowels, diphthongs, and/or consonants in the coda) and for unstressed syllables to be more simple.

For some words, stress has a very important meaning distinguishing function. Consider the word *object*. With stress on the first syllable ['ɒbdʒɪkt] we are looking at a noun, with stress on the second syllable [əb'dʒɛkt] we see a change in vowel qualities and we are looking at a verb. Another example would be *present* as a noun ['prɛznt] and as a verb [prɪ'zɛnt]. The same applies to the difference between single words and homophonous (same sounding) phrases: *black berry* [blak'bɛri] versus *blackberry* ['blakbəri]. Similarly, the stress pattern of a word may depend upon the things we attach to it: *occupy* ['ɒkjʊpʌi] – *occupation* [ɒkjʊ'peɪʃ(ə)n]. These issues are discussed in greater detail in the section of morphology.

There are a number of rules that determine stress placement in English. However, these rules are fairly complex since they make use of several phonological and morphological concepts. Some of these rules include:

- in a word with two syllables, the first syllable is stressed: *stagger, donkey, carry*.
- in a word with three of more syllables, check whether the penultimate syllable (the second one from the right) is complex, heavy with a long vowel or complex coda. If it is heavy, it is stressed. If it is light – with a short vowel and/or no coda – the antepenultimate syllable (the third one from the right) is stressed.

As we have seen before, there are numerous exceptions to these rules. With *present, object* etc. stress placement depends in word class. Prefixes (items which are attached before the word, like *re-, un-* or *im-*) can also interact with the rules and maybe call for different stress placements: *recoil, recess, resist* etc. should be stressed on the first syllable, but obviously aren't.

Stress also operates on the phrase and sentence level. Here, stress usually signals emphasis or contrast as in *The RED dress looks fantastic!* Here, putting stress on the adjective *red* usually signals that more than one dress is at issue and that, out of the set of available dresses, the red one looks particularly good. We call this contrastive stress.

2.4.5 Intonation

The last topic we need to touch upon briefly is **intonation**. This term refers to patterns of pitch or melody. While most people probably have a good intuition about intonation and how to use it, the description and analysis is still somewhat difficult. While most approaches agree upon the three central factors of pitch as pitch range, height, and direction, many of them differ in terms of what their object or unit of study actually is and how it can be studied. We will therefore restrict ourselves to some of the basic issues. Intonation (and with it prosody, a term loosely used for pitch, loudness, rhythm etc.) plays an important role in the grammar of spoken language where it can signal sentences, clauses, clause types, etc. In that respect it is a little bit like punctuation in writing. One important example for English are relative clauses. These are usually differentiated into restrictive and non-restrictive. The former are necessary in order to identify the antecedent properly, the latter only give additional information. In writing, the two are usually distinguished by commas. Compare:

(a) The girl who had the cheesecake left without paying.
(b) Carla, who had the cheesecake, left without paying.

In (a) we would not be able to identify which girl left without the restrictive relative clause which tells us that we are talking about the one who had the cheesecake. When we use a personal name as in (b) we usually assume that the hearer will know who we are talking about. In that case, the non-restrictive relative clause does not give vital information, but something additional. The two can be distinguished by commas and very brief pauses.

Intonation also has a pragma-syntactic function in that it helps us to give new or **additional meaning to fixed grammatical structures**. For example, we can turn a simple declarative sentence (SVO) into a question without changing the word order, just by using a different intonation contour. Declarative statements have a so-called **falling intonation**, i.e. their intonation level goes down at the end, while questions have a **rising intonation**, where the level goes up. When we combine this intonation contour with a declarative sentence, we arrive at an intonation question.

(a) John is coming to the party.
(b) Do you like parties?
(c) John is coming to the party?

This may be formalized as follows. H* is a so-called 'peak accent', i.e. the syllable is in the middle or slightly above the middle of the speaker's pitch range. !H* stands for a 'stepped accent' is the same as H* but lower than the preceding H*. L* is a 'low accent', with the accented syllable in the lower part of the speaker's range. Finally, L*+H has a low accented syllable that is followed by a rise to the middle or upper part. L+H* consequently refers to a low (but not as low as L*) syllable followed by a steep rise to the peak accent. Intonational boundaries are usually marked by phrasal accents H⁻ and L⁻: Boundaries tones (H% - rise - and L% - fall -) mark the last syllable.

So, declarative, information questions can, for example, have one of the following intonation patterns:

H* H⁻H%: peak accent followed by an intonation phrase with a H tone boundary

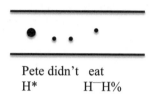

Pete didn't eat
H*   H⁻H%

L* H⁻H%: low accent followed by an intonation phrase with a H tone boundary

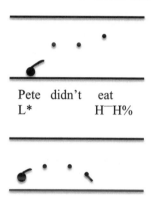

Pete   didn't   eat
L*   H⁻H%

Pete   didn't eat
L*   H⁻L%

Note that this notational system is extremely complex and actually varies from study to study. One attempt to arrive at a more uniform approach is the development of ToBI (Tone and Break Indices, see http://www.ling.ohio-state.edu/~tobi/; cf. Cruttenden 1997). ToBI systems are not like the International Phonetic Alphabet und universally applicable. Rather, they are developed for individual languages, and sometimes even single varieties. The point is that the notational systems as such are conventionalized so that language and varieties become comparable, even though their ToBI systems may differ for language internal reasons.

But we must not forget that intonation is more than just a complex technical detail of suprasegmental phonology. It is also very helpful in **conveying** speakers' attitudes, emotions, perspectives, and so on. Depending on how you pronounce it (intonation-wise!), the line *Peter kissed Paul* can mean so many different things: neutral and factual description, contrast, surprise, anger, pride, sarcasm, happiness etc. Unfortunately, we still know very little about this whole issue. Yet, in fact, there is reason to believe that these expressive and interpersonal functions and their related structures are at least as important as the communication of meaning that is made explicit by the choice of words and sentence structures. And there is still a lot of room for future research in this domain.

2.5 Exercises

1. Explain the difference between a *phoneme*, *allophone* and a *phone*.

2. Show that /p/ and /b/ are phonemes of the English language.

3. Characterize the following sounds:
   Example: [ʃ]   (post-)alveolar, voiceless, fricative

[m]	[ɔ]
[k]	[ə]
[ʤ]	[ɪ]

4. What is the phonological rule for the distribution of [k̡], [k̡] and [k] as in [k̡ɪt], [k̡ʌt], and [kæt]? Are [k̡], [k̡] and [k] allophones or phonemes of English? Give reasons.

5. Divide the following words into syllables:
   Example: including - in.clu.ding

   derive, youngster, dream, stumble, hugging, sun, phonology

6. How do you syllabify *elephant*? Give reasons.

7. Have a look at the distribution of [p], [t], [k] and [pʰ], [tʰ], [kʰ] in the
    following data set. What can you say about the distribution of these sounds
    and their phonological status?

[pʰʊt]	'put'	[spɪt]	'spit'
[tʰɪps]	'tips'	[stɪk]	'stick'
[kʰɪn]	'kin'	[skɪn]	'skin'
[tʰræv(ə)l]	'travel'	[ɪnstənt]	'instant'
[kʰat]	'cat'		
[pʰʊʃ]	'push'		
[ɪmpʰəlaɪt]	'impolite'		

3 Morphology

3.1 Introduction

In the chapter on phonology we have seen that the smallest meaning differentiating units of language, its building blocks, are sounds, or better phonemes. The obvious question to ask now is if there is anything else between the phonemes as the smallest unit and the word as a much bigger unit of language. Most people would intuitively say that words such as *multinational* seem to have several different parts that mean something or do something special: *multi* (many) + *nation* + *al* (an adjective ending). The same applies to other words, such as *swims* or *kissed*. In these cases, one part of the word carries 'the meaning as such' (*swim* and *kiss*) while the other part does 'the grammatical job' (*-s* and *-ed*). Note, however, that all these parts such as *multi-, -al, -s,* and *-ed* do not constitute words themselves, but only parts thereof. This seems to suggest that there must be some sort of structure between phonemes and words. This is what we study in morphology, the topic of the present chapter.

3.2 Defining morphology

Morphology, a Greek term meaning the study of the form or shape of an organism or part thereof, essentially deals with words and the elements that combine into words. It looks both at grammatical phenomena, such as the formation of plural nouns out of singular nouns (e.g., *cat* > *cat-s*), for example, and lexical phenomena, such as the creation of completely new words out of old ones (e.g., *information* + *entertainment* > *infotainment*). The latter is also referred to as **word-formation**. This raises an important question: what is a word? We can look at many different criteria here: spelling, sound, form or meaning, for example. However, none of them is entirely satisfactory. In terms of spelling we find <baby>, which is uncontroversial, of course, but also <babyshower> next to <baby shower>. Clearly, we want to regard <baby shower> as one word just like <babyshower>. But how do we distinguish between <English teacher> (a teacher of English, probably one word) and <English teacher> (a teacher from England who teaches physics, or something else, probably two words)? And how about so-called phrasal verbs and idioms such as <put up> or <kick the bucket>? Spelling is not always reliable here. Hyphenation also causes problems: <mother-in-law> clearly should count as a word, and yet it has two hyphens. How do we treat 'apostrophe s' as in <John's>

(and is there a difference between <John is stupid> and <John's car>?), or the form of <am> in <I'm>? Phonology is another problem. As we have seen in the phonology chapter, there are no clear word boundaries in connected speech. The only thing we can say is that words usually, but not always, have one main stress. But again this can lead to problems with more complex idioms if we wish to include them, and it still does not tell what is part of a word and what is not. Meaning is also a very tricky issue. If we want to claim that one word only has one meaning, we have to explain why <English teacher> in the one sense 'a teacher of English' is a word, and in another sense 'a teacher from England' is not. In order to overcome this problem, the notion of **lexemes** was introduced. This is defined as **the smallest unit of meaning in the mental lexicon** of speakers. Lexemes can be smaller than words, as we can see with *un-* in *unreal* but also much bigger, as, for example, phrasal idioms show (e.g., *head over heels*). But lexemes are a semantic unit (we will return to this in the section on meaning in language) and do not help to answer the question what a word really is. In sum, we can say that there is no simple, single satisfactory criterion that helps us to define what a word is. Nevertheless, speakers seem to have a fairly good intuition in this respect and about the criteria in combination, so it seems worthwhile to try and find out what it is that underlies our intuition.

3.3 Morphemes and allomorphs

As the concept 'word' is so difficult to grasp, morphology, just like phonology, also uses a basic level unit of analysis. But here this is not called a phoneme, but a morpheme. **Morphemes are defined as the smallest meaning bearing units of language**. Meaning bearing means that in contrast to the phoneme, which only distinguishes meaning, there is actually some sort of content attached to the morpheme. While a phoneme like /t/ does not have any meaning as such, but only helps to distinguish between words like /ti:/ *tea* and /bi:/ *bee*, a morpheme like {ment} signals that it turns verbs into nouns (*entertain* > *entertain-ment*), while {s} can signal that its carrier is meant to be seen as a plural noun (*word* > *word-s*). In that sense, morphemes actually have meaning, and this meaning can be described.

Some words just consist of one morpheme, e.g. *cat*, others have two, e.g. *cat-s*, where the lexical morpheme, *cat* combines with some other morpheme denoting 'plural', yet others have three, e.g., *possibilities* (possible + ity + s), some others even more. Just look at *unexpectedness*. How many morphemes can you find here? Four is the right answer: *un+expect+ed+ness*. But this is only half the story. Just like in phonology, morphology also distinguishes between the **abstract units** in the language system (in phonology these are called phonemes, in morphology these are morphemes), and their **concrete**

realizations in specific contexts. In phonology, these concrete realizations are called allophones, in morphology we call them **allomorphs**. As long as we haven't classified the units as either phoneme or morpheme, allophone or allomorph we can simply refer to them as phones and morphs, respectively. Note that each of these linguistic units has its own bracketing convention: phonemes go into slant brackets, like /t/, allophones into square brackets, like [tʰ], morphemes get curly brackets, like {ment}, allomorphs again square brackets, like [z]. This can be summarized as follows:

	Phonology	**Morphology**
Abstract unit	/Phoneme/	{Morpheme}
Concrete Realization	[Allophone]	[Allomorph]
Unclassified	*Phone*	*Morph*

How do we identify morphemes and their allomorphs? Obviously, this must be a little bit more complex than the minimal pair test in phonology. Essentially, we can use two criteria. First, morphemes should have a clearly identifiable meaning or function, and all of their corresponding allomorphs should have exactly the same meaning or function as their mother morpheme. Second, allomorphs usually (but not always) share some formal properties, and their concrete form usually depends predictably on phonological factors.

Morphemes can be classified according to two different dimensions. On the one hand, we need to distinguish between **free and bound morphemes**, i.e. those which can occur independently (e.g., {and}, {sleep}) and those which need a host to attach to (e.g., {-ly}, {dis-}). On the other hand, we need to distinguish between lexical morphemes, i.e. those that carry lexical content (e.g., {swim}, {cat}, {re-}, {-ment}) and grammatical morphemes, i.e. those that carry grammatical function (e.g., {-s}, {-ing}, {and}, {of}).

In Chapter 2 we have seen how we can distinguish phonemes and allophones. How does that work for morphemes and allomorphs? Look at the following set of words: *impossible, illogical, inconsequent, irresponsible, inadequate*. What do they all have in common? Their meaning can be described, quite generally, 'as *not+x*', so *not possible, not logical, not consequent, not responsible, not adequate*. It thus makes sense to assume some underlying abstract unit which has this particular negative meaning and which combines with the base form. For the sake of formalization, let us call this morpheme {neg}. Remember that, technically speaking, it does not matter what is inside these brackets – just like with phonemes and the IPA. All we need is some sort of label that reminds us what this abstract unit means. Once this abstract unit, the morpheme {neg}, is used in a concrete environment, when it is realized, it may change its shape according to this environment. In front of a bilabial plosive like /p/ it becomes bilabial [ɪm], in front of the liquids /l/ and /r/ it turns into these liquids: [ɪl] and [ɪr], and so forth. This can be summarized as follows:

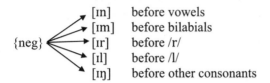

{neg}	[ɪn]	before vowels
	[ɪm]	before bilabials
	[ɪr]	before /r/
	[ɪl]	before /l/
	[ɪŋ]	before other consonants

Figure 3.1: Allomorphs of the negative prefix.

Note that the realizations of {neg} are rule-guided, i.e. they do not occur randomly, but rather follow a certain pattern, just like allophones. And they all belong to one single morpheme. Exactly the same can be seen with grammatical morphemes, i.e. morphemes which do not have any lexical meaning, but which tell us something about the grammatical function and form of the word they attach to. We usually talk about '3rd person -s' in English when we refer to the inflection of English verbs in the third person singular indicative active simple present, as in *sing – sings*. But when we look at it from the viewpoint of morphology, this is not entirely accurate. Apparently, only a few words actually show '3rd person -s' in their pronunciation, many others don't. What we really hear is *kick – kicks* [kɪks], *swims* [swɪmz], *kisses* [kɪsəz], *can, could, may, might, must, will, would, shall, should, is* and *has*. When we usually only talk about '3rd person -s' this has to do with the fact that -s is the most common representation in writing. However, as we have just seen, this is not true for spoken language. All of this can be captured very elegantly with the tools and concepts of morphology. We can now say that the underlying abstract morpheme is {3rd person singular indicative active simple present} – remember that this is only an abstract label, we could also use an abstract symbol like ॐ! – and say that all the forms just listed are allomorphs of this underlying, abstract morpheme. Note that some of these allomorphs are phonologically conditioned, while some others are grammatically conditioned and yet some others are lexically conditioned, i.e. their form is not predictable from any rules, but has to be learned by heart. Again, we can summarize our findings as in Figure 3.2 below. Note that this summary needs to be processed top-down, i.e. only if the first rules don't apply we need to check the next. Once a rule has been applied, we stop. In other words, we only need to check for the last sound of the stem if the word is not a modal verb, for example.

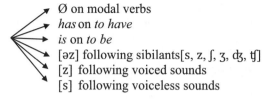

{3rd person singular indicative active simple present}

Ø on modal verbs
has on *to have*
is on *to be*
[əz] following sibilants[s, z, ʃ, ʒ, ʤ, ʧ]
[z] following voiced sounds
[s] following voiceless sounds

Figure 3.2: Allomorphs of 3rd person singular present suffix.

The last two examples have shown that the morphemes that we add to the stem can change their shape as allomorphs. But stems can change, too. We call this **stem allomorphy**. Consider the morpheme {electric}. This seems to be the root for a number of other, related words: *electrical, electrician, electricity, electrify* are some of them. In each of these cases, the root {electric} [ɪ'lɛktrɪk] changes its form: [ɪ'lɛktrɪkəl], [ɪlɛk'trɪʃən], [ɪlɛk'trɪsɪti], [ɪ'lɛktrɪfʌɪ]. This effect goes back to the morpheme that we attach to the root. Stem allomorphy is quite common in English. Other examples include *nation-national, fantasy-fantastic, atom-atomic, pronounce-pronunciation, divine-divinity*, and many more. Allomorphy of this kind can also be morphologically, i.e. grammatically conditioned. The plural of *wife* [waif] is not, as can be expected, *wifes [waifs] but rather *wives* [waivz], with a change in the root of the word. The same can be seen in *leaf-leaves* and *knife-knives, wolf-wolves, half-halves*. For historical reasons, the regular affixes do not lead to regular plural forms in present-day English, but rather to new, unpredictable forms with root allomorphy.

Another phenomenon that we find for historical reasons is **suppletion**. This is what we see with words like *good-better-best, bad-worse-worst, go-went-gone, be-am-are-is-was-were* and similarly irregular forms. From what we know about inflectional morphology, we would expect regular forms here, like *good-*gooder, bad-*badder, go-*goed-gone* etc. Or at least we could expect some more predictable irregular form, as in *cut-cut* or *sleep-slept*. But this is also not the case. Instead, we find words in the paradigms which clearly do not belong there – at least from a synchronic, present-day perspective. But there is a good explanation from language history. In Old English, before 1100 CE, we had two different words, <gōd> 'good' and <betera> 'better', which comes from <bōt> 'to remedy'. These were combined during the Middle English period, between 1100 and 1500 CE into one single paradigm and now belong to one single word as irregular forms. Similarly, *go* and *gone* both go back to Old English <gan> 'to go', while *went* stems from a different verb in Old English <wendan>, which also meant 'to go'. Again, these two paradigms were combined into one, the present-day *go-went-gone*.

In the following, we will first focus on grammatical morphology, i.e. free and bound grammatical morphemes, then on lexical morphology.

3.4 Grammatical morphology

3.4.1 Free grammatical morphemes

English as a mostly isolating/analytic language (on language typology, see below) is particularly rich in free grammatical morphemes. These are free, individual words that 'only' have a grammatical function. One preliminary list could look like this:

- **conjunctions** (*and, or, but,...*)
- **prepositions** (*on, in,* at,...)
- **articles** (*the, a*)
- **pronouns** (*he, which, that,...*)
- **negative particles** (*not*)
- **auxiliaries** (*to be, to have*)

This list is only an approximation, simply because there is a long and complicated debate about how many word classes there are and how to distinguish them. Some approaches claim there are only four, others say seven, yet some others talk about nine or even thirteen. It all depends on your perspective and how you argue your case. For example, you might want to claim that the group of pronouns should actually be divided into three or even four separate groups: personal pronouns, demonstrative pronouns, relative pronouns, which in turn may be differentiated from the invariable relativizer *that*.

In any case, the list of free grammatical items we have just developed contains only what we also call closed-class items. This means that it is very rare (but not completely unheard of) that new items are added to this group of words, in contrast to the free lexical items, as we will see below. With the latter it is very common to continually expand the vocabulary. So, while J.K. Rowling could easily invent and establish new words like *muggle* or *Quidditch*, she would probably find it harder to develop a new preposition or conjunction.

3.4.2 Bound grammatical morphemes: inflectional morphology

Apart from free grammatical morphemes, many languages also have **bound grammatical morphemes, so-called inflections**.

However, some languages have more of that than others. Typologically speaking, English belongs to the more isolating/analytic type of languages, which means that it shows grammatical functions (like subject or direct object) through word order and free grammatical morphemes rather than inflections. Latin, by contrast, is a more inflectional language, which means that word order is less important, but that inflectional morphology plays a crucial role here. This in turn means that Latin has a large number of bound grammatical (i.e. inflectional) morphemes – the long paradigms that students of Latin hate so much! – whereas English only has very few of these left. But then, Latin also has a relatively free word order, while in English the right word order is very important.

Present-day English only has eight or nine inflectional morphemes left. Practically all of these have some sort of standard, unmarked realization, which is given here in square brackets as a kind of shorthand form. Note, however, that all of these morphemes also show allomorphic variation as outlined above.

On the noun:
  - {plural} [s]
  - {possessive} [s] (perhaps, see below)

On the verb:
  - {past tense} [ed]
  - {past participle} [en]
  - {progressive} [ing]
  - {third person singular, indicative, active, simple present} [s]

On the adjective:
  - {comparative} [er]
  - {superlative} [est]
  - {adverb} [ly] (but only maybe, see below)

Two or three interesting issues need to be discussed here. First, the list shows very clearly that in English (as in many other languages!) inflectional morphemes only appear at the end of a word. We call these **suffixes**, in contrast to **prefixes**, which appear word initially. Second, there is an interesting functional difference between, e.g., {comparative} [er] and {third person singular, indicative, active, simple present} [s]. The former basically only has one single function, while the latter has seven different functions combined into one single morpheme. Third, the inclusion of the category 'adverb' is anything but clear. On the one hand, the [ly] suffix obviously changes the word class of its stem and this is something that inflectional morphemes usually do not do. It is precisely one important feature of inflectional morphemes that they only produce new word 'forms', but not new words. So, *sing* and *sings* are essentially one single word, one lexeme, albeit in two different grammatical forms. This is not quite the same for *quick* and *quickly*. However, the difference in meaning is not very prominent and fairly predictable (Brinton & Traugott 2005).

3.4.3 Somewhere in between: clitics

Consider the following phenomena *I am* – *I'm, they have* – *they've, do not* – *don't, we will* – *we'll*. The first members of these pairs (*am, have, not, will*) are not a big problem, these appear to be simple free grammatical morphemes. However, the second members (*'m, 've, n't* and *'ll*) are not that straightforward. Are these bound grammatical morphemes, inflections? Apparently not. When you compare them with {s} as in *she sings*, for example, you see that {s} is firmly attached to its host and does not have a free form. In contrast to that, *'m* as in *I'm* or *n't* as in *don't* do have related free forms. Similarly, in the previous section, we have listed {possessive} as an inflectional morpheme that modified the noun. However, this is also not completely true when you look at it more carefully. In *John's house* the 'apostrophe s' does what it should do, i.e. it attaches to the noun itself and tells us that John is the possessor of the house. But what about *the Queen of England's sofa?* Here, the 'apostrophe s' does not attach directly to the noun *Queen* itself, but rather to what we call the noun phrase, i.e. the noun *Queen* plus its modification *of England*. Inflections usually do not do that, they attach to their specific word classes. This leads us to believe that we need a new morphosyntactic category in order to capture these strange, new elements. We do not call these items 'words' or 'affixes', since they do not behave as such, but rather **clitics**, a word borrowed from Greek meaning "to depend or lean on". Orthographically, they can be represented by single letters, apostrophe forms, or even independent words. Clitics are somewhere in between free morphemes and affixes. We can distinguish between enclitics, which attach to the end of a word or phrase, and proclitics which attach to the beginning of words and phrases. Whereas affixes work on the word level, clitics operate on the phrase level (for syntactic phrases, see Chapter 4 on syntax). Morphologically and syntactically, clitics are more independent than inflectional morphemes, phonologically, however, they are dependent on their host. One such example in English would be the indefinite article: *a blue ball, an adventure story*. The article looks like an independent word, but is in fact phonologically weak and dependent on the following phrase. Note that in present-day English there are at least three allomorphs of the indefinite article: *a* [ə] and *an* [ən], depending on the following sound, and *a* [eɪ] as an emphatic, stressed form.

3.5 Lexical morphology, word formation

In the following sections, we will turn to lexical morphemes, i.e. morphemes that do not have grammatical function, but carry lexical, dictionary meaning. As with grammatical morphology, we will first look at free lexical morphemes and word formation processes and then turn to bound lexical morphemes, so-called derivational morphemes.

3.5.1 Free lexical morphemes, word formation

Free lexical morphemes are what people usually call lexical words, i.e. nouns, verbs, adjectives, and maybe adverbs. These are morphosyntactically independent elements that carry lexical, dictionary meaning. Moreover, these are also the open-class items, i.e. new nouns, verbs, adjectives (and adverbs) are very easy to create and establish. The American Dialect Society is the publisher of the journal *American Speech* which, for more than 60 years now, includes a regular collection of new words, entitled 'Among the New Words'. This is, of course, an invaluable source for anybody interested in word formation and semantics. New words, so-called **neologisms,** can be created in at least three ways:

1) There are words which are entirely invented and completely new, like *google, Quidditch, yahoo.*

2) Some words enter the language through language contact, for example *angst, fahrvergnügen, schnitzel, wunderkind, garage, wine, street, army, dine, beef, history, skirt, sky, burrito, adobe, guitar, marijuana, pizza, opera, piano, cookie, gin, punch, shampoo, bandanna, yoga, tea, chop suey, litchee, tsunami, karaoke,* and many more. You may now get the impression that there are hardly any 'English' words in the English language. And this is not entirely incorrect. Depending on how you count, you may find up to 70% of the English vocabulary to come from non-English sources. We will return to this question in Chapter 5 on meaning in language.

3) Many new words are created by using material from existing words and combining it in new ways. Examples include *Yogalates* "yoga + pilates", *mentee*

"sb. who is being mentored", *hardscape* "man-made features in nature", *abdominoplasty* "the surgical removal of excess flesh from the abdomen", *Iraqnophobia "the fear of Iraq"* and *neuticles* "testicular prosthetic implants for neutered pets". This is usually referred to as word formation and derivation.

3.5.2 Word formation

Word formation deals with the creation of new words out of existing material. At least several different processes can be recognized:

- compounding
- blending
- clipping
- back formation
- conversion
- acronyms & alphabetisms
- derivation

Compounding involves the combination of two or more free morphemes, as in *bookshelf* or *cross-trainer*. Note that, technically speaking, there is no upper limit for compounding lexemes into new words in English. Geoffrey Pullum, author on *language log*, for example, reports on what he terms one of "the most spectacular compound nouns": *Amy husband bribery plot landlord cleared*. The compound actually consists of the first five nouns (*Amy husband bribery plot landlord*) in this newspaper headline. The newspaper article deals with the trial of a pub landlord who was accused of being involved in a plot by accepting a bribe from the husband of Amy Winehouse, hence it was 'The Amy husband Bribery plot landlord' who was cleared (for a full discussion, see http://languagelog.ldc.upenn.edu/nll/?p=279).

In English, all free lexical morphemes can be combined, albeit with different degrees of productivity. Productivity refers to the frequency and likelihood with which new lexemes are built in a certain way. The more new words are formed with a certain pattern, the more productive is this pattern or process:

Table 3.1: Possible ways of compounding in English.

	Noun	Verb	Adjective
Noun	book cover	brain drain	skin-deep
Verb	sunshine	sleepwalk	letdown
Adjective	hot spring	broadcast	bitter-sweet

While noun-noun compounding is by far the most productive word formation process, i.e. used most often to create new lexemes, adjective-adjective and verb-verb combinations are rare, verb-adjective combinations practically non-existent.

In most compounds we are able to identify one element as the more important, central one (we call this the **head**), and the other as the less important one that gives additional information (we call this the **modifier**). So, in *book cover* we talk about a special kind of cover, not a special kind of book. *Book* only tells you what cover we are talking about. *Hot spring* has *spring* as its head, while *hot* as modifier tells you what kind of spring is meant. Note that the head also tells you what word class the compound belongs to: *skin-deep* has the adjective *deep* as head, and is therefore also an adjective. In English, the head of a compound usually is the second, right-hand element. So, ordering is important. *Birdcage* is a kind of cage, *cage-bird* is a kind of bird. There are some compounds, however, where we cannot identify one single head. These are called **coordinative compounds**. Examples include *bittersweet* and *actor-director*. Here, *bitter* does not modify *sweet,* it is equally important. Similarly, an *actor-director* does both, act and direct, and would probably refuse to say that he is a director who acts a little bit on the side, or vice versa. The same applies to **reduplicative compounds**, like *easy-peasy, boogie-woogie, hodge-podge, zigzag, mumbo-jumbo,* where for pragmatic purposes two somehow rhyming or phonologically corresponding elements are combined. However, none of the two elements can be identified as the central one, the head.

But not only free lexical morphemes can combine. Consider the following items: *drive-in, take-away, sleep-over, mother-in-law, undergraduate, intake, outreach.* As it seems, the combination of verb and prepositions or adverbs (in either order) also seems possible and even somewhat common. Note that many of these forms apparently stem from former free combinations. The unusual compound *mother-in-law* illustrates this quite nicely. Before the combination lexicalized, i.e. turned into a fixed lexical item, the three elements were independent just like *breakfast in bed* is today.

Compounds are particularly interesting because they can also illustrate the differences between morphology/lexicon and syntax/grammar – and show that this distinction does not always lead to clear results. On the contrary, there are some very fuzzy edges. Look at the two items *sweetheart* and *sweet taste*. One of them is one word, a compound, the other one an independent and free grammatical combination of two words which we call a noun phrase (see the section on Syntax). The most prototypical compounds are (i) spelled as one word, (ii) have one initial stress, and (iii) are not internally modifiable. All the criteria apply to *sweetheart* but not to *sweet taste*. The former is spelled as one word, the latter as two. *Sweetheart* is stressed on the first syllable, *sweet taste* is stressed on *taste*. You can't modify *sweetheart* internally (**sweet lovely heart*), but you can modify *sweet taste: sweet cherry taste*. Still, these three criteria unfortunately do not always work. *English teacher* as a compound (with stress on *English*) needs to be distinguished from *English teacher* as a noun phrase (with stress on *teacher*), despite the fact that both of them are spelled as two words. Similarly, *full stop* (as a word for the orthographic sign <.>) is a compound, but receives stress on the second syllable.

Semantically speaking, we can distinguish between several types of compounds. There are **endocentric compounds** where the meaning of the compound is predictable in some sense by looking at the parts. The meaning of the parts is usually in a 'kind of' relationship: *bookshelf* is a kind of shelf, *honeybee* is a kind of bee, *smalltalk* is a kind of talk. In contrast to this, **exocentric compounds** are not readily predictable in their meaning: *white-collar* is not a kind of collar, *sunset* is not a kind of set (or sun), a *skinhead* is not a kind of head. However, the latter examples nicely show that exocentric compounds often develop out of endocentric ones. At some point, *skinhead* used to refer to neo-nazi followers who shaved their head. The aspect of being bald, however, was lost over time and the term is now usually perceived as neo-nazi follower, which is something you could not predict without any knowledge of the development of the word. A special type which cannot really be classified as either exo- or endocentric are coordinative compounds like *secretary-treasurer, maidservant, bitter-sweet, freeze-dry* which we have just discussed. Here, both elements are equally important and neither of them can be identified as the head. *Bittersweet* is not just a kind of sweet, but equally a kind of bitter. A *secretary-treasurer* is someone who is both a kind of secretary and a kind of treasurer. So the question of endo- versus exocentric is more tricky in these cases.

Another interesting and productive word formation process is **blending**. Here, two or more independent morphemes are blended (like a cocktail) into one single form. Examples include *neuticles, celebutante, blog*. In *neuticles* the verb *to neuter* is blended with the noun *testicles,* in *celebutante* we find *celebrity* and *debutante, blog* comes from *web* and *log*. Perhaps blends are so popular (at the moment) for the simple reasons that they are very economical in the sense that a complex concept can be expressed not with two or more, but with one single, abbreviated word without loosing the origins completely, and maybe also because they can be very creative uses of language. In some blends, one of the bases remains intact (*newscast, email*), in others both bases are modified and shortened. While being a very productive process in general, the occurrence and mechanism of blending is still fairly unpredictable, i.e. we cannot tell beforehand what will be blended and what not, or what the blend will look like.

Clipping is a word formation process which is somewhat similar to blending. In clipping, some morphological material is simply clipped away from an existing word to make it shorter: *advertisement > ad, refrigerator > fridge, telephone > phone, omnibus > bus, influenza > flu, Lieutenant > Loo*. In blending, two forms are combined into one and you always begin with the first element of the first form and end with the last of the second form. In clipping you may have one or more items and you can take away from the beginning (*phone*), the end (*ad*), or both (*flu*).

In what we call **back-formation** we take an existing usually morphological complex word and make it morphologically more simple, by clipping away some affixes. Examples include *headhunter* > *to headhunt, editor* > *to edit, underachiever* > *to underachieve, television* > *to televise.* In contrast to clipping, where some more or less random material is taken away (usually phonologically motivated), back-formation is the deletion of what we identify as morphemes (such as {er}, {or}, and {ion} in the examples above). Back-formation is not always easy to attest and is usually not recognizable to native speakers without any linguistic training. What we need to do in order to diagnose a back-formation process is to look at the history of the word in question: which form is the first, historically speaking? According to the Oxford English Dictionary (OED), *editor* was first attested in 1649, *to edit* in 1791. With *use* and *user* it is the other way round: *to use* was first attested in 1300, *user* somewhat later, in 1400. This means that *editor* >*to edit* is back-formation (the reduction of morphologically complex forms), whereas *to use* > *user* is affixation (the creation of morphologically complex forms, see section 3.5.3 below).

Conversion (also referred to as zero derivation) is a word formation process by which words can change their word class without any visible or audible changes to their form. *Butter* used be a noun and was then turned into a verb *to butter.* Conversion can apply to:

verbs > nouns: *read, smile, go, cheat, laugh*
nouns > verbs: *eye, ski, panic, water, finger*

adjective > noun: *comic, daily, private, drunk, regular*
noun > adjective: *fun (He is such a fun person)*

adjective > verb: *blind, empty, free, narrow, slow*
verb > adjective: *entertaining, boring, stunning, amused, bored, stunned*

Verb adjective conversions are different from the other examples, simply because this is a much more productive, almost derivation-like process in which the {ing} suffix, originally a marker for progressive aspect, is used (as a gerund-participle) to convert verbs into nouns. Similarly, {ed} or {en} – the past participle form of a verb – can be used in verbal constructions (*She has given him the book*) or in the conversion of verbs to adjectives (*the broken window*). This is another area where grammar becomes complex and sometimes fuzzy. In

It was broken by John out of spite, broken clearly is a past participle form of a verb, in *It didn't seem to be broken,* it is a past-participle adjective, in *It was broken* we can't tell which of the two *broken* it actually is. It could be either a verb or an adjective.

While conversion, strictly speaking, means change of word class without any overt changes to the form, there are some minor conversion types where this does not strictly apply, but which nevertheless show obvious similarities to prototypical cases such as *(to) butter*. On the one hand, conversion may also involve a shift within the word class, i.e. changes in the morphosyntactic properties of the word in question. This is what we see in *beer* and *coffee,* for example. *Beer* and *coffee* used to be mass nouns, i.e. uncountable. Now, however, you can easily order *three beers* or *two coffees*. In other words, these items are still nouns, of course, but have become countable. The same can happen with verbs. *To smile* is an intransitive verb, i.e. it usually does not take any objects, in contrast to *to eat,* for example: *she smiled* versus *she ate two cookies*. Adele Goldberg in her work on constructions (see also Chapter 6) discovered an interesting use of 'smile' in the work of Douglas Adams: "She'd smiled herself an upgrade" (Douglas Adams 1996: 642, see also Goldberg 2006: 6). This is, of course, a perfectly comprehensible sentence, despite the fact that *to smile* is used here as a transitive verb with an object. Again, this can be regarded as word-class internal conversion. Another minor, less prototypical type of conversion can be seen in the change from the noun *object* to the verb *to object* (and, similarly, *torment, insult, permit, convict, compliment, estimate, belief/believe, house*). In all these cases, we see more or less small phonological (and sometimes also orthographic) differences that accompany the shift in word class. In *object, torment, insult, transfer* we only see a stress shift, in *permit* and *convict* we see a stress shift and vowel change, in *compliment* and *estimate* there is only a vowel shift, and in *belief/believe, house* there is a change in the word final consonant.

	Noun	**Verb**
object	/'ɒbdʒekt/	/ɒb'dʒekt/
torment	/'tɔːrment/	/tɔːr'ment/
insult	/'ɪnsʌlt/	/ɪn'sʌlt/
transfer	/'trænsfɜːr/	/træns'fɜːr/
permit	/'pɜːrmɪt/	/pər'mɪt/
convict	/'kɒnvɪkt/	/kən'vɪkt/
compliment	/'kɒmplɪmənt/	/'kɒmplɪment/
estimate	/'estɪmət/	/'estɪmeɪt/
belief/believe	/'bəliːf/	/'bəliːv/
house	/'haus/	/'hauz/

Conversion in all of its guises is particularly common and productive in English. One of the reasons for this lies in the morphosyntactic typology of English itself. As an analytic/isolating language, English has lost most of its inflectional morphology, which makes shifts back and forth between word classes very easy and convenient (in contrast to German, for example, where verbs are heavily inflected and even as infinitives are usually marked by an {en} suffix: *singen, tanzen, spielen*).

Initialisms, like acronyms and alphabetism, are a way of making words shorter. In acronyms like *ROFL* "rolling on the floor laughing" or *IKEA* "Ingvar Kamprad Elmtaryd Agunnaryd" (Swedish home furnishings retailer founder's initials and location), the initial letters of the words are taken and used to form a new which is then pronounced as a regular word. Some acronyms go back to proper names, such as *IKEA* and *NATO* "North Atlantic Treaty Organization", while some others abbreviate some more or less complex phrases like *AIDS* "Acquired Immune Deficiency Syndrome" or *TEFL* "teaching English as a foreign language". Some acronyms are fairly transparent, yet some others are so well-established that we do not recognize them as acronyms anymore: *laser* "lightwave amplification by stimulated emission of radiation", or *radar* "radio detecting and ranging". In contrast, the letters in alphabetisms are pronounced individually, and not as a regular word: *USB* "universal serial bus", *VIP* "very important person", *DNA* "deoxyribonucleic acid", *DVD* "digital versatile disc", *AKA* "also known as", e.g. "exempli gratia", *i.e.* "id est". Alphabetisms are extremely productive and are used very often in professional contexts, such as technology, science, business administration, and in digital discourse – though one might add that the frequency of rather opaque alphabetisms such as *YMMV* "your mileage may vary" in online discourse is usually overrated (see Bergs 2009).

3.5.3 Bound lexical morphemes, derivation

This final section is concerned with bound lexical morphemes, i.e. morphemes which carry some sort of lexical meaning (in contrast to inflections!), but which nevertheless cannot stand alone and need a host to attach to. Some examples have already been mentioned: {entertain}+{-ment} or {dis-}+{illusion}. **Affixes that attach to the beginning of a word are categorized as prefixes, those that are attached to the end of a word are called suffixes**. In some languages we also find so-called infixes, i.e. morphemes which are inserted in the middle of a word. But this process is rather rare in English and is mostly restricted to some expletive inserts like {bloody}, {bleeding}, or {fucking}. Some examples of affixes are:

Affix Types

Prefix	Infix	Suffix
un-cover	abso-**bloody**-lutely	nation-**al**
pre-view	un-**fucking**-believable	king-**dom**
re-read	extracu-**bleeding**-ricular	wet-**ness**
de-frost	a-**whole**-nother	scarc-**ity**

With derivation we enter into a vast and complex domain, simply because it touches upon many different linguistic levels, ranging from phonology to syntax and even pragmatics. First of all we need to recognize that derivational affixes may stack, i.e. we can apply several derivational processes to a base. One of the most famous textbook examples stacks one prefix and three affixes onto a single base: *establish > establishment > establishmentarian > disestablishmentarian > disestablishmentarianism*. Note, however, that there appear to be complex factors which determine both the possibility of affixation in general (not all affixes go with all bases), and of the ordering of affixes in particular. When certain combinations are ruled out this is usually referred to as 'blocking'. Some factors in blocking that need to be considered are:

• the word class of the base: {ity} only attaches to adjectives, {re} usually occurs with verbs, hence {complex} > {complexity} but {read} > *{readity}, {read} > {re-read} but {complex} > *{re-complex}.
• the etymology of the base: Germanic bases tend to go with Germanic suffixes, as in {king}+{dom}, but not *{king}+{ness}, Romance bases tend to go with Romance suffixes, as in {encourage}+{ment}, but not *{encourage}+{ness}.
• the etymology of the suffix(es): Germanic suffixes tend to be further away from the root than Romance suffixes. Hence we find {nerv}+{ous}+{ness} with Germanic {ness} following Romance {ous}, but not *{care}+{ful}+{ity}, with Romance {ity} following Germanic {ful}.
• the semantics of the base and its affix: we usually do not find combinations which are morphologically possible if there already is an existing word that has the same meaning. So it is generally claimed that {steal}+{er} does not exist because of the existing word {thief}. Note that this is a very problematic way of arguing, since equivalence in meaning is hard to establish objectively. And in the case of *stealer* we find that, according to the OED, this word was actually in use until the late nineteenth century and can still be found occasionally in present-day English.

So far, we have mostly looked at the classification of affixes into free and bound, grammatical and lexical. But bases also pose some interesting questions. Look at the following data set:

durability	author
duration	tutor
endure	professor
dureless	administrator
durable	inventor
dureful	debitor
durant	acto

Some identifiable invariant elements become visible here. On the one hand, there is -*dur(e)*- which appears in a number of combinations and whose meaning is something like "long time". On the other hand, we find a clearly identifiable suffix {or} (in the sense of 'somebody doing something') in the right hand data set. Both these diagnoses in themselves are not a problem, but their consequences are very interesting. If we agree that -*dur(e)*- is a morpheme and the base for all these words, this would mean that this is a bound base which does not have any free, independent form. If we agree that {or} is a regular suffix, then we must ask what sort of bases {auth-} and {tut-} are. Again, the two do not have any free, independent form, but only appear in combinations. English has a number of these bound bases (or bound lexical morphemes). Most of these come from Latin or Greek, where they used to be free lexemes (cf. *augere* "to increase, to promote" and *durare* "to harden" and *durus* "hard"). Interestingly, *to dure* used to be an English word, but is now considered archaic and dialectal. Some affixes allow combinations with bound bases, e.g., {dis-}, {pre-}, {-or}, {-ous}, others require free bases, e.g. {un-}, {-ful}, {-ness}, {-ly}.

A similar problem occurs with the so-called **cranberry morphemes**. When you look at *cranberry, raspberry, strawberry, blackberry* etc. it becomes obvious that {berry} is a morpheme and a regular base (head), which is modified by the preceding element in a compound like fashion. However, *cran*- does not have any identifiable meaning, function, or special etymology. It is related to *crane*, but this is not reflected in any other form. In fact, it only appears in one single word: *cranberry*. Nevertheless, it must have some sort of meaning as it helps to distinguish the different types of berries and we somehow need to deal with it structurally as we recognize {berry} as a morpheme. Elements like {cran} are referred to as unique or cranberry morphemes. The phenomenon is extremely rare in English. *Lukewarm* may be another example, but *luke* used to be very mildly productive in Middle and Early Modern English: *luke hot, luke hearted, lukely, lukeness.*

This concludes our section on morphology, i.e. word structure and word formation. What most students find difficult and frustrating in morphology is the mass of terminology that it brings, especially since some of it comes from Greek or Latin (unfortunately, the same will happen again in the section on Semantics). However, morphology is also one of the most popular domains since it is very close to our daily language use and our intuitions. Words and their structure are something that most speakers seem to have a very good intuition about: many actually enjoy playing around with words, even though they haven't heard anything about morphology! One of the best examples probably comes from the 1990s US sitcom Seinfeld which brought us a huge number of interesting new words: *sidler, spongeworthy, regifter, shusher, shushee,* and *unshushables, breaker-upper, close-talker, pimple popper,* to name but a few.

3.6 Exercises

1. What are the different allomorphs of the past tense morpheme? On what does the usage of the allomorphs depend?

2. Find the plural of the following nouns, indicate what the plural morpheme is:

Noun	Plural	Plural Morpheme
apple	apples	suffix -s
sheep		
tooth		
child		
louse		
peach		
man		

3. Divide the following word into morphemes:
   Example: unpalatable   {un} {palate} {able}

   impossible, degenerate, cats, characterizes, played, illegalize, mistreatment

4. Identify all free and bound morphemes in the following example. Which of these are lexical and which are grammatical morphemes?

   Few things are harder to put up with than the annoyance of a good example.
                                   (Pudd'nhead Wilson's Calendar, Twain 1894)

5. Identify all inflectional morphemes and all derivational morphemes in this example:

   While the girls were singing the boys sat down unhappy and watched them enviously.

6. Give three examples for each of the following word formation process:

   Clipping:
   Blending:
   Conversion:
   Acronyms:

7. Describe the morpheme {en} in *oxen* and *wooden*. What is the difference?

8. Which word formation process led to the formation of *downright*? Discuss the word classes are involved. There may be more than one answer.

4 Syntax

In the last sections on phonology and morphology, we have seen that the smallest building blocks of language, phonemes, are combined into the smallest meaningful units, morphemes, which in turn can be combined into words. When we move one level further up now, we see that words can of course be combined into phrases, clauses, sentences. This level of language is dealt with in syntax.

4.1 What is syntax? What is grammar?

Sometimes, there is some terminological confusion regarding the terms syntax and grammar. Syntax can be defined, quite simply, as **the study of sentence structure**. When it also looks at the relationship of (inflectional) morphology and syntactic patterns, this is sometimes referred to as **morphosyntax**. Grammar is a much more complex term. Quirk et al. (1985: 12-15) list at least four different readings:

1) Grammar as syntax and inflection
Here, the term roughly grafts onto what other frameworks would call morphosyntax. Grammar in this sense simply looks at everything that has to do with syntax and morphology. Quirk et al. (1985: 12) also point out that grammar in this sense leads to the common misconception that some languages have more or better grammar than others. Latin, for example, is usually considered to be a language with a lot of grammar, English as a language with hardly any. This fairly narrow view of grammar as complex inflectional morphology is of course untenable in the light of modern linguistic theory, especially when this view is paired with the idea that complex grammar equals better languages. It is correct to say, though, that English has little inflectional morphology in contrast to Latin.

2) Grammar as rules
This sense is somehow related to the one just discussed. Here, grammar equals language rules of all kinds. In this case, it is not just syntax or the morphology that are at issue, but rather the language and its perception from within and outside the individual speech community. Some languages are perceived as having more rules, as being more complex, difficult and restrictive in their use than others. English, for example, is usually seen as very tolerant and lenient towards linguistic variation and non-conforming behavior (which, of course, might have to do with its large number of speakers, combined with the historical

development and colonial expansion of the language). All this might be reflected in the fact that English does not have a Language Academy or an Academy Grammar, such as French with its Académie Française. French is often regarded as very complex and strict in terms of rules and norms. German seems to be somewhere in between, as it does not have an Academy, but the Duden still holds a very strong position with regard to the codification of grammar and vocabulary.

3) Grammar as codification
Grammar is also the term that we use for the books, descriptions and analyses that deal with grammar. So, people say things like *Have you seen my modern French grammar?*. Similarly, theoretical approaches are characterized as grammars: in linguistics we find generative grammar, head-driven phrase structure grammar, construction grammar, lexical-functional grammar, etc. Here the term refers to particular theoretical approaches and viewpoints regarding not only syntax, but often the linguistic system as a whole.

4) Grammar as prescriptive rules
Within a language speakers may sometimes refer to something as 'good grammar' or 'bad grammar'. Using multiple negation, as in *I haven't done nothing!* is usually seen as 'bad grammar', and some people claim this should be avoided. Sometimes this understanding of the term grammar even extends to spelling and pronunciation.

5) Grammar as language
In some theoretical frameworks, e.g. generative grammar as developed by Noam Chomsky, grammar is treated as a short hand form which is more or less synonymous with 'linguistic system'. Syntax is treated as the fundamental core component of the linguistic system, and thus a careful and comprehensive analysis of the syntax of a given language equals an analysis of its grammar, and, ultimately, its system as a whole.

While it is important to be aware of these different understandings of the term grammar and their respective implications, in the following we will more or less work within the first definition, i.e. grammar means morphosyntax, and this will be what the present chapter is about.

4.2 Syntactic frameworks

While all language levels are approached from sometimes fundamentally different viewpoints, there are few domains where the variety of theoretical approaches is as visible as in syntax. Some of the current frameworks that you might discover when you go to the library or just browse through the web include:

- Chomsky-style Generativism, including Extended Standard Theory, Principles and Parameters, Government & Binding, and Minimalism (see Radford 2004)
- Head-Driven Phrase Structure Grammar (Pollard & Sag 1994)
- Lexical-Functional Grammar (Bresnan 2001)
- Word Grammar (Hudson 2007)
- Construction Grammar (Goldberg 1995)

These approaches share many viewpoints and ideas, but they sometimes also differ radically from each other (for a brief and insightful outline and comparison, see Kreyer 2010, Sells 1985, Moravcik 2006a/b). Both **Chomskian Generativism** and **Construction Grammar**, for example, claim to be 'generativist' in the sense that they 'generate' an infinite number of sentences out of a very finite and small inventory of rules or patterns. However, we have numerous concepts in Chomskian Generativism, such as 'deep structure' versus 'surface structure' or 'movement' and 'derivation', which are not shared by Construction Grammar. And the same applies, of course, the other way around.

For many students, this is a difficult and frustrating experience. And one can indeed be tempted to think that there must be one viewpoint which is right, while the others are wrong. Unfortunately, in the arts and humanities, this is rarely the case. Whereas most of the natural sciences see their object of study as fixed and given, many disciplines in the arts and humanities see their object of study as being dynamic and in need of construction in academic discourse. In other words, we first need to agree upon what we regard as the material and the problem we are interested in. Our perceptions can differ quite a bit here. We have seen this in our discussion of word classes in Chapter 3 (cf. Section 4.6 below). There is no natural class of adverbs in this world, independent of us as researchers. We as researchers identify and define this class according to some principles and ideas that we develop. This is different in biology, in physics, or in chemistry. A given chemical substance is there, a particular kind of bird exists, and the apple falls downwards, no matter whether we as researchers take notice, or even exist. So the object of study in the arts and humanities is usually not independent of the researchers, in the natural sciences it is. Moreover, we can offer different explanations for a given problem or question, and these in turn are often influenced by the premises and basic assumptions that we make. So if I posit that there is a hidden, underlying deep structure, I can use this concept in my explanations. But I may also work in a different framework and, for some good reason, not share this basic assumption of an underlying deep structure.

Neither does this invalidate the idea of deep structure as such nor does this make my approach less valid.

Essentially, there seem to be at least two or three criteria for evaluating theories in the arts and humanities: **plausibility** (i.e. consistency in argumentation), **falsifiability** (a good theory needs to be falsifiable), and **explanatory scope** (a good theory has a certain reach). Needless to say, all of the above mentioned syntactic frameworks pass these three tests. Since it is nearly impossible (and unnecessary) to familiarize yourself with the details of all of these frameworks, we will concentrate in the following on some of the major aspects of syntactic theory and some phenomena of English syntax. We will try to keep this as theory neutral as possible. You should be aware, though, that there are many different approaches to syntax available, and that all of them have something interesting and special to offer.

4.3 Spoken language, written language

One of the founding fathers of structuralism and modern linguistics, Ferdinand de Saussure, demanded that linguistics should primarily investigate spoken language, as this is the more natural, direct form of speech which gives us better access to the actual linguistic competence, and hence also the linguistic system, of speakers. In syntax, this leads to some very interesting theoretical and practical problems. One of the basic notions in syntax is that of the **sentence** as the **possibly largest structural unit of the linguistic system**. In terms of grammar, sentences are not dependent on any other grammatical element; they are not part of any other grammatical constituent (in contrast to phonemes and morphemes, for example). Most speakers usually think that sentences minimally consist of a subject and a verb. They begin with a capital letter and end with a punctuation mark. In spoken language, they usually show one full intonation contour and they are separated from other sentences by certain pauses. Unfortunately, all of this only works in theory. Recent research has shown that there may be units in the linguistic system (the grammar) which are actually larger than the sentence: **discourse chunks, phrases, texts**. The structure and well-formedness of actual sentences may depend on these larger units (see Esser 2009), but we need more research into that. Another issue is that spoken language often does not show the kind of sentences we would like to see as theoretical syntacticians. Example (1) below comes from actual spoken language. Obviously, spoken language does not have any capital letters or punctuation marks, so these were deliberately removed from the sample.

(1) it's a diploma so you how much could get that yeah as well i'll give you
    twenty for it how much you give me for it thirty mm ill go hundred yeah but

you got ta remember you could buy it for fifty you got ta remember you can
buy them for fifty if you land on it that's true yeah so shel can sell it for a lot
more than that mm cos if you remember mike used to go to bloody stupid
yeah but he he he well he five hundred didn't he he probably thought he
was it because he was the new salesman salesman director and I used to take
the piss out of him and we'd turn round and say well keep it what have got
go up to i'll go to hundred go on then i don't thi i didn't buy any property
either did I aye excuse me i'm so that means what do i need now then
[BNC, KCU, Conversation, punctuation and capitalization removed]

As we can see in example (1), there are false starts, interruptions, repetitions,
incomplete sentences, sentences loosely embedded in other sentences, and so
much more which we would consider 'bad grammar' or 'unacceptable' in written
discourse. This means that when we look at what speakers actually do in spoken
language, the traditional notion of 'sentence' is somewhat problematic. But does
this mean that there are no traditional sentences in language? Obviously not,
since the sentences as such can be found in written language – and written
language is one form of actual language that we need to deal with. Second,
while spoken language is sometimes not organized in traditional sentences, a
whole lot of it is. Recent studies (cf. Miller 2006: 679) suggest that about 90%
of the utterances in casual, non-academic conversation follow the usual syntactic
patterns of English. And one also can assume that utterances such as (1) above
are actually based on some underlying patterns which give some basic form to
them. If there were absolutely no basic underlying patterns (such as sentences)
we could expect a much greater bandwidth of variability. However, this is not
the case. Even in 'non-sentential' spoken language there is some underlying
basic order which gives some shape to the linguistic product. You cannot simply
jumble the words in (1) and still arrive at an equally acceptable utterance.

What does this mean for our study of syntax? One the one hand, this means
that we can look at 'ideal' sentences (as we can find them in written language,
for example) and investigate their structure as the basis for what we often find in
spoken language. On the other hand, we also need to be aware of the fact that
the syntax of actual spoken language may be very different from what we
discover in our study of ideal sentences. This, of course, also needs to be
considered and investigated.

4.4 Constituency

Syntax looks at **what is happening between the word level and the sentence
level**, and one of the fundamental questions is what kind of systematic units, if
any, we can find between these two levels. Consider the following example:

(2) i remember when certain critics were objecting about that movie Pocahontas did you see that? that it wasn't historically accurate, and Mel Gibson said for God's sake there's a raccoon in it that talks [MICASE, LES300SU103]

At least two things become apparent here. First, this example comes from spoken language, a university lecture on American literature. There is more than one grammatical, ideal sentence here. Between what seems to be a complex, ideal sentence, *i remember when certain critics were objecting about that movie Pocahontas [...] that it wasn't historically accurate, and Mel Gibson said for God's sake there's a raccoon in it that talks,* we find another grammatical, ideal sentence inserted, the question *did you see that?* The second thing that we might notice is the fact that certain units in this utterance somehow 'belong together'. Most people would probably agree that *certain critics* and *that movie Pocahontas,* for example, would go together, and so would *about that movie Pocahontas* and *that talks.* These sub-sentential units are called **phrases** and **clauses**, and they are of central interest. There are a number of tests that help us to find out if there are any other units between the word level and the sentence. These tests involve:

- substitution
- movement
- questions

In the **substitution test**, we try to substitute complex elements by simpler ones. So, for example, *certain critics* may be successfully substituted by *they* and *that movie Pocahontas* can be substituted by *it.* For clarity's sake, let us fully explore this option on the basis of an invented sentence:

The small children	played football	with a blue rubber ball.
The small children	played football	with a blue rubber ball.
They	played it	with it.

The resulting sentence certainly does not sound very good or elegant, but grammatically it is fully acceptable. This is not the case when we try to substitute other elements:

The small children	played football	with a blue rubber ball.
*The small children	played football	with a it.
*The small they	played football	with a blue rubber ball.
*They small children	played it	a blue rubber ball.

So after the substitution test we can identify *the small children, football* and *a blue rubber ball* as possible candidates for higher level units.

Let us try the **movement test** next. In the movement test you try to re-organize the sentence into a different order while using as many of the same words as possible. Note that sometimes you have to add a few (grammatical) elements in order to arrive at a grammatical sentence:

The small children played football with a blue rubber ball.
With a rubber ball, the small children played football.
Football was played by the small children with a blue rubber ball.
What the children did was play football with a blue rubber ball.
Play football with a blue rubber ball is what the small children did.

Many movements, in contrast, are not possible:

*The blue rubber ball was played football with by the small children.
*Play football the blue rubber the small children with ball.

And so, again, a number of candidates emerge. Note, however, that some of them are new: *with a rubber ball, the small children, play football, play football with a blue rubber ball.*

In the **question test** we simply ask for individual elements or constituents:

Who played football with a blue rubber ball?
                                        The small children.

What did the small children play football with?
                                        A blue rubber ball.

What did the small children do?
                                        Play football with a blue rubber ball.

What did the small children play with a blue rubber ball?
                                        Football.

What did the small children do with a blue rubber ball?
                                        Play football.

Note that we cannot ask for other elements in the sentence without introducing new concepts such as color into the question (e.g. *What color did the rubber ball have?*).

So eventually, we can identify a number of elements that surface in all three tests as somehow belonging together: *the small children, football, play football, play football with a blue rubber ball, with a blue rubber ball, a blue rubber ball.*

These phrases form the units between the individual words and the sentence level. Note that the phrases we have just identified do not all look the same: *the small children, play football, with a blue rubber ball* somehow seem to belong to different types of phrases. *The small children* is classified as a noun phrase (NP), *play football* as a verb phrase (VP) and *with a blue rubber ball* as a prepositional phrase (PP). There are at least two more types of phrases: adjective phrases (AP) as in *a very tall building* and adverb phrases (AdvP), e.g., *very quickly*. That we can distinguish between different phrase types has to do with the fact that in syntactic phrases, just like in morphology (see Chapter 3), we also need to distinguish between **heads and modifiers**. Heads are the most important, central elements and determine the morphosyntactic behavior of the element in question. They also give the name to the phrase. So, noun phrases are headed by nouns, verb phrases by verbs, prepositional phrases by prepositions, and so on. In the latter case we can argue that the preposition determines the morphosyntactic form (case marking) on its modifier, e.g., we can only say *to them*, not *to they*. Similarly, the verb in the VP determines the number and types of modifiers (sometimes also called complements) that it takes: *play* takes one simple NP (as direct object) *play football, sleep* does not need any complement, *put* needs an NP and a PP *put the book on the table* or an NP and an AdvP *put him there*. Note that in the case of noun phrases there is an ongoing debate about whether the noun or maybe the determiner (article, demonstrative, quantifier, etc.) is the central morphosyntactic element. The latter assumption is called the Determiner Phrase (DP) Hypothesis (Abney 1987). One of the main arguments here is that the determiner apparently selects its noun phrase complement and that by assuming D(eterminer) to be head of a DP we also have so-called functional projections in the DP/NP domain, not only in the Verb Phrase. Note that when there is only a pronoun, this fills the determiner slot. Some DPs may also have an empty D-position, e.g. some plurals like *dogs* in *Dogs bark* (for a much more extensive treatment, see Coene & D'Hulst 2003; Alexiadou et al. 2007).

Phrases come in various shapes and sizes. They can be very small and can consist only of their head, as in *Dogs scare me*, where *dogs* and *me* are both full NPs, or *Susan talks* where *talks* is the entire VP. On the other hand, they can also be very big, with pre- and postmodifiers as in *The tall man with blond hair who forgot his suitcase at the airport two months ago was arrested* where *the very tall man with blond hair who forgot his suitcase at the airport two months ago* is indeed one single noun phrase, headed by *man*. *Very tall* is a premodifier, the prepositional phrase *with blond hair* and the relative clause *who...ago* are postmodifiers. The whole phrase can easily be substituted by a pronoun: *he was arrested*. Moreover, this very large phrase shows that phrases can be nested, i.e. included in each other. Within the big NP *the very tall man with blond hair who forgot his suitcase at the airport two months ago* we can identify at least two adjective phrases (*very tall, blond*), two prepositional phrases (*with blond hair, at the airport*), one verb phrase (*forgot...ago*), and four NPs (*blond hair, his suitcase, the airport, two months ago*). This complex nesting can be represented in different ways, e.g., through bracketing, as illustrated in the following example. The small subscript labels identify the phrase type. Note that the following analysis is already somewhat simplified and that some more phrases could be identified.

[the [[[very tall]_{AP} man]_{NP} [with [blond hair]_{NP}]_{PP} [who [forgot [his suitcase]_{NP} [at [the airport]_{NP}]_{PP} [two months ago]_{NP}]_{VP}]_{RC}]_{NP}

Obviously, this bracketing is not the most elegant and readable way of describing or presenting the different phrases and their relationships. Another popular way of doing this is by developing a so-called **syntactic tree**, such as the following.

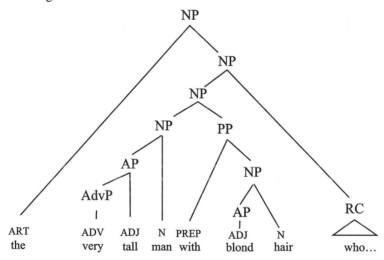

Figure 4.1: Syntactic tree "the very tall man with blond hair ...".

This tree essentially gives the same information as the bracketing above. Some people find this more readable, especially with regard to which phrase immediately contains which other phrase(s). Eventually, however, both representations contain the same information. What is important at this point is to remember that the tree diagram itself does not constitute any theory or any theoretical aspects; it is merely one way of representing what certain syntactic theories claim about the structure of sentences.

Before we continue with other issues in syntactic theory, two more points regarding constituency and syntactic theory need to be addressed, not in the least because the tree diagram above shows these two related problems very clearly. First, the tree gives a hierarchical ordering and there are only binary branches in the tree, i.e. every node has two daughter nodes. This helps a great deal in illustrating which parts of the sentence have a closer relationship than others. If all constituents were presented on the same level, we might miss the chance of showing their complex dependencies. Second, we have introduced a number of intermediate NPs such as *very tall man* and *very tall man with blond hair*, which are not immediately recognizable as such: they cannot be moved, they cannot be questioned. And yet, it seems desirable to be able to say that *very tall man* is some kind of core which is modified by *with blond hair* which in turn is modified by the relative clause, etc. This is comparable to the Russian doll principle, where inside the doll you find yet another doll, and yet another one, and so on. Since we do not want to assign the same label to the intermediate levels that we assign to the phrase as a whole, we need a new category. Many syntactic theories have opted for so-called **bar-level categories** and have introduced labels such as **N-Bar** and **V-Bar** in order to be able to identify the intermediate level without confusing it with the highest phrase level as such, but this will not concern us in any more detail here. A more detailed exposition on formal syntactic theory is offered in Radford (2004), Moravcik (2006) and Kreyer (2010).

One very last issue needs to be addressed here before we can go on. Through both bracketing and tree diagrams we can easily show that constituency is not just some fancy question of representation, but that it also plays an important role in our interpretation. There is a fundamental difference between [small [car dealer]] and [[small car] dealer]. In the former, where *car* and *dealer* form a unit modified by *small*, it is the *car dealer* who is *small*, in the latter case, where *small* and *car* form a unit that modifies *dealer*, this is a *car dealer* of any size who deals with *small cars*. This difference in interpretation can easily be explained when you consider phrasal constituency, and not just simple words.

4.5 Form and function

One of the most fundamental distinctions in linguistics is that between form and function. As we have just seen, we can establish a number of **different forms (word classes, phrase types, clauses, sentence types)** in English. However, these need to be separated from what functions we have in language. **A function is what you can do with a given form**. So, for example, knife, fork and spoon are forms, their functions are cutting, picking up solid food and picking up more liquid food, respectively. Note that some of these three forms can be used in more than one function (you also pick up solid food with a spoon), while other forms have clear restrictions on their possible functions (you can't eat soup with a knife or cut your bread with a spoon). The same principle applies to language. One such function, for example, is 'subject'. The subject of a given sentence can be defined as the argument about which something is predicated. Very often, but not always, it is 'the doer' of some action. Now look at the following sentences:

(3)   Bianca ate all the cheesecake.
(4)   A girl called Bianca ate all the cheesecake.
(5)   That Bianca ate all the cheesecake is a pity.
(6)   Eating cheesecake can be fun.
(7)   There is/are five more pieces of cheesecake in the fridge.

Can you identify the subject in these four sentences? In (3) it is fairly obvious: *Bianca*. In (4) things become slightly more difficult. Is it still just *Bianca*? In some practical sense it is of course, since *Bianca* is the person who actually ate the cheesecake. But grammatically, it must be something else. Look at sentence (4a) and (4b) in contrast:

(4a) A girl called Bianca is eating all the cheesecake!
(4b) Two girls called Bianca are/*is eating all the cheesecake!

The scenario in (4b) may sound weird, but the sentence is, technically speaking, grammatical – as long as the verb *to be* is in the plural. The option *is* needs to be marked with an asterisk, which means that this version is not acceptable in standard varieties of English. This seems to suggest that the grammatical subject must be more than just *Bianca*. In fact, it seems to include everything preceding the verb: *A girl called Bianca* in (4)/(4a), and *two girls called Bianca* in (4b). Why can't we say that *girls* or *two girls* are the subject? These two items are in the plural and we could explain the plural verb form that way. But if we say that only *(two) girls* is the subject we cannot say which two girls – namely those called *Bianca*. But this is what the sentence actually says, it specifies the two girls that ate the cheesecake. How about sentence (5) above? Again, it makes no sense to assume that *Bianca* is the subject here, not even the practical subject, as this would render the main (matrix) sentence as *Bianca is a pity*. Rather, it is the fact that Bianca ate the cheesecake that is the subject, and the rest of the sentence predicates something about this particular fact. Unfortunately, the word *fact* does not appear in (5). Instead, what we have is the (big) clause *That Bianca ate all the cheesecake*. This clause, then, must be regarded as the grammatical subject. This is supported by the fact that no matter what we do inside the clause, the verb of the matrix sentence remains in the singular. Compare (5a) and (5b):

(5a) That Bianca ate all the cheesecake is a great pity.
(5b) That twenty girls called Bianca ate all the cheesecake is/*are a great pity.

Note, however, that even in (5) we can interpret *Bianca* as a subject – namely the subject of the embedded clause *Bianca ate all the cheesecake*. This clause shows everything we need: predication and two arguments, one of which is *Bianca* as the subject and *all the cheesecake* as the object. However, this clause is embedded inside the matrix clause which functions independently.

Look at sentence (6) now. Here, the element preceding the verb, and the argument that we say something about, is not very large, in fact, it is very small. But it is not a very good noun-like argument either. In terms of morphological form, it is the present participle (or gerund) of a verb (marked clearly with an {ing} suffix) used as a noun. Finally, in (7) the subject function is fulfilled by a pronoun-like dummy element *there*, just like in *it might rain tomorrow,* where the pronoun *it* has a similar dummy function. You might want to argue that this is an inverted sentence and that the subject actually follows the verb: *Five more pieces of cheesecake are (there) in the fridge.* This could indeed be the case, but then it would be hard to explain why many varieties allow for *there is*, with a singular verb form, even when the following NP signifies plural entities (as in 7). So we can also assume that *there* is the semantically empty, dummy subject here. The existence of these dummy subjects has to do with the fact that in English we need something to fill the subject slot. In languages like Italian overt subjects are not always required, as, for instance in *Ti amo* (literally: "love you"). This is, of course, not permitted in English.

In sum, we can say that the syntactic function of 'subject' can obviously be fulfilled by a number of different forms: proper nouns (names), bigger elements like noun phrases, clauses, even nominalized verbs and dummy pronouns. Alternatively, consider the noun phrases as one particular form in language. What kind of functions can this form fulfill? What can we do with it? Noun phrases in English can be used in subject and object function and as complements. **Complements** are syntactic elements that are neither subject nor object, i.e. the verb does not really predicate anything about them and still they are needed to complete the sentence or phrase; they are required for a full grammatical utterance. We can distinguish between three types of complements:

- adverbial complements
- subject complements
- object complements

Adverbial complements usually appear in complex transitive constructions. These have one regular object plus some prepositional phrase which does not really qualify as an object of any kind: *put the book on the table; donate money* *to charity. The book* and *money* in this case are easily identifiable as the direct objects (in German they would have accusative case marking). But what is *on the table* and *to charity*? They do not behave as NPs, which, superficially, look very similar: *give the boy some money.* Here, we have an alternative passive construction: *some money was given to the boy.* This option is not available for the prepositional phrases *on the table* and *to charity*: *?*on the table was put the book;* *?*to charity money was donated* (these two are only acceptable as highly marked structures in very special contexts). This means that the two constructions *donate money to charity* and *give the boy some money* need to be treated as different constructions. Hence, *give the boy some money* is a regular ditransitive construction with a direct and an indirect object, while *donate money to charity* should be analyzed as Verb-Direct Object-Adverbial Complement.

Subject complements are elements that occur with so-called **copular verbs** like *to be, to seem, to appear.* Compare the following two sentences:

(8) Peter read a good book on flyfishing.
(9) Peter is a Wall Street agent.

In (8) we find a regular sentence with subject-verb-object ordering. *Peter* is the subject, *a good book on flyfishing* is the object. The two are separate entities and exist independently of each other. In (9), however, we find a sentence with subject-verb-'subject complement' order. *Peter* is again the subject, but the noun phrase following the verb is not the same kind of thing as the object noun phrase in (8). *A Wall Street agent* tells you something very crucial about the subject, *Peter*. The two basically refer to the same thing, they are **co-referential**. So, in a way they are not two separate entities, but in a way one and the same thing. Which is why *a Wall Street agent* would not be called an object, but rather a subject complement. The verb *is* in example (9) is also very special. We call this a copular verb as it links the subject and its complement. *To seem* and *to appear* can do the same thing. Note that *to be* not only appears not as a copular (full) verb but also as an auxiliary, as in (10).

(10) Andrew is sleeping on the floor.

Here, *is* does not have any independent meaning apart from its grammatical function in the construction of a present progressive form *is sleeping.* As an auxiliary, *to be* only has a helping function and cannot stand alone. As a copula it functions more or less like any regular full verb, i.e. it can stand alone.

Essentially the same can be seen in **object complements** as in example (11):

(11) She considered Edna a fool.

In example (11), *She* is the regular subject, *Edna* the object – but how do we categorize *a fool?* Again this is not like a regular ditransitive sentence with direct and indirect object, as in (12).

(12) William gave them $299.

In (12), *William* is the subject, *them* is the indirect object (the recipient or benefactor of the action) and *$299* is the direct object (the directly affected, i.e. transferred entity). In inflecting languages like German, the indirect object is often signaled by a dative marker, the direct object by an accusative marker. The two objects clearly are separate entities. In (11) above this is different. *Edna* and *a fool* are co-referential, i.e. *a fool* characterizes and specifies *Edna*. This is what we call an object complement. In German, object complements are usually also marked by accusative morphology: *Friedrich nannte ihn einen Schweinehund.*

Another good example for the difference between form and function comes from **adverbs** and **adverbials**. 'Adverb' is a word class, a form, characterized by morphological, syntactic and semantic features. 'Adverbial', on the other hand, is a syntactic function, just like subject, object, and complement. Adverbials tell us something about place, time, reason, quality etc. The function of adverbials can be fulfilled by many different forms:

(13) Yesterday I bought a Porsche.
(14) At night, the Porsche is usually parked in the garage.
(15) Three times a Porsche disappeared overnight.
(16) Because of that, no insurance company is willing to cover that risk.

In (13) the adverb *yesterday* functions as an optional adverbial, in (14) it is a prepositional phrase that does the same job, in (15) it's a noun phrase, in (16) it is even a clause. Usually, adverbials are very flexible with regard to their position in the sentence. They can appear at the beginning, in the middle or the end of a sentence. Note, though, that some are more flexible than others:

(17) (Eventually) I (eventually) bought a Porsche (eventually).
(18) (Yesterday) I (*yesterday) bought a Porsche (yesterday).

Moreover in contrast to complements, the omission of adverbials does not lead to ungrammatical sentence.

4.6 Word classes

One of the tasks in syntax and morphology is the classification of words. This can be done on the basis of semantic, morphological, and syntactic criteria. Semantic criteria look at the prototypical meaning of a given word class. So, usually, nouns denote things, people, places, or ideas; verbs denote actions or states; adjectives denote qualities of somebody or something; adverbs denote qualities of actions or adjectives. While this is very clear and straightforward it is obviously also highly problematic and numerous counterexamples can be found: nominalized verbs denote actions (e.g., *swimming*), some things expressed by verbs do not readily lend themselves to the classification as either event or state (e.g., *She suspects something*: should we speak of a state of suspicion? *He got a C+ in the test* – what is the action, what is the state?). Eventually this means that semantics needs to be supplemented by morphology and syntax. In the section on morphology, we discussed in how far some word classes have their own, specific morphological markers. It was shown that inflectional morphology, despite not being very rich in present-day English, can already help in the classification: grammatical elements like prepositions and conjunctions have no overt morphology at all, adjectives can show gradation, verbs can show some person/number marking, or tense, nouns can have plural inflection. However, this also has its problems. In every word class we find a number of exceptions to these rules: the uninflected grammatical marker *if* can have plural marking when it is converted into a noun, e.g., in the phrase *ifs and buts*. Some adjectives are not gradable: *alive, asleep, dead.* Some verbs, like the modals, do not have person marking, mass nouns do not have plural inflection. So morphology alone also does not offer the solution to the word class problem. In syntax, we look at the syntactic function and specific behavior of word classes. Consider the following examples:

(19)   The/An/This/Every **apple/*swims** helps.
(20)   The very fresh **apple/*swims** helps.
(21)   The **apple/*swims** that you gave me helps.
(22)   The **apple/*swims** on the table helps.

Nouns – in contrast to verbs or adjectives – can be preceded by definite and indefinite articles, demonstratives, quantifiers, and by one or more adjectives, which in turn can also be modified. They can be followed by relative clauses or prepositions. Verbs, in contrast, can be preceded or followed by nouns, they can be followed by prepositions. Adjectives can have preceding or following adjectives and adverbs, and so on. The idea is that word classes have special syntactic behavior, i.e. specific syntactic environments in which they occur. This however, is also not 100% foolproof, since, for example, both nouns and adjectives can be preceded by adjectives as in *heavy red book* where the noun *book* is preceded by the adjective *red* and the adjective *red* is preceded by the adjective *heavy*. Note, however, that in terms of modification, both adjectives actually modify the head noun. If you really want to modify an adjective you need an adverb to do so: *very heavy, strongly recommended*. Eventually, only the three tests (semantics, morphology, syntax) taken together can help us to determine the word class of a given element.

4.7 The syntax of English

There is certainly not enough room in a short book like this to describe the syntax of English in any greater detail. For much fuller descriptions, readers are referred to the standard, authoritative handbooks on English Grammar: Quirk et al.'s *Comprehensive Grammar of the English Language* (1986) and the more recent *Cambridge Grammar of the English Language* (2006) edited by Huddleston, Pullum et al. A shorter and reliable survey is now available in Aarts (2011).

4.7.1 Word order and information structure

English superficially looks like German when it comes to word order, i.e. we usually find subject-verb-object ordering. However, German is a so-called V2-language, where the verb always comes as the second constituent in the sentence, no matter whether the first element is the subject or an adverbial. Compare the following examples:

(23)   Der Junge las ein Buch. (SVO)
(24)   Gestern las der Junge ein Buch. (AdvVSO)

In English, the verb follows the subject, at least in canonical, unmarked sentences:

(25)   The boy read the book. (SVO)
(26)   Yesterday, the boy read the book. (AdvSVO)

In German, however, inflections give us much greater flexibility when we do not want to begin the sentence with the subject. In English it is highly problematic to put something else in subject position, simply because this can easily lead to misunderstandings.

(27)   Ein Buch las der Junge. (OSV)
(28)   ?*A book read the boy.

This does not mean, however, that English does not have any ways to change the **information structure** of a given clause. Studies on information structure look at the ways in which information is conveyed in the clause and sentence. In daily life we often distinguish between old and new information. However, when we look at this more closely, we can discover that there seem to be many nuances of these notions. So, for instance, we may want to distinguish between information that is old and cannot be recovered versus information that is old but recoverable. There is also a difference between speaker new information and hearer new information. Then there is information that is neither old nor new but is actually available through context (when you are eating at a restaurant, for example, you can say 'Pass me the menu, please', even though nobody has talked about a menu before. That does not make 'the menu' new or exciting. It simply belongs to the context of eating at a restaurant). Finally, we can also distinguish between the categories **"old/given"** and **"new"** versus **"topic"** and **"comment"**. A topic need not be new or old, it is simply something the speaker would like to talk about (i.e. comment on). Only think about phrases such as "Now that you mention gummibears, have you heard the news that they are good for your health?". "Gummibears" is, technically speaking, given information, since the other speaker obviously has mentioned them before. And yet, it's the topic of the sentence "Now that you mention...". A similar effect can be reached by "as for" or "apropos" clauses and similar devices.

Usually, we like to start our sentences with given or old information, which also serves as the topic. This helps hearers to connect the new information, or comment, to what we have already talked about. However, this need not always be the case. Despite the fact that English has a rather fixed word order with subject-verb-object it also has a number of devices available that give speakers a chance to produce special effects, such as contrast, to begin new topics, to highlight certain aspects or even to hide particular facts. Only think about passives: usually you would start a sentence with the subject. The subject is often the actor, the doer of the action ('My son broke my glasses last night'). If you turn that into a passive sentence, you can hide the actor ('My glasses were broken last night'). Similarly, you also have several choices in such a case to stress that it was your son, and nobody else, who did it. So, some of the most common **information structuring devices** are:

- **Passivization**:
  The dog bit the man > The man was bitten (by the dog).
- **Fronting**:
  The dog bit the man > The man the dog bit.

- **Left dislocation**:
  The dog bit the man > The man, the dog bit him.
- **It-clefts**:
  The dog bit the man > It was the man the dog bit.
- **Wh-clefts** (pseudo-clefts):
  The dog bit the man > What the dog did was bite the man.

All of these different constructions have very specific, individual meanings and functions. Fronting, for example, can express surprise, contrast, maybe even disapproval (e.g. *Did you hear what he bought for himself? A Porsche he bought!*). Left dislocation is used on the one hand to reintroduce and reactivate material into the discourse, which was previously mentioned and is in the background. On the other hand, it can also express contrast. It-clefts and wh-clefts mark given information as new and surprising, commonly contrastive. However, the given information in it-clefts may be inactive; in a wh-cleft it is active, but backgrounded. This becomes clear when you try to begin a new story with these two structures.

(29)   It was a knock on the door that awoke him from a nightmare….
(30)   What awoke him from a nightmare was a knock on the door….

It-clefts can be fine as first sentences in a new story, wh-clefts usually sound very weird in this position.

Note that this brief paragraph can only scratch the surface of this huge and fascinating field of study (for example, we haven't even mentioned the Prague School concepts of Theme and Rheme, for reasons of space). An excellent introduction to information structuring in English can be found in Birner, Ward & Huddleston (2002) and in Horn & Ward (2004).

4.7.2 Periphrastic constructions

One of the most striking features of English syntax is probably the abundance of **periphrasis**, i.e. the number of constructions that somehow 'work' around grammatical features. English as an **analytic language** has lost almost all of its inflections. As inflections signal constituency and grammatical functions, it had to develop alternative strategies for these. Some of these alternatives are a rather fixed word order (with the exceptions just mentioned), the frequent use of auxiliaries and (associated with the auxiliary use) the development of a complex system of periphrastic constructions. For example, as has been mentioned before, the morphological function of comparative and superlative can be expressed morphologically (with the suffixes {er} and {est}) and syntactically (with *more* and *most*). The perfect in English, just like the progressive and the passive, requires auxiliaries. Only compare Latin *amatur* (one word, the verb *amare* inflected for present tense indicative passive) to its English equivalent *He/She/It is loved.* This is perhaps most noticeable when it comes to **negation** and **question formation**.

While English has a number of different ways to negate a sentence, one of the most common ones is to add the clitic *not/n't* to an auxiliary (if present). So, *I can dance* becomes *I can't dance.* Matters become more complicated of course if there is no auxiliary to which we can attach the clitic. In that case, English requires the use of an operator, or dummy auxiliary, *do.* So, *I dance* becomes *I don't dance.* This dummy auxiliary or operator is semantically empty and its only function is to build this specific construction. Note, however, that we also have *do* as a full, lexical verb: *He does his homework* and as a quasi-modal: *I do like broccoli!* These different functions should not be confused with the dummy auxiliary. The same dummy is also used in yes/no question formation. Instead of fronting the full verb like in German, English only allows auxiliaries to be fronted. *You can dance* becomes *can you dance?* Problems again arise when there is no auxiliary in the corresponding declarative, so, *You dance* does not become **Dance you?.* Instead, dummy *do* is inserted and fronted: *Do you dance?.*

Interestingly, English did not always have this periphrastic construction. Until about Early Modern English, i.e. Shakespeare's time, English used structures not unlike those of modern German: *Sleepest, or wakest thou, jolly sheperd* (*King Lear*, iii.6) and *I speak not to disprove what Brutus spoke* (*Julius Caesar*, iii.2). It was during the Early Modern period that English gradually developed the periphrastic structures with auxiliary *do* as we know them today (there are numerous studies that deal with this development in detail. For a full account of the development, see, e.g. Stein 1992 or Han & Kroch 2000).

4.8 Exercises

1. Identify the parts of speech (word classes) in the following sentence:

   For the next eight or ten months, Oliver was the victim of a systematic course of treachery and deception.

   (Dickens 1838)

2. Identify the phrases in the following sentence, use bracketing to label the different phrases:

    The naughty boy threw a ball through the window pane.

3. Draw a phrase structure tree for the following sentence:

    A present from grandma is in the box behind the sofa.

4. What is the function "a very good cook" in the following sentence?

    Paul seems to be a very good cook.

5. What is the function of "in the kitchen" in the following sentence?

    The children ate some apples in the kitchen.

5 Meaning in Language

Semantics is one of the two disciplines in linguistics that explicitly deal with meaning. The other one is pragmatics. While semantics looks at meaning independent of context or speaker intention, in pragmatics we study exactly that: meaning in its dependence on context and speaker intention. The general difference between the two approaches can be easily illustrated. The utterance *Do you have the time?* is usually used by people who want to know the time; their intention is to provoke the addressee to tell them what time it is. But this is already context dependent and based on speaker intention. It's not what the speakers actually say. What they could say instead is *Tell me the time!*. In terms of semantics, regardless of all these factors, all the utterance *Do you have the time?* does is asking a 'yes-no' question. The speaker asks the addressee if he or she has the time. Not more, not less. The rest is up to the hearer. In the following section we will focus on the basics of semantics first before we turn to pragmatics.

5.1 Semantics

Semantics is usually divided into at least two different approaches. On the one hand, we need to look at the meaning of words, or lexical items. This is usually called **lexical semantics**. On the other hand, we also need to investigate the meaning of larger units, i.e. sentences. This is usually referred to as **sentence semantics**. Semantics can be characterized as a hybrid discipline with close connections to other fields of study, such as philosophy, semiotics, logic, and cognitive science, not in the least since all of these are also very much interested in meaning as such.

5.1.1 Lexical semantics

How do we describe the meaning of a word? And what is the meaning of a word, anyway?

Consider a simple lexical item like *book*. On the one hand, this item has some independent, definable meaning, some sense, which distinguishes it from other lexical items such as *car* or *hippopotamus*. This **sense** can be seen as an abstract mental representation of the item. The ancient Greek philosopher Plato coined the term 'idea' for something like this, and Ferdinand de Saussure, one of the founding fathers of structuralism talked about the linguistic sign as a combination of **signifier (form)** and **signified (meaning)** (see section 1.5). 'Sense' as one 'abstract representation', Plato's 'idea', and de Saussure's 'signified' are very similar in many respects. Yet another important technical term for sense is intension. **Intension is the sum of all features that characterize one particular item.** So, for *book* this would comprise features such as being inanimate, being made out of paper, with several pages etc. Note that all lexical items have sense, or intension. If an item had no sense, it would simply be 'nonsense'. One example of that can be found in Lewis Carroll's poem *Jabberwocky,* which begins like this:

> Twas brillig, and the slithy toves
> Did gyre and gimble in the wabe;
> All mimsy were the borogoves,
> And the mome raths outgrabe.   (Lewis Carroll, *Jabberwocky*, 1871)

Note that the poem is perfectly 'grammatical' and that the words even somehow seem to fit into the syntactic slots. And yet, they lack sense, or meaning; in other words, we do not have any definition for *brillig, mome, borogroves,* and most of the rest. They are just 'empty shells', forms without content. But, interestingly, one might add, many of the nonce words in this poem are very 'suggestive' due to their special phonetic form!

Lexical items do not only have sense, or an intension. They can also have reference, or an extension. **Reference**, quite simply, is the relationship between a linguistic expression and the non-linguistic world of experience. This can either be definite, or specific, when we have a very concrete entity in mind, or it may be indefinite, or unspecific, when the reference is more general and abstract. However, the relationship between definiteness and specificity is anything but straightforward and is still a matter of debate. It is quite easy to show, for example, that both definite and indefinite noun phrases can refer to both specific and nonspecific entities. Look at the following examples.

(1) I am looking for the man who stole my laptop.
(2) I am looking for the perfect man.
(3) She wants to marry a Norwegian.
(4) I am looking for a DVD which I forgot here yesterday.

In (1) the noun phrase *the man who stole my laptop* refers to somebody very concrete and very specific, in (2) the noun phrase *the perfect man* may not refer to somebody the speaker already knows, but we can still assume that the speaker has somebody specific in mind. However, in both cases the noun phrases contain the definite article *the*. Example (3) is ambiguous between a specific and a nonspecific reading. *A Norwegian* may either refer to someone specific who is from Norway (the speaker may just have forgotten the name), or to the fact that whoever she wants to marry must be from Norway. Finally, in (4) the speaker is again looking for something quite specific. However, in both (3) and (4) the noun phrases contain the indefinite article *a*. This leads us to the conclusion that the relationship between morphosyntactic definiteness and semantic specificity is anything but clear and requires some further investigation.

Having discussed both the terms sense and reference, it is also worth pointing out that reference as such does not equal meaning. One only needs to think about the two names 'Mark Twain' and 'Samuel L. Clemens'. You may know both these names (i.e. you may be familiar with their senses). You may think that Mark Twain is the author of *The Adventures of Tom Sawyer*, while Samuel Clemens is the author of *A Yankee at King Arthur's Court*. So you may be tempted to think that the two mean different people. Only when you realize that the two books, *Tom Sawyer* and *A Yankee...* were written by one and the same author you can see that both expressions, Mark Twain and Samuel L. Clemens, actually have the same referent in this world, i.e. Samuel Langhorne Clemens (November 30, 1835 – April 21, 1910). So, one thing in this world may have different senses, but still one and the same referent: However, this approach and distinction is also not without a few pitfalls. One may object, for instance, that treating 'sense' in this way makes it very difficult to argue for sense as the 'objective meaning' part of expression in a given langue (the conventional language of a speech community). But this is beyond the scope of this introduction.

Now that we have established some of the key concepts and also some problems of the concept of 'meaning' as such, we can turn to the question how we can actually capture and formalize 'meaning' on the word level. Traditionally, we have about three different approaches at our disposal: sense relations, componential features, and prototype theory. In the following, we will discuss each of these in turn.

5.1.2 Sense relations

One of the oldest and best ways of describing meaning is to look at so-called sense relations. **Words, or rather their senses obviously do not exist in isolation**. Rather, they are somehow related. Words can

- mean the same (more or less), or
- mean the opposite (more or less), or
- be parts and types of each other.

This is what we study in sense relations. Since this approach goes back at least to ancient Greek philosophy, many of the terms we use today are still based on Greek. Students usually find this very confusing, or even annoying, but you will get used to these five or six terms very soon. Just try to use them as often as you can.

Let us begin with one term that is probably already familiar: synonymy. **Synonymy essentially means that two words mean the same thing**. They are synonyms. Examples include *couch* and *sofa*, *height* and *altitude*, and, of course, *drunk, inebriated, pissed, blotto, blasted, wasted* (and so many more – if you are interested, you may want to look up a few words in a good thesaurus, i.e. a dictionary of synonyms, such as *The Oxford Thesaurus of English,* or *Roget's Thesaurus*). The three examples just mentioned perhaps already show what the problem is. Are they really synonymous? Do they 'really' mean the same thing? If this were so, we should be able to substitute them for each other just as we like. This is clearly not the case. There is nothing that keeps us from telling the judge that we were *fucking blotto* that night when we urinated into that convertible Porsche, but it is perhaps wiser to use *extremely inebriated* instead – even though the words somehow mean the same. Also, why should a linguistic system have two or more expressions that mean the same thing, or do the same job? That would be a waste of precious brain capacity. The point is that many synonyms actually have **the same propositional content**, i.e. their sense (intension) is indeed the same. But they differ quite a bit in terms of **connotation**, i.e. what we associate with them, what kind of register and style they are used in, what kind of person (gender, age, education etc.) uses them in what context and so on. Sometimes these differences are rather obvious (see above), sometimes they are more subtle, as, for example, with *sofa* and *couch*. The former is usually associated with a better style and education. So the Queen of England probably watches 'telly' not on a couch, but on a sofa. In January 2002, former US President George W. Bush had a bad accident when he was watching a football game on TV, eating pretzels. Apparently he chocked on a pretzel, fainted, and fell off some piece of furniture. Most reports now say he fell off the... *couch*. Ouch. Similarly, even almost identical synonyms like *handsome* and *pretty* obviously do not operate in the same way. *Handsome* usually goes with male head nouns, such as *boy, guy,* or *man. Pretty* on the other hand goes with female head nouns, such as *girl, chick, woman, lady* and the like. Again, the propositional content is the same, and yet the words are not synonymous, strictly speaking. Which is why most scholars today would agree that total synonymy does not exist in language, or at least is extremely rare. What we find quite often, however, is near synonymy.

The opposite of synonym is antonym. **Antonyms mean the opposite of each other**. Examples include *on* and *off, dead* and *alive, hot* and *cold, fast* and *slow*. When you look at these examples very carefully, you may notice some interesting, subtle differences. The former two are binary opposites, i.e. they are complementary with no gradation in between: either – or. The latter two are gradable opposites, i.e. there are various steps between being *hot* and *cold* (*hot, warm, lukewarm, tepid, fresh, cool, cold...*), or between *fast* and *slow* (*slower* and *faster...*). Also, with gradable antonyms, the negative part of the pair does not necessarily entail the other one: *the water is not hot* does not mean that it is *cold*; *my car isn't slow* does not mean that it is *fast*. This is very different for non-gradable antonyms: *He is not alive* means that he is *dead*. *The lights are not on* means that they are *off*. Note, however, that non-gradability is not that simple a phenomenon when you look at it in detail. Before we had stand-by switches on our TVs, people had a different idea about *on* and *off*. Similarly, neurologists and other people in the medical profession may have a different opinion about *dead* and *alive* than for example priests and philosophers. And there is no need to talk about the *male – female* issue today anymore.

Another important sense relation is **hyponymy**. This refers to a 'type of' relationship between senses. Alsatian is a type of dog, rose is a kind of flower, Chevy is a kind of car. The superordinate term (*dog, flower, car*) is called the **hyperonym**, the subordinate term (*Alsatian, rose, Chevy*) is called the **hyponym**. If a word has more than one hyponym (most of them do) these are called **co-hyponyms**: *Basset* and *Greyhound* for *dog, tulip* and *lily* for *flower, Ford* and *Jaguar* for car. Needless to say, every hyponym can also be a hyperonym, and vice versa. *Dog* (hyponym) is one kind of animal (hyperonym), and *rose* is a hyperonym for more than 30.000 different kinds of roses (hyponyms): *gallicas, damasks, albas, centifolias...* Usually, hyponymy can be elegantly described in tree-like diagrams:

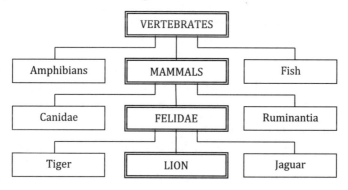

Figure 5.1: Hyponymy vertebrates.

We need to distinguish hyponymy from meronymy, although the two look very similar at first sight. **Hyponymy is a 'kind of' relationship, meronymy is a** '**part of**' relationship. *Finger* is part of your hand, not a type of hand. *Tire* is a part of a car, not a type of car. *Petal* is part of a flower, and so on. We can say that *finger*, *tire*, and *petal* are **meronyms** of *hand*, *car* and *flower*, respectively.

Some more terms need be discussed here, even though they do not hold the same status as the aforementioned. These are **polysemy, homonyms, homophony,** and **homography.** They do not really express sense relations, but rather deal with the linguistic form as such and how it relates to content, or sense.

The term **polysemy** is used in cases when one single lexical item can refer to several, apparently unrelated things: the *head* of an animate being and the *head* of an organization. Nevertheless, the two uses of *head* are actually related and they go back to one and the same source (namely Latin 'caput'). We can even see this when we look at the actual uses. The head is somehow the most important, dominant thing on an animate being, in that it gives it direction, and so the head of an organization. But what about *mole*? There is the mole on your skin, the mole in the harbor, the mole as a unit in chemistry, and, of course, the mole that digs tunnels and holes in your garden. All four of them are described by one and the same word: *mole*. Are they related? Even with the widest stretch of imagination we cannot claim that the mole in your garden has anything to do with the mole in the harbor and neither has this one anything to do with your skin. And this is also supported by the **etymology**, the source and history of the terms. The mole on your skin comes from Old English *mal* 'spot, mark', especially on cloth or linen, which in turn comes from Proto Germanic **mailan* 'spot, mark' which again goes back to the Proto-Indo-European base **mei-/*mai-* 'to stain, defile' (cf. Greek *miainein* 'to stain, defile'). The mole in the harbor comes from Middle French *môle* 'breakwater', from Latin *moles* 'mass, massive structure, barrier', which goes back to Proto-Indo-European **mo-* 'to exert oneself'. The chemical mole actually comes from German *Mol* (1900), short for *Molekül*, and the name for the animal probably comes from obsolete *mouldwarp,* lit. 'earth-thrower', which may be derived from Old English *molde* 'earth, soil'. In a word, they all have different etymologies, they have nothing to do with each other. This is what we call **homonymy.** For some historical reason, or accident, completely unrelated words have come to be spelled and pronounced alike. In contrast to that, polysemy refers to different senses of one and the same word. Homography and homophony refer to special cases of homonymy. In **homography,** the words are only spelled in the same way, but the pronunciation is different. In **homophony,** the words are pronounced the same way, but the spelling is different. One example for homography is *wind* [wind] and [waind], one example for homophony is [thru:], spelled either <threw> or <through>. The relationship of homonymy, homography, and homophony can be illustrated as follows:

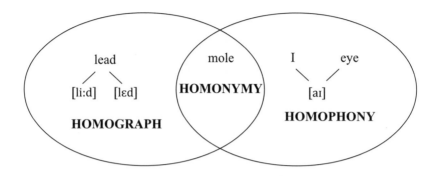

Figure 5.2: Relationship of homonymy, homograph and homophony.

5.1.3 Componential features

The very basic idea behind **componential feature analysis** is that every lexical item can be decomposed, broken down into smaller elements of meaning, the sum of which characterize that particular item and no other. These features should be as basic and simple as possible, so e.g. [+/– animate] is a way better feature than [+/– mauve colored after heavy rainfalls during springtime]. Some researchers suggest that there are a number of universal primitives which cannot be further broken down and which form the building blocks of more complex concepts. This notion, however, is not uncontroversial. Moreover, the features that we identify should be necessary and sufficient, i.e. we should aim at describing a given concept with not more and not fewer features than we actually need. Features are usually regarded as binary, i.e. as either being present (+) or absent (–). If necessary, one might even say a given feature is (+/–), either present or absent. This is mostly interesting when we need a certain feature to distinguish some members of a given set of concepts, but not all of them. Eventually, we can develop a tableau which contains both the features and the set of concepts that we wish to describe and distinguish. Table 5.1 which analyzes the word field *'relationships/relatives'*, is one such example. There are a few things you might notice when you study the table. First, the initial three rows (animate, human, related) seem superfluous and obviously contradict our principle of 'necessary and sufficient'. This is true for this tableau, but these three features are so fundamental that they actually apply to practically all things we ever encounter. So, for completeness sake, they were also included here, since they help us to distinguish between *brother* [+animate, +human, +related], *tree* [+animate, –human, –related], *stone* [–animate, –human, –related], and *boss* [+animate, +human, +/– related]. The second thing you might notice is that we only have [male] in the table, not female. This has nothing to do with any mysogynism or chauvinism, but simply with the fact that in this case, [+male] automatically entails [–female] and vice versa. However, as male and female also belong to the very fundamental features that we mentioned in the beginning, we could also have added [female] for completeness' sake. In this case, however, we opted in favor of a very neat and tidy table without redundancy in this respect. Finally, some cells have a [+/–] to show that the features could be there or could not be there. So, a cousin may be either male or female, which means that this feature simply does not matter in defining the word *cousin*. Things are more tricky with the terms *parents* and *sisters and brothers*. These are plural and they 'require' both a female and a male part. If you only have sisters, you call them *sisters*, not *sisters and brothers*. This is why we opted for [0] as a feature value in this case. In sum, the table nicely captures the similarities and differences between the individual complex concepts in this word field.

The same kind of analysis can also be carried out with verbs. Verbs are really heavy duty elements in language. Not only do they grammatically specify the number and type of arguments in a sentence and the thematic roles of these arguments, they also have to describe what the situation that the sentence describes is like. Some events or situations are rather static, others are dynamic. Some have a fixed endpoint, some don't. Look at the following examples:

(5) Lord Winterbottom loves red wine.
(6) TJ booked a flight to Hawaii.
(7) The fire alarm beeped.
(8) The fire alarm beeped until the batteries had died.

In the first sentence we find a **static verb**, *love*, which usually expresses more or less permanent states. Some other verbs in this category are *have, be, know,* and *like*. In contrast to that, the second sentence illustrates a **dynamic verb**, *book*. This process has definable beginning and end, and in many cases we can intentionally influence the process (in contrast to states). Also, these processes usually require some energy input from an agent or force. Other verbs in this category are *read, kill, eat, play*. Note that the boundaries are not always 100% clear-cut. A big international food chain invented the marketing slogan "I'm loving it" – with a dynamic use of a formerly stative verb.

Table 5.1: World field 'relationship/relatives' (based on Bierwisch 1969).

	relative	parents	father	mother	sister	brother	brothers and sisters	child	son	daughter	uncle	aunt	cousin	nephew	niece
animate	+	+	+	+	+	+	+	+	+	+	+	+	+	+	+
human	+	+	+	+	+	+	+	+	+	+	+	+	+	+	+
related	+	+	+	+	+	+	+	+	+	+	+	+	+	+	+
Directly related	+/-	+	+	+	+	+	+	+	+	+	-	-	-	-	-
same generation	+/-	-	-	-	+	+	+	-	-	-	-	-	+	-	-
older	+/-	+	+	+	+/-	+/-	+/-	-	-	-	+	+	+/-	-	-
male	+/-	0	+	-	-	+	0	+/-	+	-	+	-	+/-	+	-
plural	-	+	-	-	-	-	+	-	-	-	-	-	-	-	-

In the third sentence, the verb *beep* denotes something that happens only once, or maybe even had some unspecified duration, in the fourth one there is a clearly definable end or goal (like in *John read the book*, which usually means that he finished it). In a very influential study, Vendler (1967) distinguishes between four different situation types on the basis of whether the action is stative, durative, telic or voluntary: STATES, ACTIVITIES, ACCOMPLISHMENTS and ACHIEVEMENTS.

We can go even further and try to capture some of the meaning in seemingly meaningless elements, like modals. These, as members of the closed class of grammatical words, are first and foremost associated with function, not with lexical meaning. And yet, we see something like meaning in them when we take a closer look. This meaning can be identified as modality. **Modality** is essentially about how we see and how we describe the world and what happens around us. For example, we can be very certain about some facts, or rather uncertain. We can express that something should happen or that we think it happened. The two major types of modality in English are epistemic and deontic modality. Both terms come from Greek. Here, 'episteme' refers to knowledge in general, 'déon' refers to 'that which is binding'. Hence, **epistemic modality** is about our thoughts, beliefs, conjectures, while **deontic modality** is about rules and laws. Interestingly, although one and the same modal verb can be sued in both ways, the difference is very easy to see:

(9)   That must be John (uttered upon hearing the door slam)
(10)   You must be home by seven (father to daughter)

In the first sentence, the modal verb *must* expresses that the speaker believes, on the basis of hearing a door slam, that there is a person called John approaching. This is about the speaker's knowledge or beliefs. In the second sentence, the same modal verb *must* expresses that the speaker commands the addressee to be home by seven. This is about laws and rules, and hence a case of deontic modality. Note that the two are not always easily distinguishable and that modal verbs and their analysis have a long and very productive history in linguistics. For instance, there is an ongoing debate about different types of modality, such as root modality and dynamic modality and how these relate to the traditional categories epistemic versus deontic. Similarly, it is far from clear whether one modal verb, such as *must*, should be treated as being **polysemous**, i.e. equipped with two or more related meanings or if the two functions of *must* warrant the idea that this is a case of homonymy, which means that the two are not related in any way.

Componential feature analysis, like many other ideas in semantics, goes back to ancient Greek philosophy, but it had its heyday in 20th century structuralism. If the tableau reminds you of phonetic features, you are absolutely right; both phonetic features and semantic features represent the attempt to develop a neat and tidy system of primitives that help us to uniquely define more complex elements (phones and concepts) as matrixes of pluses and minuses. This is indeed one of the big advantages and fortes of componential feature analysis. It is a very stringent and systematic approach to the analysis of meaning. On the downside, however, it also has various problems. On the one hand, there is no reliable and universally accepted way of identifying semantic primitives or even semantic features. As the system that we need is way more complex than in phonology (the largest phoneme inventories of the world's languages have only about 140 phonemes, large lexical inventories easily go beyond 1,000,000 words), we need more features. And these features are necessarily very difficult to establish, since we need to take cultural, historical, philosophical, anthropological factors into account. Therefore, we only have a number of studies in very carefully delimited domains such as family relations, color terms, military ranks, verbs of movement, etc., that support this method as such. Another problem that we have to face with this approach has to do with the status and nature of semantic features. The system we arrive at may be very convincing, but it does not necessarily reflect actual language use and speaker competence. Speakers are very good at classifying tricky cases. For example, what are the features that we need for a bird, apart from the obvious [+animate, –human]? Feathers? A beak? The ability to fly? How do we find features that capture robins, eagles, penguins, hummingbirds, ducks, ostriches...? Ludwig Wittgenstein, an influential philosopher of the early 20th century, pointed out a similar problem: How do we define the word *game*? He was able to show very convincingly that there is no unique set of features to include everything that we as speakers would classify as games. Instead, all the things that we classify as games share features in sub-groups. And still we recognize a conceptual family of games here. This is one of the reasons why, from the 1960s onwards, researchers in psychology and cognitive science began to develop a counter program to the componential feature approach: prototype theory.

5.1.4 Prototype theory

The essential idea of prototype theory goes back to Wittgenstein's analysis of the term *games* that we just mentioned. Here is a longer quotation translated from the original Wittgenstein text:

> 66. Consider for example, the activities that we call "games". I mean board-games, card-games, ball-games, athletic games, and so on. What is common to them all? – Don't say: "They *must* have something in common, or they would not be called 'games'"– but *look and see* whether there is anything common to all. – For if you look at them you won't see something that is common to *all*, but similarities, affinities, and a whole series of them at that. To repeat: don't think,

but look! – Look, for example, at board-games, with their various affinities.

Now pass to card-games; here you find many correspondences with the first group, but many common features drop out, and others appear.

When we pass next to ball-games, much that is common is retained, but much is lost. – Are they all 'entertaining'? Compare chess with noughts and crosses. Or is there always winning and losing, or competition between players? Think of patience. In ball games there is winning and losing; but when a child throws his ball at the wall and catches it again, this feature has disappeared. Look at the parts played by skill and luck; and at the difference between skill in chess and skill in tennis.

Think now of singing and dancing games; here we have the element of entertainment, but how many other characteristic features have disappeared!

And we can go through the many, many other groups of games in the same way, can see how similarities crop up and disappear.

And the upshot of these considerations is: we see a complicated network of similarities overlapping and crisis-crossing: sometimes overall similarities in the large and in the small.

67. I can think of no better expression to characterize these similarities than **"family resemblances"**; for the various resemblances between members of a family: build, features, colour of eyes, gait, temperament, etc. etc. overlap and cries-cross in the same way. -And I shall say: 'games' form a family.

(Wittgenstein 1978 [1953]: section 66-67)

In the 1970s, a psychologist, Eleanor Rosch, began to put Wittgenstein's thoughts into practice with the explicit aim of developing a model of meaning and meaning description that is cognitively plausible and reflects how speakers actually think. Instead of using necessary and sufficient features in order to uniquely define a given concept, prototype theory regards concepts as graded and fuzzy. **Categories** can have one central, prototypical member which satisfies most or even all criteria of the category and which is regarded as the model par excellence of this particular category by the speech community. Other members of the category are less central, less (proto-)typical to various degrees. The central, most prototypical member of the category 'pet', for instance, could be a *hamster*, a *guinea pig*, or maybe a *cat*. Slightly less typical might be a *rabbit*, a *dog*, or a *canary bird*. Even less typical is perhaps a *rat*, a *snake*, or a *chameleon*. Even stranger, but still somehow a pet, is Michael Jackson's monkey Bubbles, or George Clooney's potbellied mini pig Max. This can easily be visualized by concentric circles: This categorization is, of course, very culture specific (see Figure 5.3). People from Africa, Asia, or the Arctic may have very different items in their circles.

One of the big advantages of this approach is its testability and empirical foundation. Speakers can be asked about their prototypes, or how they would rate and classify this or that object. Labov (1973), for example, carried out a fascinating experiment with cups, mugs, and bowls. He presented subjects with 19 different pictures of 'containers', i.e. cups, mugs, bowls, glasses, goblets, vases, with and without handles, wide, narrow, tall, small, square, round, triangular... and asked them how they would call the different items. The result was not a clear-cut boundary between cup objects and non-cup objects but rather a graded scale of 'cuppiness'. This depended for the most part on the ratio of height and width, but also on the material (if given by the researcher) or the thing that was said to be in the container. For example, if the container was roundish and had a handle, a height to width ratio of 1.0 was sufficient for a classification as 'cup', but if the width-height ratio increases to 1.5, 15% of the respondents rather opted for 'mug' or 'bowl' than 'cup'. Nevertheless, prototype theory sometimes still suffers from the cliché of being somehow soft and fuzzy, and lacking the explanatory power of other approaches such as sense relations and componential feature analysis. This may be partly true, but especially some more recent approaches have aimed at combining the strengths of the structuralist methods and approaches with prototype theory. It was suggested that the prototype of a given category has a number of semantic features, much like componential features. However, in contrast to traditional componential feature analysis, the other members of the category need not share all of these features. So, instead of being necessary and sufficient for a valid definition, features in prototype theory are violable and need not be present in order to define a given entity as member of some category. In other words, not all birds need to fly, just like some mammals rather look like fish (or vice versa...). But, not unlike componential feature analysis, prototype theory also suffers from the vastness of data it has to cover, and so far there are only very few analyses of selected, clearly defined lexical fields available.

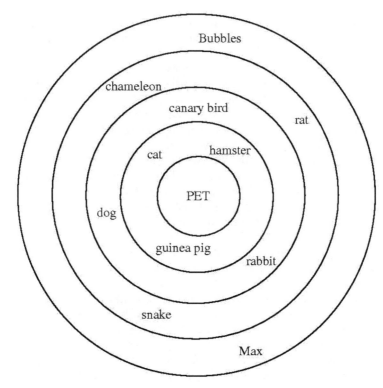

Figure 5.3: Prototype diagram "PET".

5.2 Sentence semantics

Semantics not only deals with the meaning of words. It also looks at the meaning of sentences. However, the **study of meaning** in sentences is not as clearly defined as that in words. Some of the topics that are being discussed include sentence propositions and entailments, thematic roles, and verb semantics. We will touch at least briefly upon each of these.

5.2.1 Truth conditions, entailment, presupposition

When we study the meaning of sentences, we are faced with some problems we already know from lexical semantics. One of these is the question of propositional content and propositional equivalence. In order to describe the meaning (or propositional content) of a given sentence, we usually turn to its so-called truth conditions. **Truth conditions** are the facts that need to be true in order for the sentence to be true. So, the sentence *It rained last night* is true if and only if it actually rained last night, i.e. the night before the utterance. It was claimed by scholars like John Lyons that "[s]entences have the same propositional content if and only if they have the same truth conditions" (Lyons 1995: 148). Typical examples are active and passive sentences. We usually think that they mean the same, i.e. it does not matter (proposition-wise) whether I say *The cat stole the fish* or *The fish was stolen by the cat*. However, apart from all intuition, Lyons's theory would require us to seriously consider whether there are any circumstances in this world in which one of the two sentences could be true, and the other not true. This may sound easy at first, but Lyons (1995: 148) challenges his readers to show that the two sentences "That man is unmarried" and "That man is not married" do *not* mean the same thing. This would require that one could show that there is a context in which the man is married and not unmarried – at the same time.

Closely linked to propositions are the concepts of 'entailment' and 'presupposition'. Examine the following sentences:

(11) Peter broke the vase.
     The vase is broken.

(12) Bartholomew managed to repair the car.
     Bartholomew tried to repair the car.

The first sentence, Peter broke the vase, logically entails the second. If the first one is true, the second one must also be true. If the second sentence is false, the first one must also be false. This relationship between two propositions is called **entailment**. Entailment as such is a phenomenon of propositions and logic and is absolutely context independent. The second set of sentences illustrates a slightly different relationship between propositions, namely **presupposition**. The first sentence presupposes the second sentence, i.e. Bartholomew cannot have managed to repair the car if he did not try in the first place. Verbs like *manage* (a so-called presupposition trigger, just like definite noun phrases or emotive verbs like to *regret* or *be sorry*) presuppose that something was deliberately tried. But you need to be very careful before you jump to conclusions about entailments. This is illustrated by the next example.

(13) a. Tim broke the vase.
     b. The vase is broken.

At first sight we might be tempted to think that proposition (13a) entails proposition (13b) and vice versa. But this is clearly not the case. Sentence (13b) may be true, i.e. the vase may be broken, but on the other hand, somebody else could have dropped it, i.e. sentence (13a) could be false. And so, even if (13b) is true, (13a) may be false. When we look at it from this direction, there clearly is no entailment. The entailment and presupposition only holds in one direction. Somebody else may have broken the vase, and Bartholomew may have tried to repair the car, but he could have failed. When we try to distinguish between entailments and presuppositions there is one very important test: presuppositions survive negation, entailments do not. Compare:

(14) a. Bartholomew managed to repair the car.
     b. Bartholomew did NOT manage to repair the car.
     c. Bartholomew tried to repair the car.

Both (14a) and (14b) obviously presuppose (14c), despite the fact that (14b) is a negated version of (14a). This is obviously not the case with entailments, as the following set of examples shows:

(15) a. Tim broke the vase.
     b. Tim did NOT break the vase.
     c. The vase is broken.

Sentence (15a) entails (15c), but there is no such relationship between (15a) and (15b). Sentence (15b) says nothing about the state of the vase, i.e. it could be broken (because somebody else broke it), but it need not be.

5.2.2 Thematic roles and verb semantics

Two other topics in sentence semantics are **thematic roles** and **verb semantics**. Thematic roles go back at least to the 1960s when Charles Fillmore investigated what he called "deep semantic cases". The idea is simple and yet intriguing: the arguments in a given sentence not only have morphological case like nominative or accusative, and they do not only fulfill grammatical functions like subject or object. Rather, there is also a third layer in which these arguments somehow relate to situations and the roles they play in these situations. These are thematic roles or deep semantic cases. One simple example may help to make this clear:

(16) Priscilla opened the door with a crowbar.

In this sentence, we find three different entities, or arguments: the traditional subject, *Priscilla,* the traditional object, *the door,* and one adverbial of manner, *with a crowbar.* What do they do, what do they tell us about the situation?

Priscilla can be characterized as the initiator and doer of the action, as the agent who performs something deliberately. *The door* is not actively involved but acted upon. It undergoes whatever action is performed by the agent. We might want to call this the patient. *With a crowbar* tells us how the action is performed, by what means or instruments. We might call this the instrument role. When we look carefully at a number of utterances we can recognize quite a number of these different roles:

Agent/Actor: the (deliberate) initiator and doer of some action
Elvis has left the building.

Patient: the entity undergoing some action, usually with some change of state
Bruce baked a cake.

Experiencer: the entity experiences the action or state, but has no control of it
Mary loves cheesecake.

Beneficiary: the entity benefits from the action
Peter cooked her dinner.

Recipient: the entity who received something through the action
Mrs. Smith gave Mr. Jones a new tie.

Instrument: the means by which the action is performed
Maxwell signed the contract with a new pen.

Location: the location of some entity or action
The books were kept in the great library.

Source: the entity from where something originates, either physically or metaphorically
The crown was stolen from the tower.

Goal: the entity towards which something moves, either physically or metaphorically
He pointed them towards the next police station.

Obviously, one could develop even more different roles, or one might lump together one or two of them (such as goal, recipient, beneficiary, for example). This was and is indeed the topic of many debates and we cannot discuss this in any detail at this point. It is more important to understand the fundamental difference between this particular approach and the more traditional, grammatical approaches that we have discussed before. One of the consequences, for example, is that the position in the sentence cannot determine thematic role of a given argument. Look at the following examples:

(17)   John opened the door.
(18)   The key opened the door.
(19)   The wind opened the door.
(20)   The door opened.

In the first sentence John is clearly the actor, i.e. the entity that deliberately initiates the action. The key in the second sentence, although it is also the subject, grammatically speaking, cannot be the agent/actor. Rather, it seems to be something like an instrument for an unmentioned agent/actor. Is the wind also an instrument? Probably not, at least not in the same sense as a key or a tool. This difference should be reflected in another syntactic role. We might need a new role to capture this, maybe force. And what about the last sentence? The door in this case does not really fit into any of the categories we have discussed so far. A neutral term like 'theme' probably captures best what is described here. It has been suggested in the literature that there is an implicational hierarchy of thematic roles, i.e. speakers across languages seem to tend to put certain thematic roles more often into the subject slot than others, given a choice. This hierarchy looks as follows:

Agent > Recipient/Benefactive > Theme/Patient > Instrument > Location

This hierarchy represents two findings: (a) speakers prefer the roles further to left as subjects in unmarked sentences and (b) if a language allows for any of the roles in this hierarchy to appear in subject position, then it also allows for all the other roles to the left of this particular role to appear in subject position. So, if a language has instruments in subject position it will also have theme/patient, recipient/benefactive and agent arguments in the subject position, but not necessarily location. English, for example, allows for basically all roles in subject position, though examples with location are rare and usually only work with **mediopassive** constructions such as in *This tent sleeps ten people*.

It is usually assumed that thematic roles are somehow associated with the semantics of the verb. They build a link between syntax and semantics. Thus it seems possible to develop thematic grids for individual verbs and verb classes. Some examples of these grids are:

V: <agent, patient, instrument>, *Peter played the piano with his toes.*
V: <agent, theme, recipient>, *The boy gave the rubber duck to the toddler.*
V: <agent, goal>, *The girls went to London.*

5.2.3 FRAMES and SCRIPTS

Charles Fillmore was one of the key figures in yet another (similar) approach to meaning in language. In so-called **Frame Semantics** it is assumed that we do not understand or determine the meaning of a word in isolation, but that all the relevant, essential encyclopedic knowledge that is associated with that word is also activated. For example, upon hearing or uttering the word *buy* one activates a wide range of concepts including somebody who sells, somebody who buys, and a commercial transaction (with all its details, such as the relationships between buyer, seller, the goods, and the money). The central idea is that we do not fully grasp the meaning of a word or concept if we do not understand all the other concepts that are attached to it. Thus, all concepts can be found within **semantic frames**, which are based on experience, and which in turn form a coherent network. Interestingly, many frames allow us to view and portray a given situation or concept from different perspectives. The frame for *buy* highlights the action from the point of view of the buyer, the frame *sell* looks at the same action, but this time it focuses or highlights on the viewpoint of the seller. Frames and Frame Semantics find their most powerful use in the open-access Berkeley website *FrameNet* (http://framenet.icsi.berkeley.edu). Here you can access a very large database with frames, frame elements, and lexical entries, and you can study their relations. Below you can see a screenshot for *sell* in the Frame *Commerce_sell*. Words that belong to this frame are defined as "describing basic commercial transactions involving a buyer and a seller exchanging money and goods, taking the perspective of the seller. The words vary individually in the patterns of frame element realization they allow. For example, the typical patterns for SELL: SELLER sells GOODS to BUYER for MONEY. Robin sold a car to Abby for $5,000" (FrameNet, s.v. *commerce_sell*). Typical or core Frame Elements (FEs) are BUYER, SELLER, GOODS. Non-core FEs can include DURATION, MANNER, MEANS, and others. The typical lexical entries for this frame include: *auction*.v, *retail*.v, *retailer*.n, *sale*.n, *sell*.v, *vend*.v, *vendor*.n.

A similar and somehow related concept is that of so-called scripts. In 1977, the IT specialist Roger Schank and the social psychologist Robert Abelsohn extended the static idea of frames and made it more dynamic and diachronic. They tried to capture the meaning of events and actions, and what our knowledge of these might look like. So, for instance, what do we know, what kind of knowledge do we activate when we think about going to the movies? First, you need to decide which movie theater, which movie, and what time.

Possibly coordinate this with friends. Get dressed. Get there. Buy ticket. Go inside. Possibly buy drinks and food. Go to the theater where the movie is shown in time. Find your seat, sit down. Enjoy the show etc. A common misunderstanding is that all actions and events have a script. This is not the case. For instance, there is probably no 'hard drive crash' or 'buy books online' script or anything like that. The concept of script first and foremost applies to highly conventionalized, ritualized, stereotyped events and actions.

5.3 Pragmatics

In this section, we will turn to the second major approach in linguistics that deals with meaning: pragmatics. As has been pointed out above, **pragmatics is interested in meaning in context and in speaker intention**. So, it is not so much about what is said but about what is intended. This is so pervasive in our everyday life that we sometimes find it very hard to leave this perspective behind and look at the semantics of a given utterance. For example, can you see any difference between the semantics and the pragmatics of the following utterance?

(21)   If you keep an eye on my seat, I'll get you a cup of coffee.

Naturally, we would understand the *if*-part (protasis) of this *if...then* clause as being a necessary and sufficient condition for the *then*-part (apodosis) to happen. However, this is only the case, strictly speaking, for 'if and only if', short hand, (iff) clauses. Compare:

(22)   If and only if you keep an eye on my seat, I'll get you a cup of coffee.

Here, it is fairly clear that the apodosis crucially rests on the fulfillment of the protasis. But in the first example, this is not so. There is no reason why the speaker should not get the hearer a cup of coffee even though nobody kept an eye on the free seat. Semantically speaking, protasis and apodosis are more or less independent. To be precise: the fulfillment of the condition calls for the promised reaction; but what happens when the condition is not fulfilled is left open, semantically speaking. It is only in the pragmatics of this construction that we think there is an 'if and only if ' link between the two. Most people find it very hard to see beyond this very conventional – but still not semantic – link between the two.

Some approaches differentiate between micro- and macropragmatics. **Micropragmatics** deals with the smaller level units of communication, i.e. utterances, and how meaning is produced with and within these.

Macropragmatics, on the other hand, looks at higher level constructs, such as texts, conversations, discourse, and how they are organized and structured on the basis of pragmatics. In other words, macropragmatics is rather interested in the organization of utterances. In this sense, it becomes almost synonymous with the terms **discourse analysis or conversation analysis** (see Chapter 7). Issues such as emotions and politeness are also usually grouped within macropragmatics although they have their repercussions in the micro-structures of language, e.g., speech acts.

Within pragmatics we can usually identify a number of problems or 'hot topics' that continually surface here: implicatures, deixis, speech acts, the cooperative principle, and politeness. In the following, we will discuss each of these in turn.

5.3.1 Implicatures

In the previous section on semantics we discussed the phenomena of entailment and presupposition. It was shown that entailments establish a logical, context independent relationship between two propositions. **Presuppositions** (sometimes also called conventional implicatures) are also context-independent and semantics-based, but in contrast to entailments, they survive negation. So, *My car is red*, presupposes that I actually have a car, and so does the negative counterpart, *My car is NOT red.*

Pragmatics offers yet another type of implicature, namely **conversational implicatures**. Some examples of this type are given in (23) to (25):

(23)   Many students left the room.
(24)   A: Do you like spinach? B: Do fish have lips?
(25)   A: Did you bring the cookies and the milk? B: Oh, I brought the cookies.

All three sentences imply something which is probably not visible at first sight. *Many students left the room* implies that some stayed and that not only a few left. The somewhat strange answer *Do fish have lips* implies 'no', and *I brought the cookies* implies that the speaker only brought the cookies, but forgot about the milk. These implicatures, however, are not semantic in the strict sense, i.e. they do not depend just on logic or some conventional linguistic triggers, i.e. there is nothing in *many* that logically implies 'not all', nothing about *fish and lips* that implies 'no', and nothing in the verb *bring* that implies 'bring A but not bring B'. This is something that we read into those utterances during a given conversation. One feature of implicatures of this kind is that they can be cancelled, i.e. corrected:

(26)   Many students left the room, in fact, all of them did.
(27)   A: Do you like spinach? B: Do fish have lips, ah, in fact, yes, I do.
(28)   A: Did you bring the cookies and the milk? B: I brought the cookies...
        and here's the milk.

Another interesting facet is that some seem to depend heavily on context, i.e.
shared world knowledge, while others are fairly context independent. So, it's not
important in which context you speak of *many students* – it will usually imply
that not all of them left. On the other hand, look at the following example:

(29)   A: What's the time? B: The evening news just started.

Here the answer is very much context dependent since you need to know when
the evening news are actually on: this could be 7pm, 8pm, 9pm, or even much
later, depending on the context in which you live, i.e. your place of living, your
favorite TV channel, etc.
       On another level, we can see that some of these implicatures arise in regular,
standard conversational routines, as, for example, when using the quantifier
many. *Many* just like *some*, or *warm* and *a bit* signifies something on a scale as
represented in the following:

none	few	some	many	most	all
cold	lukewarm	warm	hot	boiling	roasting
not	bit	little	ok	lot	totally

The fact that a given term by implicature excludes more or less on the scale is
something pragmatic. It depends on the so-called **Gricean maxims** (see below).
As hearers, we trust that speakers will give us the most precise information
available to them. So if they use *many* we believe that they mean 'many'. If they
meant 'all' they would have said so. In that sense, **scalar implicatures** are
pragmatic phenomena, just like the example with milk and bread above. If a
speaker replies *I brought the bread* to the question *Did you bring the bread and
the milk?* we believe that he did not bring the milk, since that is something he
would have mentioned in the reply. On the other hand, not giving precise
information here is also not lying in the strict sense. Since 'many' and 'some' are
included in 'all', you do say the truth when you claim that some left when in fact
all had gone. Also, the speaker who mentions the bread but not the milk cannot
really be called a liar, even when he forgot to mention the milk that he brought.
Note, however, that this is not the case with the most extreme endpoints on
scales. If you say *none* this semantically means 'none', just like *all* semantically
means 'all'. Hence, you cannot cancel anything in the cases:

(30)   ?None of the students left, in fact, some left.
(31)   ?All of the students left, in fact, some did not leave.

This means that here we actually do lie if we talk about *all* when only *some* were affected. So, the extreme endpoints of a scale have semantic importance, whereas the middle terms are pragmatically interesting. These phenomena are usually subsumed under the headline of 'scalar implicatures'. On the other hand, some implicatures arise because they do not really follow what can be expected. So, *do fish have lips* and *the evening news just started* are, strictly speaking, not valid answers to the questions, but rather off-topic. They violate or flout what we call the Gricean maxims of conversation (see below). It's the hearer's job to figure out what the speaker actually means when he or she says something that apparently does not fit into the context.

5.3.2 Deixis

The term deixis comes from Greek *deiknymi* which roughly means 'show' or 'point'. The central idea is that we not only point with our fingers, but also with our language. Consider the following utterances:

(32)   I want some of this, that, and that!
(33)   Let's meet again next week.
(34)   Why don't you come here more often?

Can you decode, i.e. truly understand what the speakers actually mean? Probably not, because some elements in these utterances are heavily context-dependent pointers: *I* ('pointing' towards the speaker), *this, that, and that* (pointing towards entities visible to the speaker and addressee), *next week* (pointing towards some time that depends on the time of the utterance), *you* (pointing towards the addressee), *here* (the place where the utterance was made) and also *come* (move towards the place where the utterance was made). Note that for all these deictic elements we have one starting point, the 'I, here, now' **deictic center** (or *ego, hic, nunc origo*) which we need as background knowledge in order to decode the messages. Every unmarked utterance that we make starts from this origo. This is not to say, however, that every utterance has its starting point in *ego, hic, nunc*. There are various linguistic ways to shift this center and take a different viewpoint on what is told. This can be seen for example in indirect, reported speech or in narrative texts:

(35)   "Meet me here tomorrow with a book about this thick"
(36)   John told me to meet him there at the restaurant the following day with a
        book about 2 inches thick.

In English, we can identify at least three different central, i.e. common, types of
deictic elements (the list of examples is, of course, not exhaustive):

Table 5.2: Central types of deixis in English.

Spatial Deixis	Temporal Deixis	Person Deixis
this, that, these, those...	then, now, soon...	I, you, he, she, it...
here, there...	present, actual, next...	
come, go, bring, take...	yesterday, next year...	

Apart from these three more central types of deixis we also find a number of
more marginal examples. Social deixis in English is mainly expressed by terms
of address such as *Sir, Madam, Ms, Dr.,* but also first versus last name or titles
such *Mr. President.* Other languages and language communities apparently
attach more value to social deixis and implement this more strongly in their
linguistic system. German and French, for example, have the so-called T-V
pronouns. *T* stands for *tu* ('Du'), *V* for *vous* ('Sie'). The use of these pronominal
forms reflects social deixis quite strongly. Note that English also used to have T-
V pronouns (*you* and *thou*) up until about 1700. Another more marginal type of
deixis in English is manner and degree deixis. These are usually accompanied
by gestures of some sort: *He twisted it like that/so. The pizza was this/so big.*
Finally, the third marginal type of deixis is discourse deixis. This is slightly
more complicated than the other because it very closely resembles so-called
phoric elements in language. The difference between the two goes back to the
difference between context and co-text that we discussed before. Compare the
following two examples:

(37) As mentioned before, pizza definitely does belong to the group of healthy
     foods.
(38) I just read Dan Brown's *Angels and Demons.* It's a story about the order of
     the Illuminati.

In the first case, the clause *as mentioned before* itself actually refers to some
external referent – the relevant utterance made before. In the second example,
the pronoun *it* does not in itself refer to Dan Brown's novel. In the first place, it
is co-referential with the previously used noun phrase "Dan Brown's *Angels and*

Demons". It is this noun phrase which actually refers to the language external object. The pronoun is co-referential with the noun phrase and thus only refers indirectly. This is different for the (discourse) deictic element in the first example. This directly refers to the outside world (even though this may be textual). In other words, discourse deixis is linked to context, phoric elements to co-text.

Deixis is also interesting because it is usually regarded as a bridge between semantics and pragmatics. Deictic elements are Janus-headed beasts: on the one hand side, they have an invariable, semantic component. For example, the pronoun *he* can only refer to male entities, *this* can only refer to single entities. On the other hand, they are also very much context dependent and only 'make sense' in the right context where they can refer to the right entity and are decodable for the respective participants. This clearly is a pragmatic problem. It is thus hardly surprising that discussions of deixis can be found both in textbooks on semantics and on pragmatics.

5.3.3 Speech Acts

Just like semantics, pragmatics with its focus on meaning in context did not originate in linguistics, but rather in philosophy. From the early twentieth century onward, beginning with Ludwig Wittgenstein, some philosophers were dissatisfied with the way philosophy treated meaning in language, particularly everyday, natural language. Philosophy and logic were and are very successful in describing and analyzing meaning in terms of propositional content, truth conditions, and the like. But much of everyday language cannot be captured with these tools. What, for example, are the propositional content and the truth conditions for utterances like

(39) *Good morning.*
(40) *Sorry.*
(41) *I'm hungry.*

These utterances are not about propositions, i.e. exchanges about the state of the world. *Good morning* expresses the feelings (wishes) of the speaker, and so do *sorry* and *I'm hungry*. The latter, however, can also be understood as the speaker's question if anybody would like to join him or her for lunch. With none of these utterances you could apply a simple 'true-false' test. "Good Morning!" – "That's false!" is not an acceptable exchange. The philosophers John L. Austin and John R. Searle developed the concept of speech acts in order to capture utterances like these. The basic idea is that you can 'do things with words': you can express your feelings, you can order people to do things, you can commit yourself to doing something, you can describe facts, or you can even really change the state of the world by saying something – given the appropriate context.

These five different types of actions were mapped onto five different types of speech acts:

Table 5.3: Types of actions.

Action	Speech Act	Example
Describe the world	Representative	He was already dead when I arrived!
Order sb. to do sth.	Directive	Give me that!
Commit yourself to sth.	Commissive	I will help you with linguistics.
Express feelings and thoughts	Expressive	I feel so lonely.
Change the world	Declarative	This meeting is adjourned.

Speech acts have several different parts, but the most important one is certainly their **illocution**, i.e. the speakers' intended meaning. The illocution may be very explicit *(Get me Meyer on the phone right now!),* in which case the speech act is said to be direct. Many direct speech acts contain explicit direct speech act verbs such as *order, ask, apologize, promise* etc. In that case it is usually quite easy for the addressee to see the speaker's intention. But there are other cases in which the intention is hidden and needs to be (re-)constructed by the hearer: *Would you like to tell me where your little sister is?* is not a question about whether the addressee would like to tell the speaker about this, but rather a command, an order: *Tell me where your little sister is.* This roundabout way of making your intention clear is called an **indirect speech act**. How do addressees know how to decode these, how to look beyond the literal meaning?

First, languages provide us with so-called Illocutionary Force Indicating Devices (IFIDs). These include intonation and stress, word order and sentence type, and lexical devices such as *please* or performative verbs. Consider the following two examples:

(42)   Hello? (with a rising intonation upon picking up the phone)
(43)   Can you help me, please?

The rising intonation indicates that this initial *hello* on the phone is not meant as a greeting, but rather that it functions as a form of summons and identification, or that it perhaps shows insecurity on part of the speaker. The word *please* in the second example is actually semantically incompatible with the question *can you help me?*. This becomes clear when we substitute *can* by *be able to: ?are you able to help me, please?* sounds much less felicitous. Since it is incompatible with the actual meaning, it helps addressees to look beyond the actual meaning of the utterance for what is really intended by the speaker: in this case, this is more like a directive speech act and not a simple question.

Indirect speech acts are not only decodable with the help of IFIDs. Another important factor involves the so-called cooperative principle, developed by the philosopher Paul Grice in the 1970s. This will be the topic of the next section.

5.3.4 The cooperative principle

The idea is that speakers and hearers tacitly agree to be 'cooperative', i.e. to follow certain rules in the coding and decoding of messages. Grice put it this way: "Make your contribution such as required, at the stage at which it occurs, by the accepted purpose or direction of the talk exchange in which you are engaged" (Grice 1975: 45).

Note, first of all, that the cooperative principle, though it may look like an explicit rule, is not meant to be a prescriptive norm for communication in the 'do this', 'don't do that' style. Rather, it is simply a hypothesis about what could be underlying all of our communicative acts. It is also important to stress that the basic assumption behind all communication is that speakers are trying to 'make sense' while hearers are doing their best to understand what speakers mean. We have to trust that what speakers are doing must be meaningful somehow, no matter how strange a given utterance may sound, and as speakers we have to trust that our listeners are not deliberately trying to misunderstand us and that they try to find our intention within our utterances. That they actually do so even in the face of difficulties may well have to do with the general psychological principle of 'effort after meaning' that was proposed in the 1930 by the psychologist Frederick Bartlett. 'Effort after meaning' means that we always try to make sense of this world somehow; people usually do not accept that something might be nonsense.

The Cooperative Principle can be broken down into the so-called Gricean maxims. These are:

The maxim of **Quality**: Only say what you believe to be true
The maxim of **Quantity**: Say as much as is required, not more, not less

The maxim of **Relevance** (or **Relation**): Be relevant
The maxim of **Manner**: Be orderly and clear

Again, like the Cooperative Principle itself, the Gricean maxims look like prescriptive rules, but in fact they are not. Rather, they describe the tacit agreements that speakers and hearers follow or at least base their communication on. So, hearers have to trust that speakers do not intentionally lie, that they give all the relevant information that they have, that what they say is somehow relevant for the topic being discussed and that they structure their contribution in an orderly fashion, e.g., start at the beginning. It is obvious that we do not always follow these maxims. Actually, most of the time we don't. If we were to strictly stick to the maxims, there would be no figurative speech, no vaguely hinting at something, no being brief and sketchy... just plain, straightforward, exact talk. This, obviously, is not what we do everyday. And yet our communication functions very well most of the time. How can this be when the maxims are frequently flouted? The trick is that despite the violations there is still cooperation between speakers and hearers. When we realize that someone does not follow the Gricean maxims we do not stop our processing, but instead try to find out what the real intentions are. So, somehow, flouting one or more maxims is a bit like a huge IFID – only that we don't know what the illocution is. Rather, the flouting itself serves as a signal to the hearer that there is a hidden meaning to be uncovered. And this is essentially how indirect speech acts work. Imagine the following conversation:

(44) Speaker A: Do you want to come to my party tonight?
     Speaker B: Sorry, pal, I have to work.

Quite obviously, Speaker B flouts the maxim of relevance. The only appropriate answer (i.e. the second turn in the adjacency pair Invitation-Acceptance) would have been either 'Yes' or 'No'. Instead, Speaker B begins with an apology and talks about his obligation to work. This, superficially, has nothing to do with the invitation. However, this is a perfectly normal speech exchange and there is no obvious communication problem between A and B. It should be clear for A that Speaker B actually means 'No'. This raises two questions: how can A arrive at this conclusion and why does Speaker B not simply say 'no' but instead chooses to take the roundabout way?

     First, Speaker A has to see that B's answer is irrelevant here, i.e. that B flouts the maxim of relevance. Then, following the effort-after-meaning principle, A needs to ask himself what B really did want to say. So A has to infer that because B has to work, he won't come to the party. This implication, however, is not something that is logical here. It is based on pragmatics, on world-knowledge, and common sense. When A takes all that together he can see that B actually meant 'no'. Why didn't B say so, then? There are a number of reasons for using language in a roundabout way. First, it is usually regarded as very impolite and direct if we simply say what we mean, particularly when it is something negative. We like to hide bad messages as much as possible so that we do not offend our interlocutors. Second, humans have been described as *homo ludens,* the 'playing man'. We simply like to play with language. And we like to say things in new, innovative ways. Or in very elaborate, ornate ways. Using language creatively in such a way usually gives us a social advantage: we are regarded as witty, intelligent, interesting. This means that the simple information aspect of language is backgrounded, while the social and affective aspects are strengthened. In fact, indirect speech acts, despite the fact that they flout one or more maxims are much more common than direct ones, and the amount of indirect speech generally exceeds by far that of direct speech.

5.3.5 Politeness

As we have mentioned before, language is not only a means to transmit simple, propositional information. This is something computers can do. Language is also the main tool that helps us to establish and maintain social relationships. As social beings, we have several different socio-psychological needs. Two of the major ones are **positive and negative face.** 'Face' is a socio-psychological concept that is not very different from the original use of the term in Japanese culture. On the one hand, we like to be acknowledged as competent, nice, acceptable and accepted human beings. We love to be loved, desirable by at least some others. This is what we call positive face. On the other hand, we also love to be independent, we like to make our decisions without influences from outside, and we like to have as much leeway as possible whenever we say or do something. This is called negative face. Language can help us to maintain somebody's positive and negative face. For example, we can make people feel good directly by giving them compliments, by saluting their decisions or by hedging our criticism, as in the following example:

(45)   A: I think governments should not interfere with economical issues.
        Let business and the market sort it out.
        B: OK, I see your point there, BUT…

Negative face means that people want freedom to decide, they do not want to be influenced in any way. So, it makes a big difference whether you use (46a) as a command or (46b):

(46)   (a) Close the door.
        (b) Excuse me, would you mind closing the door?

(46a) is a directly face-threatening act in that it forces the hearer to either react according to the command and close the door or respond in a more or less directly negative, open way. The latter means, of course, that the hearer has to threaten the former speaker's face by opposing his command. And this again is something that we do not like to do. In other words, the hearer of (46a) is drastically limited in his or her choices in the situation, which is why (46a) is usually considered rude and offensive. (46b) on the other hand, is not much different in terms of its illocution or speaker intention (namely, *close the door*), but this is wrapped in a message that is much less threatening and leaves more room for the addressee to say no. Upon hearing (46b) hearers still have a chance of politely declining, without loosing too much face by opposing the first speaker. The speaker of (46b) first gives a signal that he acknowledges the hearer's need for positive face by excusing him or her for the command, and then asks – at least on the literal level – for the hearer's evaluation of the situation: *Would you mind---*. (46a) does not do anything of this kind. However, one might also say that the apology *excuse me* is of course a threat to the speaker's negative face in that it puts the speaker into an inferior position towards the hearer.

In linguistics we can identify certain **face-threatening acts** (FTAs) with regard to both positive and negative face on the hearer and the speaker. Obvious FTAs to the hearer's positive face are insults, disapproval, belittling, deliberate misidentifications. Threats to the speaker's positive face include apologies, acts of self-humiliation, accepting a compliment. The hearer's negative face is threatened when speakers give orders, express compliments, or wishes, hopes, offers or promises since all of these deprive hearers of free choice. Similarly, the speaker's negative face is threatened when he or she expresses thanks or excuses, or reacts towards some violation of the conversational maxims or even commits himself or herself to something he or she does not want to do. All these acts delimit the speakers' choice of action.

Language provides us with a large number of politeness strategies that help to save face or minimize face-threatening acts. These politeness strategies can be categorized into four different groups:

- Positive politeness
- Negative politeness
- bald on-record
- off-record

Positive politeness strategies tend to the hearer's (and speaker's!) positive face and are intended to generally make them 'feel good'. Positive politeness strategies include, among others, solidarity markers, offers and promises, compliments and interest in the other person, avoidance of disagreement and jokes. **Negative politeness strategies** are meant to limit the imposition on the hearer and to give him or her more room to move and decide. These strategies include: indirect speech acts, hedges, passivization and generalization, apologies, and plural or general pronouns (*we, one*).

Bald on-record means that there is virtually no minimizing of the face-threat. We usually do this when the situation urgently requires action and/or we are very familiar with the other interlocutors. In other words, in talking to close friends and family members, we may sometimes rather go bald on-record than use elaborate politeness strategies (*Don't forget to close the door, Watch out!, Leave it.*).

Finally, **off-record** refers to strategies which are so indirect that it is completely up to the hearer to decide how to interpret them. Instead of saying *Come on, let's go eat* (which would threaten the hearer's negative face) or *You look hungry, you don't want to go for lunch by any chance* (which would use a positive politeness strategy) one might also say *Gee, I haven't had anything to eat since 5 am* as a simple statement and wait for the hearer to interpret this as an indirect speech act with the illocution *I am hungry, come and join me for a meal*. Obviously, off record strategies carry the greatest risk of being misunderstood.

In the previous sections we have discussed various aspects of meaning in language, from simple lexical semantics through sentence semantics to micropragmatic issues such as implicatures and speech acts to politeness. The literature on all these topics is vast and such a short introduction as this one can obviously only scratch the surface on a few selected topics. I therefore wholeheartedly recommend that anybody interested in meaning in language should have a look at some of the standard textbooks, such as Mey (2008) or Yule (2006), or, for the very brave, Stephen Levinson's *Pragmatics* (1983) and Sir John Lyons 2-volume *Semantics* (1977). The latter two are tough reading for the beginner, no doubt, but they are also great classics in the field.

5.4 Exercises

1. Give synonyms for *fast*.

2. List possible antonyms of the following words. Which of them are gradable antonyms?

    large; love; hot; dead; dark; easy; evil; short.

3. Find co-hyponyms of flower.

4. Find meronyms of *house*.

5. How could a prototype analysis for *chair* look like?

6. Identify all deictic elements in the following sentences, to which type of deixis do they belong?

    a) I think they will meet tomorrow at ten in the small restaurant over there.

    b) Can I have that now, Mommy?

7. Which of the Gricean Maxims is violated in the following examples?

    a) A: What will you do tomorrow?
        B: I went to Spain last year.

    b) A: Did you go out last night?
        B: Yes, Johnny, Clare, Suzi, Dan and I went to a very nice and cosy bar not far from here– we could not decide for quite some time where to go and first we had some burgers while thinking about places to go, I suggested a bar down-town but Dan did not like it there and Suzi did not want to go that far, so Johnny suggested to go to that bar, but it took us some time to convince Clare because her ex used to work there. It's really a nice place, they have comfortable sofas to sit on, it's almost a lounge, the walls are painted green and yellow and there are a lot of pictures of movie stars. Each of us had about four cocktails and Dan ordered some tacos and we stayed very long.

8. Try to explain the following situation using the concept of speech acts:

Teacher: Who wants to talk about the importance of punctuation for essay
writing?
James eagerly holds up his hand.
Teacher: Yes, James?
James: No one?

9. Identify the speech acts used:

a) I hereby pronounce you husband and wife.
b) Go and get some milk!
c) Thank you very much for your invitation.
d) There is a cat on the cupboard.

10. Identify all thematic roles:

a) I gave Peter a cookie.
b) Timothy sliced the bread with a knife in the kitchen.
c) Fran was bitten by the dog.

11. Match the sentences (A – D) with the correct politeness strategy (1 – 4):

Situation: You are in a room and want Lisa to shut the window.

A: Shut the window, Lisa!
B: It's freezing in here, isn't it.
C: You look cold, Lisa. Should we close the window?
D: Excuse me, could you probably do me a favour and close the window?

1. Off record
2. On record
3. Negative politeness
4. Positive politeness

6   On doing things differently:
a construction grammar approach to language

6.1 Introduction

What has been described in the previous sections is a fairly conventional, structuralist approach to English grammar and language in general. This approach assumes that there is an inventory of linguistic symbols (words) which are put together by grammatical rules into higher level units such as phrases, clauses and sentences. But, as we said before, this is not the only way to do things. Syntax in particular offers a variety of different approaches, concepts, and theories. Some of these are complementary, some are rather contradictory and force us to make informed decisions on certain issues. One such approach, which is not always compatible with other mainstream frameworks, but nevertheless has become increasingly popular over the past twenty years or so, is Construction Grammar (henceforth CxG). The key idea is that syntax (and language generally) is not organized as items plus rules, but rather that syntactic units essentially behave like lexical items. Both are subsumed under the label of "constructions". **Constructions are then defined as form-function pairings** (de Saussure discussed a very similar idea under the heading of the inseparable signifier/signified nature of the linguistic sign, see Chapter 1) at all levels of linguistic structure, including lexicon, morphology, and syntax, as long as their meaning or function is not directly predictable from their components (they must show holistic properties), or they occur with sufficiently high frequency. Knowledge of language thus no longer means that we know the rules and words, but that we know the constructions of a language. Constructions do not exist in isolation, but, just like lexical words, form a structured inventory. The whole idea partly grew out of dissatisfaction with the way many traditional approaches handle idioms. In most traditional frameworks, such as Chomskian generativism, it has been assumed that certain structures are related in some sense, and that one structure can be transformed into the other. One such textbook example is active versus passive voice (see Chomsky 1956; Freidin 2007: 228-253). Compare sentences (1a) and (1b), active and passive.

(1a)   The boy gave the girl a cookie.
(1b)   The girl was given a cookie by the boy.

We can say that (1b) is derived from (1a) in that the indirect object is moved into the subject position, while the subject turns into a facultative *by* adverbial. At the same time, the active verb form *gave* is changed into the periphrastic passive verb phrase *be* plus past participle, i.e. *was given*. So far, so good. However, this analysis is not uncontroversial.

If we try the same with the superficially similar structure in (2a) below, we end up with a much less felicitous passive (2b).

(2a)   The boys spilled the beans.
(2b)   *?The beans were spilled by the boys.[1]

Note that (2b) is, technically speaking, the passive of (2a), but that the semantic relationship between (1a) and (1b) is different from the one in (2a) and (2b). You can predict the meaning of (1b) on the basis of (1a), but (2a) in one reading also means "The boys revealed a secret" whereas (2b) only means "The boys spilled the beans". In other words, there is an idiomatic reading of (2a) which is not available in (2b). Hence, the two should not be treated in the same way as (1a) and (1b).

A similar phenomenon can be observed with so-called fronting. In regular English structures, you can usually front the object in order to signal special information value, such as hot news or contrastiveness (cf. Birner & Ward 2002). (3a) and (3b) show such an example.

(3a)   I hate bean soup.
(3b)   Bean soup I hate.

(3b) essentially implies that there is some other soup that the speaker likes. It could be used as an answer to the question "What kind of soup would you like? Bean, tomato, or pumpkin soup?" – "Bean soup I hate" would imply that both tomato and pumpkin soup are alright, and that only bean soup is not. (4a) and (4b) show similar structures and therefore should work along the same lines.

(4a)   Another one bites the dust.
(4b)   *The dust another one bites.

---

[1] This is a great chance for a remark on methodology (cf. Chapter 1). Some scholars working with introspection as a method have claimed that some sentences like (2b) are actually alright, while others have claimed that these are not possible. A brief search for the string "beans were spilled" in both the British National Corpus (BNC, 100 million words) and the Corpus of Contemporary American English (COCA, 450 million words) did not show a single hit for this string. This suggests that even if this is theoretically somehow possible, it would also be extremely rare. Only compare the figures for the string "spill the beans": 0.13 per million words in COCA, 0.23 per million words in BNC. Not a lot, but more than nothing.

Again, like with examples (1) and (2), (4b) is not the transformed equivalent of (4a) in the way (3b) relates to (3a). In fact, (4b) is very infelicitous and it is hard to think of a context in which it could be used.

We could do the same for many other tests in syntax: tough-movement, extraction, clefts, embedding, nominalizations, and so on, and all of them would lead to the conclusion that there's always the odd idiom which does not show the syntactic behavior it is supposed to show. And the same applies to some constructions which are superficially ill-formed and yet in wide current use:

(5)   Jodie won't eat chocolate, *let alone* lard.
(6)   The harder it gets, the better you fail.
(7)   all of a sudden, by and large
(8)   Him, a doctor?
(9)   What are you doing eating all that pizza?

None of the sentences in (5) to (9) is actually grammatical in the sense that English grammar provides us with rules that help to construct these. On the contrary, we actually have to learn them and their meaning or function as chunks, like words, despite the fact that they look like regular syntactic constructions! This, of course, is also a problem for many traditional frameworks, which usually do not allow for items beyond the word level to be stored and processed like words. Factors like these led scholars in the 1970s (perhaps most notably Paul Kay and Charles Fillmore) to work on a syntactic framework that explains exactly these (hitherto marginalized) phenomena. Their reasoning was surprisingly simple and yet convincing: if the new syntactic theory could explain the margins and exceptions, it would not be hard to capture the simple regularities later on. This, in a way, was the birth of Construction Grammar.

6.2 Construction Grammar in practice

Constructions have been defined as conventionalized form-meaning pairings. However, within this definition, we can identify several different subtypes.

First, there are simple words like *house* and *eat*. Their meaning cannot be predicted from their parts, and they obviously exemplify conventionalized form-meaning pairings. In fact, this was already discussed by de Saussure in early 20th century structuralism (cf. Chapter 1).

But CxG takes this idea beyond the word level and applies it to other levels of language structure. As we have just seen, there are more complex units that, nevertheless, seem to operate like words: *idioms*. Examples include *spill the beans*[2] ([spɪl ðə biːnz] = 'divulge a secret'), *head over heels* ([hɛd ovəɹ hiːlz] = 'very excited'), and *nothing to sneeze at* ([nʌθɪŋ tə sniːz æt] = 'not to be underestimated'). Again, quite obviously, their meaning is unpredictable and they couple form with meaning. The idioms just mentioned are completely fixed or filled, i.e. they do not have any variable slot. Other idioms have such slots and are only partially filled: *give X a hard time, Y never got round to doing Z.*

Finally, constructions may also exhibit different degrees of concreteness. *House*, for example, is a simple, concrete construction, NOUN (as a word class) is also simple, but certainly less concrete. And the same applies to syntactic, i.e. complex, constructions: *spill the beans* is complex and concrete, the ditransitive (two object) construction is complex, but abstract. All this can be summarized as in Table 6.1 below.

Table 6.1: Construction Types

	Simple	**Complex**
Concrete	*house*	*spill the beans* (filled)
		give X a hard time (partially filled)
Abstract	NOUN	DITRANSITIVE CONSTRUCTION

In the following, we will focus on some case studies from a CxG perspective in order to illustrate how this theory can be put into practice. But before we can do this, we need some more theoretical background on how constructions can actually be described, once we go beyond the general classification in Table 6.1 above.

First, it was mentioned above that constructions are conventionalized form-meaning pairings. What does that mean in detail? Most analyses assume that a given construction has a "form side", or structure, which can contain information about its syntactic properties (how many objects it requires, for example), its morphological properties, and its phonological properties. The corresponding "meaning side", or function, can contain information about the semantics of the construction, its pragmatic properties, and discourse-functional aspects. This can be visualized as in Figure 6.1 below.

---

[2] For ease of exposition, we will present these constructions simply as FORM [IPA phonological transcript] = FUNCTION/MEANING 'semantic paraphrase'. Needless to say, a complete analysis would require many more details.

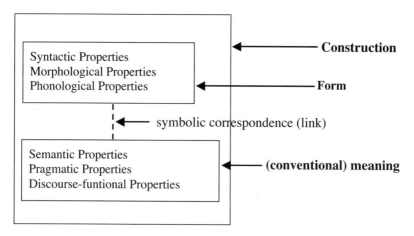

Figure 6.1: The symbolic structure of constructions (Croft and Cruse 2004: 258; Reproduction with kind permission of Cambridge University Press).

The symbolic correspondence (link) in Figure 6.1 is nothing but the symbolic nature of the linguistic sign. The signifier and the signified in language are linked this (arbitrary and conventional) way and thereby constitute a symbol. As has been outlined above, the construction in Figure 6.1 contains a form and a conventional meaning side. These together make up the construction.

The important point to remember is that all of the sub-properties can, but need not be part of the constructions. Some constructions have special phonological properties (such as the Mad Magazine sentences *Him, a doctor? Tom, a linguist? Alex, a sexgod?*, i.e. *X, a(n) Y?* in more abstract terms, which need the subject to be the obligatory intonation center), other constructions have peculiar pragmatic properties (such as *What's that shoe doing on that table?* which expresses annoyance on part of the speaker because of the fact that the shoe is on the table, contrary to what was to be expected), yet others show discourse functional-properties (the future with *will*, for example, is much more common than the future with *going to*; however, *going to,* is strongly preferred in informal discourse contexts). All this can, but need not be part of the constructional properties.

The second question that we need to address is what actually counts as a construction in the technical sense. Often, construction grammarians distinguish between what they call a "construction" and a "construct". The latter refers to the concrete realization of one or more constructions. This notion was introduced to save researchers from having to call "She gave him a cookie" a construction. Rather, this particular sentence would be a **construct**, i.e. one realization of the more abstract ditransitive constructions. The actual sentence "She gave him a cookie" and its elements do not add any special meaning to the construction as such. The ditransitive construction means something like "Agent X causes Y to have Z". The example just given does not influence or change that in any way. Therefore, construction grammarians usually claim that constructions, in contrast to constructs, must either have holistic meaning, or be sufficiently frequent. Holistic, i.e. non-compositional meaning means that we cannot tell the meaning of the construction just by looking at its parts. This is very obvious for many idioms. Nobody can even imagine what *to kick the bucket* or *to face the music* refer to if they haven't learned (by heart) what they mean ('to die' and 'to face the penalty', respectively). The same applies to more abstract constructions such as the resultative construction: *she baked him a cake* looks like a regular ditransitive *she gave him a cake* but actually means something else: 'she baked a cake so that he could have it'. Neither is this clearly obvious from either the verb *to bake* (which normally is a simple transitive verb; cf. *She baked a cake*) nor from the form *Subject-Verb-Object1-Object2*. The combination of both leads to that reading and has to be learned as such. We call this **holistic or non-compositional meaning**, i.e. the whole means more than just the sum of its parts. Alternatively, even compositional constructs which are extremely frequent may turn into constructions over time, simply because psycholinguistic tests have shown that these construct(ions) are not assembled online (as other less common non-compositional constructs are), but are rather stored as big chunks in the mental lexicon. One example here might come from morphology. One of the most common regular verbs in the English language is *look* (rank 85 on the list of the most common words in American English, based on the 450 million word Corpus of Contemporary American English, COCA, see <http://www.wordfrequency.info/free.asp>). It seems plausible to assume that the forms for *look*, i.e. *looks, looking, looked* are not mentally assembled online every time we use them, but rather that we have the combined forms ready in our mental lexicon, even though they are completely regular, transparent, predictable and therefore also compositional. Things may be very different for a verb like *extramuralize*.

Another issue that we need to look at is how constructions are stored in the mental lexicon, or **constructicon**, as some scholars call it. It is usually agreed upon that constructions do not exist in isolation but rather form a network, a structured inventory of constructions. This network is organized via so-called inheritance relations, i.e. lower ranking constructions can inherit some or all of the features of higher ranking constructions. Essentially, this is what you see in your family. People can inherit (physiological) traits of their parents and grandparents. What is more important, however, is that constructions cannot have features in violation of their mother-node constructions (again, it is highly unlikely that a child of 'purely' Asian decent will have red hair, or that 'purely'

Irish children will have Asian eye features). However, the details of these constructional networks are still a matter of debate and most recent analysis (Goldberg 2006) point towards the possibility that daughter-nodes can override mother-nodes. What is important to remember is that constructions are always in some kind of relationship with each other, and that we need to identify their place in the constructicon, so that we know where their particular features may come from. This may be illustrated by the *is to* construction, identified by Goldberg and van der Auwera (in press). This construction is illustrated in examples (10) to (13) below.

(10)   The match is to begin at 11pm
(11)   Arguments are to be avoided [...]
(12)   You are to recall each detail [...]
(13)   Junior was to become a lawyer and the chairman [...]
                (all examples taken from Goldberg & van der Auwera, in press)

Goldberg and van der Auwera show that *is to* should be regarded as a non-compositional construction in the strict sense, since it has one peculiar syntactic feature, namely that the copula must be finite. Apart from that, the finite form of *to be* behaves like any other auxiliary. In terms of its semantics, we can see that the copula appears to be subject raising, i.e. the subject of the *to be* clause is actually the subject of the subordinate clause: (10) means that the match begins at 11pm, (11) means that arguments must be avoided, (12) that you need to recall each detail and (13) that junior became a lawyer. The construction as a whole can signal prearrangement (10), predetermination (13), indirect command (12), and suitability/advisability (11). Note that all four meanings also share some overlapping areas, as for example in (14).

(14)   Your grandfather is to see the doctor next week.
                                        (Goldberg & van der Auwera, in press)

Furthermore, the *is to* construction is also pragmatically constrained and mostly used in specific (more formal or perhaps even archaic) registers and styles.
    Goldberg and van der Auwera find that the *is to* construction is linked to (or motivated by) a number of related constructions:

-   the predicative complement (*Bob is a kindergarten teacher*),
-   the *to* infinitive as a possible marker of future orientation (*She stopped to go* = "*in order to go*"),
-   modals such as *should/must* (*She is to see a doctor* = "*must*"/"*should*")

Note that *is to* of course does not qualify as a core modal (not unlike *ought*) since it has the NICE (negation, inversion, code, emphasis) properties of auxiliaries but lacks other features of core modals, such as the bare infinitival complement and the lack of (proper) inflection and tense marking.

All this leads Goldberg and van der Auwera to suggest that the *is to* construction can be represented "within a default (non-monotonic) inheritance hierarchy [...] such that daughter nodes inherit all non-conflicting information from their mother nodes. [...] we can understand the inheritance relationship to capture the notion of motivation: the existence of the mother nodes motivates the daughter node, making it more likely to exist and presumably easier to learn and use" (Goldberg & van der Auwera, in press). Eventually, this fact can be summarized in Figure 6.2 below.

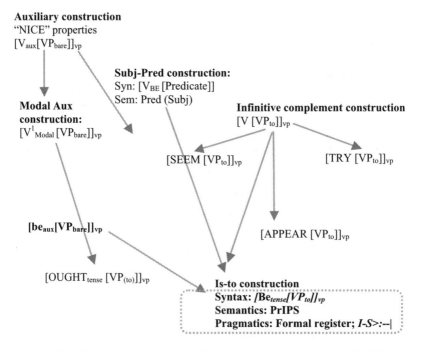

Figure 6.2: The inheritance network of the is to construction (Goldberg & van der Auwera: in press; Reproduction with kind permission of Professor Teresa Fanego).

This example shows that constructions (like words in word fields and semantic networks) do not exist in isolation but form a complex inventory with diverse relations between the single items at various levels.

6.3 Case studies

Having described some of the basic ideas of CxG, we will now turn to some exemplary case studies that can illustrate in more detail how constructional analyses actually work. We will discuss three different problems: idiomatic expressions that are fully spelled out, semi-concrete constructions, and abstract complex constructions like the ditransitive construction.

6.3.1 What's that fly doing in my soup?

Our first case study is a complex idiom in English. This can be illustrated by an old joke:

(15)   Diner: Waiter, *what's that fly doing in my soup?*
       Waiter: Why, madam, I believe that's the backstroke.

                                                                 (Kay & Fillmore 1994)

Native speakers of English immediately recognize the ambiguity in the diner's question. On the one hand, it resembles an ordinary *what* question with a progressive form of *do*. Example (16) below illustrates one such 'regular' use.

(16)   What are you doing with the data?

The sentence in example (16) probably only asks what the addressee is planning (or currently doing) with the data. The diner in example (15) above essentially uses the same syntax, i.e. *what* + be + subject + *doing* + complement. However, the diner's line in (15) has a strong disapproving overtone. The diner wants to express his or her being annoyed that the fly is in the soup, in other words, that it does not belong there. This, however, is not unambiguously phrased. Since the sentence, at least superficially, is the same as in (16), the waiter can reply to the diner's complaint as if that complaint were a real information question. Today we recognize something like a *What's X doing Y* construction which, as an integral part of its pragmatic meaning or function, signals annoyance and disapproval on part of the speaker. It probably developed this conventional meaning through its use in particular contexts which allowed for some ambiguity and the pragmatic inference of disapproval. In terms of its grammatical features, the construction shows some interesting phenomena (as outlined by Kay & Fillmore 2009):

- it requires the use of *do*

If we substitute *do* for other possible verbs or synonymous items, the inference of disapproval etc. is usually lost. Look at examples (17a) and (17b), taken from Kay & Fillmore (2009):

(17a) What was she doing under the bed?
(17b) What activity was she engaged in under the bed?

In (17a) we find the ambiguity and the overtone of disapproval, (17b) has the same propositional content, but in contrast has no such overtone.

- the verb *do* has to be used as present participle, i.e. *doing*

If we change the form of *doing* the construction becomes ungrammatical or loses its special meaning, as you can see in examples (18) and (19), both of which are taken from Kay & Fillmore (2009):

(18)   *What does this scratch do on the table?
(19)   *What has your name done absent from the list of contributors?

- *doing* has to be used as complement of *to be*

The construction in question requires *doing* to be used as complement of *to be*. If we use another verb (such as *keep*) the result is still grammatical, but loses the special meaning of the construction. This is illustrated in (20) and (21).

(20)   What did he keep doing in the tool shed?
(21)   What was he still doing in the tool shed?

Both (20) and (21) are grammatical, but only (21) carries some disapproving overtone. (20) is an innocent information question.

- *doing* in this construction does not signal progressive aspect

Despite the fact that *doing* is morphologically the present progressive form of the verb, its use here has nothing to do with progressive aspect. This can be shown by the fact that it can be used in contexts which do not allow for progressives. (22) below is a good example of the construction in question, (23) would be the required answer to the information question. Obviously, states usually do not allow for progressive aspect, so that (23) is not possible.

(22)   What's that scratch doing on the table?
(23)   *The scratch is being on the table.

- the interrogative with *what* does not permit modification by *else*

Usually, we can add *else* to *what* questions, as in (24) below. This is not possible for the construction in question.

(24)   What else do you need?
(25)   *What else is that scratch doing on the table?

- the construction does not allow for negation of either *be* or *do*

We cannot use a negative form of the construction without losing its special meaning, as (26) and (27) show.

(26)   *What isn't that scratch doing on the table?
(27)   *What is that scratch not doing on the table?

What all this amounts to is that this combination of words shows very peculiar idiosyncratic features, which cannot be explained on the basis of regular syntactic behavior. Similarly, the meaning and use of the construction cannot be predicted on the basis of its components. In other words, the meaning (i.e. disapproval) is non-compositional or holistic and results from the very combination of these elements. All these features qualify the combination in question as a construction in the technical sense.

6.3.2 Let's go (and) see

The second case study that we will discuss now is the so-called *go-(and)*-Verb construction, as illustrated in (28) and (29) below.

(28)   You will be a martyr one day, and then you will **go and see** your dad
       (COCA)
(29)   He needed Viagra or something for erectile dysfunction. "**Go see** a doctor
       or leave me alone," she yelled, ... (COCA)

Wulff (2006) discusses these two patterns and asks in how far these two qualify as constructions and whether they should be treated as only one or two independent constructions. Wulff points out that the two patterns indeed look very similar, and that the *go-*V pattern can be analyzed as a truncated version of *go-and-*V. However, some features lead us to think that this is not the case. On the one hand, the *go-*V pattern seems to have a much closer link between the two verbs than the *go-and-*V pattern, which makes "go leave" less likely than "go and leave". However, both patterns can be found in the Corpus of Contemporary American English (COCA); the sequence *go leave* occurs eight times, *go and leave* fifteen times. Similarly, *go*-V requires an agent subject, while *go-and*-V can also have other subject types. Look at examples (30) through (32), all taken from Wulff (2006: 104):

(30a) The trucks come and pick up the garbage every Monday.
(30b) The trucks come pick up the garbage every Monday.

(31a) Pieces of drift wood come and wash up the shore.
(31b) *Pieces of drift wood come wash up the shore.

(32a) The smoke fumes go and inebriate the people upstairs.
(32b) *The smoke fumes go inebriate the people upstairs.

Wulff then proceeds and checks what verbs can actually fill the slots in the *go*-V and *go-and*-V constructions. She finds that in the 100-million word British National Corpus (BNC) a small number of verbs (such as *get, see, sit, fetch, buy, pick, check, look, find, put, tell, ...*) can occur in both constructions, while there are 92 verbs (*collect, live, visit, talk, watch, ask, sort, wash, hide, stand, stay, eat, ...*) which only occur in the *go-and*-V construction versus 25 verbs (*zoom, figure, walk, run, swim, hire, search, ...*) which only occur in the *go*-V context. It becomes clear that *go*-V does not go that often with verbs denoting accomplishments or achievements as one might expect. The action denoted by *go-and*-V is more like an event with a particular identifiable sequence, whereas *go*-V usually only signifies the beginning of an event and therefore rather goes with process verbs.

The important point here is that the constructions are not only identified and distinguished by 'traditional' syntactic behavior, but also by the word combinations that they occur in. One of the textual canons in law interpretation says *noscitur a sociis*, 'a word is known by the company it keeps', and the same applies here: constructions are known (and distinguished) by the company they keep. Constructions can show very specific patterns in their collocations, i.e. in the way they fill their variable slots or combine with other elements. Gries and Stefanowitsch (2003, 2004, and elsewhere) have been among the most prolific proponents of such a viewpoint. They developed so-called collostructional analyses. These are complex statistical procedures that measure the association strengths between words and the constructions they occur in. Two of the most widely used techniques are collexeme analysis where the association of a particular word with a particular construction is calculated. The results can show that words do not randomly fill variable slots in constructions but often with some preferences. This in turn can tell us a lot about the semantics of a given construction. Gries and Stefanowitsch analyze the "N waiting to happen" construction, as in (33).

(33)   This is just a disaster waiting to happen.

They discovered that the variable in this construction, the noun slot, is not filled randomly, but rather with a more or less clearly identifiable set of nouns: *accident, disaster, earthquake, invasion, recovery, revolution, dream, it* (sex) etc. are more likely to occur in this construction than other nouns. The method that leads to that finding looks very complex at first, but the rationale is very simple. First, they checked all occurrences of the word *accident* in clause-level constructions with a verb in the British National Corpus (8,620). Then they checked the number of occurrences of *accident waiting to happen* (14). This means that out of 8,620 a total of 8,606 occurrences of *accident* can be found in different clause-level verbal constructions. Next, they checked for all *N waiting to happen* constructions in the corpus (35). With 14 occurrences of *accident waiting to happen* this means that 21 occurrences of that construction have to be without *accident.* Finally, they also checked the number of clause-level verbal constructions in total (10,206,300). Eventually, this leads to the following table:

Table 6.2: Crosstabulation of accident and the [N waiting to happen] construction (Gries & Stefanowitsch 2003: 219).

	Accident	N (¬ Accident)	Total
[N waiting to happen]	14	21	35
¬ [N waiting to happen]	8,606	10,197,659	10,206,265
Total	8,620	10,197,680	10,206,300

The question that remains when looking at the results given in Table 6.2 is whether these figures actually mean something, or if this distribution is only random. Gries & Stefanowitsch use elaborate statistical tests, such as the Fisher exact test to check the statistical significance for the association (or likelihood) of *accident* appearing in this construction (in contrast to all others). They find that this is indeed much more likely and beyond mere chance so that we can assume that this construction and the word *accident* are closely associated for the native speaker. The same can be done for the other words listed above, and they also show high statistical significance. Does this mean that the construction N *waiting to happen* carries a negative meaning, as the Collins Cobuild English Dictionary suggests? Clearly not, since the construction also allows for *recovery, dream* and *it* (sex) to fill the N slot. Therefore Gries and Stefanowitsch

(2003: 220) suggest that the N *waiting to happen* construction should receive its own entry in the dictionary "with a more neutral definition along the lines of 'if you describe something as **waiting to happen**, you mean that it will almost certainly occur and that this is already obvious at the present point in time (often used with a negative connotation)".

The second technique developed by Stefanowitsch and Gries is distinctive collexeme analysis, which can show which words like to occur with which constructions (for example when two similar constructions 'compete' in the same domain), and how strong this preference actually is. A good example is probably the ditransitive construction (which will also be the topic of our next section). The ditransitive construction (as in *Bill gave Mary a book*) competes with the prepositional dative construction (as in *Bill gave a book to Mary*). This naturally leads to the question, if these two should be treated as one construction with different realizations, or whether the two are distinct and, for example, like to co-occur with different verbs. A distinctive collexeme analysis, which contrasts the two constructions in questions and checks which verbs occur in which construction shows that the ditransitive likes verbs such as *give, tell, show, offer, allow, cost, teach, buy* while the prepositional dative rather prefers *put, bring, add, attach, play, say, limit, take* (Gries & Stefanowitsch 2003: 240). All this leads us to believe that despite their superficial similarity and synonymy these constructions are not the same and actually show significant differences in real language use. This leads back to a building principle of language as such, namely the 'Principle of No-Synonymy' developed by Bolinger: "any word which a language permits to survive must make its semantic contribution [...] the same holds for any construction that is physically distinct from any other construction" (1977: ix-x). In other words, Bolinger already suggested that whatever is different in terms of form must also make a difference in meaning. This more abstract idea is confirmed by studies such as Wulff (2006).

6.3.3 Ditransitives

Our third case study is on ditransitives. Ditransitives in English are usually formed with verbs such as *give* and *ask*. Their defining characteristic is that they require two objects as arguments, one of which is called the indirect object, the other one the direct object. In inflecting languages these would often be marked by dative (indirect object) and accusative (direct object) case. In English they simply follow the verb, usually in a particular order: *give somebody something* (*?give something somebody*) and *ask somebody something* (*?ask something somebody*). In general we can say that they all somehow have the meaning of actual or intended transfer. We might therefore posit a so-called ditransitive construction, schematized as follows:

SYNTAX:	Subj	Predicate	Obj1	Obj2
SEMANTICS:	Agent	Predicate (Transfer)	Recipient	Theme (transferred)

Note that this construction can be combined with some fairly obvious verb constructions such as *give, bring, pass,* or *send.* With all three verbs, we usually assume that there is an agent (the giver, bringer, sender), the act of transferring an object, a recipient of that object, and the object being transferred. But we can also extend this fairly narrow view by allowing for extensions of the sense of 'transfer'. We might argue that 'transfer' is translatable into 'cause Y to have Z'. This then would allow us to include verbs such as *promise, allow, deny, bake, teach, show,* and many more. How does this work? Goldberg (1995) in her seminal study argues that all these verbs can be treated as extensions of the core transfer meaning:

- *promise*: 'satisfaction condition of the speech act' implies that agent causes recipient to receive theme (literally: *I promise you a diamond ring*; metaphorically, recipient receives the promise/guarantee)
- *allow*: Agent enables recipient to receive theme
- *deny*: Agent causes recipient not to have theme
- *bake*: Agent intends to cause recipient to have theme
- *teach* (*somebody a lesson*): communication as transfer
- *show* (*somebody something*): perception as communication as transfer

We can therefore posit a very basic general construction for the ditransitive which has the core meaning of 'X causes Y to have Z' and a basic, abstract syntactic structure of Subject-Verb-Object1-Object2. Object 1 and Object 2 usually map onto the semantic roles of recipient and theme. On that basis we find a number of 'sub-constructions' with verbs like *allow* or *bake* which are in a polysemy relation to the basic core constructions. The interesting fact here is that some of the verbs that can be found in this construction are not immediately recognizable as ditransitive verbs (e.g., *bake, cook, assign, drop, spare*) but still unify with this construction and gain a ditransitive reading: *bake her a cake, cook him dinner, assign them a task, drop you a line, spare me the details.* Note that the constructional analysis does not claim that the verbs are polysemous in any sense. On the contrary, the verbs have their own semantics which have to be compatible with the semantics of the ditransitive constructions. If the semantics of the two are compatible, the two constructions can unify, resulting in the new reading. If the verb is not compatible (e.g., *be*), the result is most likely ungrammatical: ?**he is me a friend* versus *he is a friend to me.*

6.4 Construction Grammars

So far we have pretended as if there were only one type of construction grammar. However, this is only partly true. On the one hand, the various construction grammar frameworks which are out there of course share a number of central and important assumptions about how linguistic systems work. This is why Croft & Cruse (2004) coined the term 'Vanilla Construction Grammar' for an approach that basically works with a CxG framework without necessarily committing itself to any particular technical detail. On the other hand, we have at least four or five different schools of Construction Grammars which share these basic assumptions, but can also differ a lot in the details. Some of these are:

- Radical Construction Grammar (Croft 2002)
- Embodied Construction Grammar (Bergen & Chang 2005)
- Sign-based (Unification) Construction Grammar (Fillmore, Kay, O'Connor 1988; Michaelis 2005; Boas & Sag 2011)
- Cognitive Construction Grammar (Goldberg 1995, 2006)

In the following, we will very briefly outline what some of the major tenets and strengths of these schools are.

6.4.1 Radical Construction Grammar

Radical Construction Grammar (RCxG) was developed in 2001 by the typologist Bill Croft in order to unify the strengths of (Vanilla) Construction Grammar with cross-linguistic diversity. Croft discovered that what many assume to be basic, universal syntactic categories in all languages of the world are, in fact, very language specific. What makes us identify a word in English as a verb (it is inflected for person, tense, aspect, mood) could be an adjective in Makah, a native American English, since adjectives inflect for exactly these categories in this language. Similarly, Vietnamese words are not inflected at all for these categories. What this boils down to is that, according to Croft, we cannot use the traditional categories and criteria when we want to determine the word classes and categories of other languages around the world. Croft therefore suggests that we should not see categories or relations as universal or basic, but rather constructions (Croft 2002: 46). This is possible since Construction Grammar does not make any a priori claims about what constructions are universal (if any), or what types of grammatical information or elements should be present in any given language. On the contrary, construction grammar has an explicit bottom-up approach which takes the data to be primary and lets the theory follow the data. The 'radicalness' of RCxG results from the fact that what has just been said means that there are no universal, a priori atomic, schematic units (i.e. word classes and syntactic roles). This is not to say that language can't have them, but it means that these have to be developed out of the data for every individual language. Croft also claims that RCxG only works with (complex) constructions and their component parts (without any syntactic relations) and that it does not allow for any universal constructions. This means that "virtually all formal grammatical structure is language-specific and construction-specific" (Croft 2005: 277).

6.4.2 Embodied Construction Grammar

Embodied Construction Grammar (ECxG) was developed by Ben Bergen and Nancy Chang in their seminal 2005 article. Its specific aim is the integration of an embodied model of language understanding into the general construction grammar framework. Such a model implies that language understanding is conceptually deeper than simply deciphering the speaker's intended meaning. It goes beyond that in that it asks how hearers actually know how to respond appropriately to any given utterance. Such a conceptually deep understanding can be modeled and explained by treating language comprehension processes as dynamic, i.e. procedural rather than static, and as activation of embodied schemas. These embodied schemas are "cognitive structures generalized over recurrent perceptual and motor experiences" (Bergen & Chang 2005: 147). The word (and concept) *into* for example, involves a trajectory-landmark schema (so, the movement of a trajector relative to a fixed landmark), a source-path-goal schema (a trajectory moves along a path from a source to a goal) and a container schema (a boundary separates interior from exterior, and there is a portal through which the trajectory can pass). So, whenever we say or hear *into* these schemas are activated and help us understand what the word means (as in *He went into the barn*).

ECxG adds yet another concept to this model. It claims that the mental representation thus produced is also simulated in context on the basis of more general sensorimotor and cognitive structures. By invoking this simulation, ECxG introduces a 'division of labor' between very basic conventionalized meanings and the sometimes very complex, indirect inferences that speakers can make on the basis of their simulations. "In effect, constructions provide a limited means by which the discrete tools of symbolic language can approximate the multidimensional, continuous world of action and perception." (Bergen & Chang 2005: 149). Embodied Construction Grammar develops a rather complex formalization for the description and analysis of these processes, not in the least because it also seeks to offer a computational model of language production and understanding that can be implemented on computers. The reader is referred to the excellent exposition in Bergen & Chang (2005) which details further formal aspects. The main point to remember here is that Embodied Construction Grammar is one school of construction grammar that explicitly highlights on the complex and dynamic interaction between linguistic knowledge and world knowledge.

6.4.3 Sign-based (Unification) Construction Grammar

Sign-based, or Unification Construction Grammar (UCxG) along with Cognitive Construction Grammar belongs to the older and more established schools. It actually goes back to the founding fathers of Construction Grammar, Charles Fillmore and Paul Kay, who published their first studies in this line of research in the early 1970s. It shares quite a number of assumptions with the other Construction Grammar frameworks, but it is also characterized by some specific viewpoints. Whereas most other schools in construction grammar are usage-based (which means that they start with the data and usually work with large corpora and statistical data), UCxG is not uniformly so. In contrast, most UCxG analyses assume that what is frequent and predictable need not be part of the grammatical knowledge of speakers. Thus, frequency plays a small role, if at all, and there is a distinction between grammar (i.e. knowledge of language) and language use. Second, UCxG analyses work with a unification-based formalism (hence the name) which has close links to other formal syntactic frameworks such as Head-Driven-Phrase-Structure-Grammar (HPSG). Unification-based formalisms use attribute-value matrices (AVMs), in which the grammatical attributes of a particular element may be *n-ary*, i.e. they may be realized by a finite and definable set of feature-values (a little bit like the semantic features discussed in Chapter 5). This strict and complex formalism clearly has the advantage of being very stringent, clear, and explicit. On the other hand, unification based feature-value systems are not very helpful in capturing rich lexical (encyclopedic) knowledge. Goldberg (2006: 217) also criticizes that feature-based systems also might not give us enough flexibility and freedom to capture and model the sometimes very subtle differences between individual constructions. At the same time, the more information is used or needed in a particular construction, the more complex the analysis and representation gets. This is, of course, the same for all syntactic frameworks, but unification-based models, despite their overall simplicity, can look very scary when applied to more complex problems.

$$
\text{a. } \textit{ditrans-lxm} \Rightarrow \begin{bmatrix} \text{ARG-ST} & \langle \text{NP}_x, \text{NP}_z, \text{NP}_y \rangle \\ \text{SEM} & \begin{bmatrix} \text{FRAMES} & \left\langle \begin{bmatrix} \textit{caused-poss-fr} \\ \text{DONOR} & x \\ \text{THEME} & y \\ \text{RECIPIENT} & z \end{bmatrix} \right\rangle \end{bmatrix} \end{bmatrix}
$$

Figure 6.3: Sag, Ivan (in press). Sign-based Construction Grammar: An informal synopsis (in Hans Boas and Ivan Sag, eds. Sign-based Construction Grammar. Stanford: CSLI Publications). Reproduction with kind permission of Ivan Sag.

Another aspect which is different from other constructionist approaches is that the unification-based models usually do not ask about the 'motivation' for particular constructions, i.e. they usually do not have recourse to cognitive and/or functional principles that can explain why one particular construction could be more likely to evolve than another one. In other words, their focus is not so much on why the constructional inventory looks the way it does rather than how it can be modeled. Similarly, their aim is formal explicitness and maximal generalization of their claims rather than psychological or cognitive plausibility of their stipulations (cf. Goldberg 2006: 215). On the other hand, unification-based approach might be said to have greater intersubjective validity and explicitness regarding their models and theorems. Today, they have wide currency with many CxG scholars (such as Mirjam Fried, Paul Kay and Charles Fillmore, Laura Michaelis, Ivan Sag and Hans Boas) and share lots of common ground with other syntactic frameworks such as HPSG.

6.4.4 Cognitive Construction Grammar

Cognitive Construction Grammar (N.B. this is not to be confused with Cognitive Grammar!) is also one of the older and more established lines of research. It goes back to Adele Goldberg's book *A Construction Grammar Approach to Argument Structure* (1995) and is one of the most widely received approaches in the general linguistics community today. Much of what has been said in the exposition above already describes the major tenets of this school, so that this section only briefly summarizes a few major claims.

CCxG is a usage-based model, i.e. it works with corpus data, actual language use, and it pays close attention to the frequency with which particular elements are used. Today, CCxG approaches (such as Goldberg & Jackendoff 2004) would define constructions as either elements whose meaning is non-compositional (i.e. holistic, not derivable from the individual parts) or which occur with sufficient frequency. Thus, constructions comprise not only idioms, but also highly frequent, but fully compositional patterns. This is, of course, very much in line with what we know about the processing or morphological patterns. Here we can also assume a dual processing mechanism, so that on one route patterns are analyzed and processed with their parts, and on another route (frequent) patterns are simultaneously processed and treated as chunks.

A second important aspect is that CCxG works without any a priori formalism. This means that on the basis of the data and the patterns that emerge, suitable descriptions and analyses have to be developed. This can mean a formal feature analysis, but also detailed prose descriptions of the sometimes very subtle differences in the semantics and pragmatics of a particular construction. The aim, in any case, is to develop a detailed and plausible description of a particular construction, together with its network links, that captures all and only those features which are necessary to arrive at a plausible interpretation. Needless to say, such an approach is very difficult if not impossible to implement on computers, though first attempts are being made.

Finally, CCxG really sees human cognition as its focus of interest. The aim is not to arrive at a most elegant or computationally adequate account, but rather one which is plausible in terms of actual speakers using actual language. This is part of the reason why 'motivating' certain constructions takes such a vital role in the analyses. Motivation "simply explains why the construction 'makes sense' or is natural [...]" (Goldberg 2006: 217). This is of course neither highly generalizing nor predictive. It is in line with explanations as we can find them in functional or historical linguistics, or even biology. The fact that things exist in particular ways is because certain factors motivated them. It could have been different, of course. Goldberg (2006: 218) gives a very clear example. All words in English that refer to clothing items for the lower trunk are grammatically plural: *pants, shorts, knickers, kulots, leggings, stockings, trousers, khakis, bermudas*. Why? This pattern may be motivated by the fact that all the real life items have a bipartite structure, i.e. two parts. The clothing items which do not have two parts are singular: *skirt, wrap, kilt*.... So the plural construction and the "lower-trunk-wear plural construction" share the same form and they are closely related in terms of meaning, since the formal relationship hints at the fact that we are dealing with 'bipartite' clothing items. Does this explain, in a strict law-like, predictive sense, what we find here? Of course not, since there are numerous languages where this is not the case. In German we have *Hose* (which used to be a plural by the way, *Hosen*) which is grammatically singular but still has two parts. It could have been different, like we said before. Does this invalidate the approach and the explanation? Not in the least, since the aim has never been and can never be prediction, but only plausible motivation.

6.5 Summary

As was pointed out in the beginning, Construction Grammar is a language model that can give us new and exciting insights into language structure and use. It departs from traditional language models, such as Chomskian Generativism in a number of ways, but is also very compatible with a number of well-known approaches, such as Saussurean Structuralism. While constructionist approaches have always been around, only the last fifteen to twenty years have seen a massive interest in this line of research together with a quickly growing body of publications and the development of new schools and strands. While it is absolutely impossible to summarize all of the developments in such a brief introduction, the present chapter at least gives a first overview of the basic ideas and tenets. The reader is referred to the primary literature, of course, for more details. Very good expositions can also be found in Fried & Östman (2004), Goldberg (2006), Croft and Cruse (2004) as well as the forthcoming textbook by Thomas Hoffmann, and the *Oxford Handbook of Construction Grammar*, edited by Thomas Hoffmann and Graeme Trousdale. Construction grammar in contrast to other grammatical frameworks is one of the topics of Müller (2010).

6.6 Exercises

1. Give the definition of a construction.

2. What does the form side of a construction contain, what the function side?

3. Regarding constructions, what does 'holistic' mean?

4. What is the concrete realization of a construction?

5. What can you say about *take our hair down* in "You needn't be coy, Beach. No reporters present. We can *take our hair down* and tell each other our right names" (Wodehouse, P.G. (1933), *Heavy Weather*)?

7   And what do we do with that?

7.1 Introduction

The previous six chapters of this book have mostly been about language structure: how do we describe language structure? How do we analyze it? We have looked at language from the smallest building blocks, phonological features and phonemes to the largest building blocks, phrases and sentences. We have looked at meaning out of context (semantics) and meaning in context (pragmatics). We have dissected existing words and we have built new ones. We have looked inside our heads and into corpora to find our data.

The one single question that remains is: what is all that good for? Why is that worth studying? In the very beginning we have pointed out that language is one of the most fundamental and powerful ways of communication for humans. It opens windows to our minds and thoughts, and it shapes our daily behavior in ways that we could never imagine – had we not learnt about language as a powerful tool. So, knowledge and awareness of language means one more important step towards enlightenment in the original sense. And this knowledge begins, of course, with what is there before you look at what you can do with it. This is very much comparable to playing with Lego building blocks. Only if you know what blocks you have and how they work you can enjoy looking at complex Lego buildings and can try to build these yourself. Similarly, driving a car is easy, but it is only when you understand how a car actually works that you can become an autonomous and responsible user of that particular machine.

The present chapter offers a quick glimpse at some of the domains where knowledge of language structure is put to use: **sociolinguistics, dialectology, historical linguistics, language acquisition, text linguistics** and **discourse analysis,** and **forensic linguistics.**

7.1.1 Sociolinguistics and sociology of language

Sociolinguistics looks at the use of language in society. As we have seen before, language is a system with structured heterogeneity, i.e. it is not fixed and monolithic, but rather heterogenic, i.e. variable and dynamic. This kind of variation, however, is not chaotic and random, but rather follows certain patterns and rules, i.e. it also has a structure. **Sociolinguistics is concerned with finding, describing, and analyzing those patterns and structures.** One simple example: one of the founding fathers of modern sociolinguistics, William Labov, carried out a study in New York City in the 1960s investigating the use of "postvocalic *r*", i.e. the use and non-use of *r* following a vowel. People in New York could pronounce words like *four* and *floor* with and without /r/, i.e. [fɔə] vs. [fɔɹ] and [flɔə] vs. [flɔɹ]. At first one might think that pronouncing these words one way or the other is a matter of chance. But Labov was able to show that this is not the case. He went to three different department stores: Saks (upper class), Macy's (middle class) and Klein's (lower class) and asked sales people for something to be found on the fourth floor (e.g., shoes, toys, jewelry: "Excuse me, where can I find toys?"). They of course replied with some utterance that contained the words "fourth floor", e.g. "Toys are on the fourth floor". Labov replied "pardon me?" and received a second answer that also contained the words "fourth floor". The results were quite astonishing, as can be seen in Diagram 7.1 below.

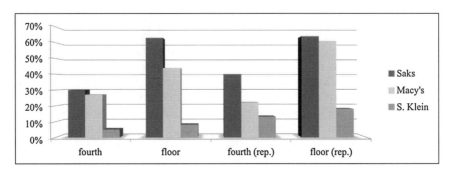

Diagram 7.1: Postvocalic r in three department stores in New York (based on Labov 1972: 52).

The sales clerks in the Saks store used *r* most often (about 50% on average), followed by those at Macy's (ca. 35%), followed by those at S. Klein's store (ca. 10%). More specifically, the Saks employees had the highest rate of *r* in both words, while the Klein's sales clerks had the lowest rate of *r* in both words. The employees at Macy's are almost on a par with those at Saks, especially with the first utterance of *fourth* and the second of *floor*. This leads us to believe that the use of postvocalic *r* in New York City in the 1960s was something that had to do with socioeconomic power and prestige. Saks on Fifth Avenue was certainly the most prestigious store with the most elite customers. If their sales assistants are the most prolific users of *r* we may assume this has to do with the fact that the use of *r* must have been a sign of being educated and well-mannered. But the study shows even more. Interestingly, the Saks people did not show a significant increase in the use of postvocalic *r* when they repeated their answer (N.B. their rate was high anyway). However, the Macy's employees showed a drastic increase in their second, repeated answers (from about 40% to 60% in *floor*). Why is that? This may have to do with the fact that Macy's is clearly middle class. Employees and customers of that store probably know what the prestigious linguistic forms sound like and try to use them if they can. However, in daily ordinary business they also sometimes forget, in other words, these are not their unmarked natural forms. But when they focus and concentrate (for example when they repeat their answer because the hearer maybe did not understand) they monitor themselves very closely and make sure that they use the most correct, educated form in an imitation of the educated, powerful upper classes. This is not the case for the employees at S. Klein – but these on the other hand probably do not have or show social aspirations the way Macy's employees and customers might do. On the other hand, we should also not forget that despite the overall low frequency of r in the Klein group, they almost triple their use in the repetition (from 5% to 18%). The reasons for this are fairly complex and cannot be discussed here in greater detail. The most important thing to see at this point is that what looks like random chaotic variation in language can often be shown to be systematic variability in the linguistic system.

This way of conducting sociolinguistic studies is called correlative sociolinguistics. In this branch of sociolinguistics we try to correlate so-called language internal, dependent variables with language external, independent variables. The aim is to find out whether there is any link between factors that lie outside the language system itself and variables in the language system. The list of language external influences is in principle infinite, but in the past some factors have been shown to be the most influential:

- **social class** (as a complex sociological concept that comprises factors such as place of living, income, occupation, etc.)
- **age**
- **gender**
- **education**

In addition to these rather stable social factors there are more dynamic **social factors** such as attitude and local group membership, which can also play an important role. For example, in a groundbreaking study of the language of high school teenagers, Eckert (2000) discovered that the social life at high school was not organized by fixed group or class membership, but rather by 'communities of practice'. These communities gather around shared interests, activities, and the construction of a shared identity. One way of constructing this shared identity is by language, so that groups dynamically build a linguistic system – which in turn gives them a further marker of identity. However, these groups are not fixed and stable, but rather dynamic and volatile, so that membership can shift, and depends again on a number of factors, such as location, time and interlocutors.

Independent language external variables are (statistically) correlated with potentially dependent language internal variables. These can come from virtually any linguistic level, from phonology to syntax and pragmatics. Labov in his New York study correlated social class with the pronunciation of *r*, others studies look at the correlation of gender and the realization of the suffix [ɪŋ] as [ɪn], so *dancin'* instead of *dancing* (e.g., Trudgill 1983). Yet others investigate the influence of social factors on the use of *ain't,* as in *I ain't seen nothing yet* (e.g., Cheshire 1981). In theory there are no limits to studies of this kind as long as some general methodological principle are kept in mind (e.g. you need enough data to be able to arrive at valid conclusions and these data need to be comparable, i.e. you need to isolate the variable you are interested in as clearly as possible).

A different way of doing sociolinguistics is so-called **interactional sociolinguistics**. Here we are not so much looking for statistical correlations between language internal and language external factors. Rather, the focus lies on the way people behave linguistically, how they interact, and how this depends on social factors, such as gender, social class and education. Obviously, there is some overlap with other linguistic fields here, such as pragmatics and conversation analysis which makes it hard to always find clear distinctions between these fields. Some of the topics that are being discussed in interactional sociolinguistics include **politeness, insult, taboo, bilingualism,** and **code-switching** (the simultaneous use of two languages or two distinct varieties). So, one might ask when and why speakers of two or more languages switch between those languages in a given conversation. For example, Pfaff (1976: 250, quoted in Muysken 2005: 6) reports the following utterance:

(1)   **Bueno**, *in other words*, **el flight que sale de Chicago** *around three o'clock.*
        Good, in other words, the flight that leaves Chicago around three o'clock.

Obviously, the speaker switches back and forth between Spanish (printed in boldface) and English (printed in italics). Why is that so? Many people believe this only happens when speakers lack competence in one language or the other, i.e. when they don't know or don't remember what a certain word or expression is in one of their languages. Numerous studies have shown that this is not necessarily the case. Even speakers who are highly competent in all of their languages sometimes shift between these languages. Studies in interactional sociolinguistics have shown that for these speakers code-switching can have a multitude of different functions, depending on the context. It may depend on the topic that is being discussed, or the time and place of language use (e.g. at home versus at school, during class or during recess etc.). Speakers may want to signal their **group membership** or their dissociation with certain groups in society. Code-switching thus not only depends on the context and social situation, but it gives social context a particular meaning at the same time.

A third group of studies that focuses on language in its social context is called **sociology of language**. Here we find a more macro-like approach in that language is seen as one important factor that shapes and influences society as the whole. In consequence, these studies are often more concerned with society and societal matters than with language and language use as such. Problems that are being discussed here include language choice and standardization (for example in postcolonial contexts), gendered language, language and power, or societal multilingualism. So, for example, Ghana in the west of Africa has a multitude of languages. There are no definite figures yet, but we can assume that no fewer than about 80 languages are spoken in this country. Needless to say, such a vast number of active indigenous languages in one single country may be a source for social, cultural and administrative problems. After all, having one common (national, official) language is a very important source of national identity. The problem that arises now is of course which language(s) should be declared official, national language(s). Various models and theories for this have been developed. One of these is so-called localized **trilingualism**. The idea is to allow both for local-identity multilingualism as well as supra-local language development, so that speakers have both local languages with which they can identify on a local basis and which they can use for cultural transfer, and one or more supra-local, national languages which allow for official administrative purposes and socioeconomic development, including education. Once such a model has been developed the next step of course is to put this into practice and to find ways to create acceptance on part of all speakers for such a model. All these are questions that are at the heart of studies in the sociology of language.

This section was only meant as a very brief introduction to the basic ideas of sociolinguistics. For much broader and more detailed accounts the reader is referred to the excellent textbooks by Hudson (1996), Chambers (2003), and Milroy and Gordon (2003).

7.1.2 Dialectology

Dialectology studies dialects, i.e. the geographical patterning of linguistic forms. It is one of the oldest sub-disciplines in linguistics and goes back to about the middle of the nineteenth century when dialectologists studied the dialects of Germany, England, France, Switzerland and Italy. Some of their studies, such as the *Deutscher Sprachatlas* (1927-1956[1]), *Atlas Linguistique de la France* (1902-1920), Ellis's *English Dialects – Their Sounds and Homes* (1890) and Wright's *English Dialect Grammar* (1905) are still of great value today. Applying various methods, such as questionnaires, interviews, telephone surveys and many more, dialectologists try to discover the isoglosses for particular linguistic features. **Isoglosses** are lines on a map that separate one area with a particular linguistic feature, e.g. southern [kʌt] *cut* from northern [kʊt]. The resulting map may look like something like Figure 7.1 below.

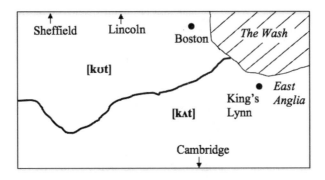

Figure 7.1: Example isogloss for [kʊt] versus [kʌt].

A single isogloss of course does not identify a dialect, though. Usually, we need several different isoglosses to roughly coincide in order to be able to identify a dialect area. We call this an isogloss bundle.

But where does the data for dialectological studies come from? Traditional dialectology focuses on so-called NORMS as informants. **NORM** is an acronym that stands for **N**on-mobile **O**lder **R**ural **M**ales. These people are particularly interesting for dialectologists (who want to describe the original dialect of a particular area) since they have rarely left the area under investigation (non-mobile), they know the traditional forms (older), haven't participated in contact-based language change (rural) and tend to be linguistically conservative (males). The items that were usually investigated were phonological variables and rural, common vocabulary, such as "What do you call the saddle of a horse?", "What do you call the insect that flies around in the summer and has a rear section that glows in the dark?". This approach has changed in more modern studies, which use all kinds of informants and also check for syntactic variables and other kinds

---

[1] The publication dates for these huge projects are usually much later than their actual production dates. The *Deutscher Sprachatlas* was devised in the nineteenth century and much of the data collection took place before 1887.

of vocabulary (see, e.g., Bert Vaux's American English dialect survey, available at http://www4.uwm.edu/FLL/linguistics/dialect/index.html), which also checks for words like "*brew thru/party barn/bootlegger/beer barn/beverage barn*" for "drive-through liquor store" or "*milkshake/shake/frappe/cabinet/velvet/thick shake*" for "drink that is made out of milk and ice-cream" (be sure you order a frappe in New York city, but a thick shake in northern California...).

A different kind of approach to dialects was developed by Dennis Preston in the 1980s: **perceptual dialectology**. Preston was not so much interested in the actual form of a particular dialect, but rather in what people think about dialects and their speakers. For example, is it true that speakers of American English usually can identify a dialect area for "Southern" or "Texan" English and associate this with a particular kind of attitude and lifestyle? Similarly, why is New York English usually regarded as uneducated and low-class, whereas the dialects around the Great Lakes are often associated with an unmarked, average kind of standard American English? Preston and his associates developed two different strategies for capturing these phenomena. On the one hand, they gave informants blank maps of the United States and asked them to identify dialect areas and to give these areas significant names. As a result, informants circled areas like Alaska and labeled it "Eskimo English", or they identified Texas as "Hillbillies/Texan". On the other hand, Preston and his associates asked informants how they would rate certain dialects in terms of (a) correctness and (b) pleasantness. The result was, for example, that most speakers rated Michigan as one of the most correct and pleasant dialects, New York as one of the least pleasant. For Texas, the reactions were more differentiated. Texans usually liked the Lakes dialects as both pleasant and correct, but rated their own varieties as quite pleasant, but not always correct. This exemplifies what Labov and other sociolinguists have described as "linguistic self-hatred", i.e. the dislike for one's own speech. Perceptual dialectology now ranks among the established methods in dialectology and sociolinguistics and is being put to use in virtually all areas of the linguistic world.

Readers are once again referred to standard textbooks on dialectology for more information. Trudgill & Chambers (1998) provide an excellent overview on traditional dialectology. Preston (1989) introduces perceptual dialectology. Some of the most recent applications of dialectological research can be found in Labov et al.'s *Atlas of North American English* (2006) and the thrilling *World Atlas of Language Structures* (WALS), edited by Martin Haspelmath et al. (2005). Note that the latter would usually be seen as work in language typology, not dialectology. Nevertheless, similar principles apply.

7.1.3 Historical Linguistics and Language Change

Historical linguistics wants to find out what languages were like at any given point in time, so for example when Shakespeare was born in 1564, when the Norman Conquest took place in 1066 or when the Scandinavian Vikings began to raid the British Isles in the eighth century. Studies in language change are interested in how languages develop(ed). Needless to say this means that both fields are theoretically distinct but practically also closely related. And both fields are way too diverse to be described here in any greater detail. Suffice it to say that historical linguistics (or better 'philology') in some sense is the mother discipline of modern linguistics. Historical linguistics and language change theory was very much en vogue in the eighteenth and nineteenth century and it was only in the twentieth century that modern linguistics left its roots behind with the advent of structuralism (namely Ferdinand de Saussure and Leonard Bloomfield) and generativism (namely Noam Chomsky).

Today, we have numerous ways and means of reconstructing and describing historical language stages, even those for which we have no evidence at all. The trick is to use documented language structures and laws as we see them today and to translate these into the past. If we can assume that the same laws and rules apply at all times (the so-called law of uniformitarianism) we have a real chance of reconstructing past (even completely unknown) language stages. At the same time, historical linguistics embraces modern studies in **language variation**, since these provide the basis for linguistic change. One of the very basic universal truths in linguistics is that there is no change without linguistic variability, but that there can be variability without change. Variation and change can be modeled just like Darwinian evolution with mutation, variation, selection, and finally change. But again everything rests on the fact that we find variability in the system.

Another important point to understand is that language change is not something that applies only to the past, for example Old and Middle English. On the contrary, language change has always been going on and will always continue. Needless to say, this has provoked many critics to say that languages are facing decay, i.e. that they might be losing efficiency and value compared to older language states. Sometimes this comes out like "Children don't speak and write properly anymore". This, obviously, is not the case. Even if there is natural and unavoidable linguistic change, the result is never in any way inferior or insufficient in comparison to older language stages. We have no account of any language ever being in danger for being non-efficient or less elegant; all existing languages are equally functional and efficient, even though they have very different ways of doing the same job. The loss of inflectional morphology, for example, as it happened in English during the Middle English period (1100-1500 CE) does not mean that the language gets 'simpler' and less elegant. We have numerous highly complex languages around the world which have few or even no inflections at all. These are called **analytic or isolating languages**. Mandarin Chinese, Burmese and Thai are good examples here, and nobody would seriously claim that these are 'simple', 'inefficient' or 'inelegant' languages. We have to accept that languages are **dynamic evolving systems**, which are shaped by their speakers according to their specific needs. And even if we have the impression that things are not improving with time, this is certainly not the case from a linguistic point of view. There may be good reason to believe that cultures and cultural values are shifting, but again, this is neither something to worry about nor business for linguists.

Historical linguistics and language change theory are a hugely complex enterprises today so that it is virtually impossible to summarize the field in just a page or two in such a handbook. The major strands today are probably **linguistic reconstruction** (which deals with the ways and means of reconstructing undocumented languages and language stages in order to describe their development), **language evolution** (which looks at how and why language developed at all), **grammaticalization** (which studies the development of grammatical items out of formerly more lexical material), **historical pragmatics** and **historical sociolinguistics**. In the following, we will briefly look into each of these in turn in order to illustrate some of the issues that historical linguistics and language change theory are concerned with today.

7.1.3.1 Reconstruction

In linguistic reconstruction we try to reconstruct past language systems for which we have incomplete or maybe no evidence at all. These we call **protolanguages**. Reconstructed forms, i.e. forms for which we have no direct evidence, are then marked by an asterisk (*). Make sure not to confuse this asterisk with the one we use to mark ungrammaticality in syntactic analyses!

We have two different techniques at our disposal in order to reconstruct lost forms: there is the comparative method on the one hand, and internal reconstruction on the other. The comparative method in essence goes back to the eighteenth century and Sir William Jones's insight that many (hitherto unrelated) languages actually look quite similar. Only look at the following comparison.

	English	French	Latin	Grm.	Gothic	Vedic	Reconstructed (Sihler)
1	one	un	unus	eins	ains	aika	*hoi-no
2	two	deux	duo	zwei	twai	dva(u)	*du(w)o
3	three	trois	tres	drei	Þrei	trayas	*trei
4	four	quatre	quattuor	vier	fidwar	catvaras	*kʷetwor
5	five	cinq	quinque	fünf	fimf	panca	*penkʷe
6	six	six	sex	sechs	saihs	sas	*s(w)eks
7	seven	sept	septem	sieben	sibun	sapta	*septm
8	eight	huit	octo	acht	ahtau	asta(u)	*h₃ekto
9	nine	neuf	novem	neun	niun	nava	*(h₁)newn
10	ten	dix	decem	zehn	taihun	dasa	*dekm(t)

Jones noticed that all these languages (and many more) show remarkable similarities. There are only three ways to explain these similarities: the languages were in contact and the items were borrowed, these items reflect some kind of universal vocabulary, or the languages go back to one common root (or mother language) which already had those items. That the languages were in contact seems highly improbable, not in the least because Vedic (Sanskrit) was spoken in Bronze and Iron Age India and developed into Classical Sanskrit by the sixth century BCE. Gothic, in contrast, was spoken in parts of the lower Danube area, in Italy, Spain and Portugal roughly between 100 CE and 900 CE. It therefore seems highly unlikely that these languages (that is: speakers of these languages!) were ever in contact with each other. That there is a universal vocabulary shared by all these languages is also unlikely, since there is a mass of languages that have other words, and since the linguistic sign is completely arbitrary. In other words, we cannot motivate such a universal group of words. Which only leaves option 3: these languages must have one common ancestor, a proto-language for which we have no direct evidence, and which gave rise to these distinct languages with obvious correspondences. This language can be called Proto-Indoeuropean, 'proto' since it is only reconstructed, 'Indo-European' since it gave rise to languages in India, Persia, and Europe, and some other parts of the world. By comparing **cognates** (similar, related words) we can try to reconstruct the actual root for these different forms. Consider the words for "three" in the table above: *three, trois, tres, drei, Þrei, trayas*. Obviously, all of these words are very similar and probably related. But what does their root form look like? Two of these forms have an interdental fricative, one of them begins with a voiced stop, three have a voiceless stop (and we can add that the majority of languages – Old Prussian, Latvian, Gaul, Greek, Umbrian, Lithuanian, Old Church Slavonic, Welsh, Russian, Albanian... – have a voiceless stop in initial position in the word 'three'). So what is the most likely initial consonant in the root? In all likelihood it was a voiceless stop. Virtually all languages have some sort of (r) following the (t). So we may want to reconstruct (tr). Reconstructing the vowel sound is a bit more complicated, but eventually it turns out that there is some good evidence that we want a closing diphthong like (ei) here. The presence or absence of a final consonant like (s) is also difficult to reconstruct. Some of the languages do have a final consonant (and most of these have (r)), while many languages do not have a final consonant. So, in the end we may want to opt for the absence of such a sound. This means that our reconstructed form could be something like *trei*. We can use the same method, essentially, to reconstruct a fairly large deal of proto-vocabulary, but also sound systems, morphology, and even syntactic patterns.

Internal reconstruction does not look at seemingly related languages and their correspondences in order to reconstruct the original, root forms, but it looks at variability in a single language in order to arrive at a valid reconstruction. Let's look at a very simple example from English. Present-day English has a number of verbs that end with /t/ or /d/: *adapt, blend, end, found, grade, greet, reflect, rent, wait...* next to *bend, bleed, cast, cut, meet, put, send, set...* The difference between those two sets of verbs is that the former uses the suffix [əd] to form the preterite (*adapted, blended, ended, founded, graded, greeted, reflected, rented, waited...*) whereas the latter group shows hardly any changes, and certainly not an affix (*bent, bled, cast, cut, met, put, sent, set...*). Now we may ask ourselves if that is sheer coincidence, or whether one of two patterns is maybe older and the other one a relatively new development. This in turn might help us to think about the original forms of these verbs and the way to form the preterite in early, undocumented stages of English and Germanic. So, what can we do? When we look at the second group of verbs (*bend, bleed, cast...*) we see that these are exclusively basic kinds of verbs. There are no special meaning verbs or verbs which are derived from nouns. The other group of verbs (*adapt, blend, grade, reflect...*) does contain such words. Second, as far as we can see, there are no obvious borrowings from Latin or French. And again, the second group includes borrowings such as *adapt* and *reflect*. Third, if we want to form a preterite out of an unknown or invented verb today, we usually automatically add the [əd] suffix to it: e.g., *miffot > miffoted, glat > glatted*. In other words: suffixless words tend to be more basic, native vocabulary and the suffix is still a very productive pattern today. This is certainly not foolproof evidence, but it still leads us to believe that the suffixless pattern may be the more basic, older pattern. In turn, this also means that the suffixation pattern may be the more recent one. This is one example of internal reconstruction, i.e. reconstruction solely based on evidence from language internal factors of one single language.

What all this boils down to is that today, after almost 200 years, we have very sophisticated tools to reconstruct language stages way beyond our direct knowledge and way beyond the evidence that we have. This not only helps us in describing the history and development of particular languages and language families (the roots of modern typology), but also in discussing the evolution of language as such. This will be the topic of our next section.

7.1.3.2 Evolution

When did language begin? And, more importantly, why did language begin? Undoubtedly language today is one of the most complex and efficient human communication systems, and equally undoubtedly it must have come into being at one point in history. Why, how, and when are the crucial questions of language evolution. So far, not one of them has been answered satisfactorily. There is good reason to believe that something like human language began with *homo habilis*, about 1.4 million years ago, while other pieces of evidence rather point towards a much later date and species, *homo sapiens* who lived 70,000 to 50,000 years ago. In any case it appears quite safe to say that language did not develop before about 1.4 million years ago and no later than 50,000 years ago. This is still a very long time, but considering the fact that we only have circumstantial evidence, if any evidence at all, this is not so bad a guess. Which leaves us with the question why language as we know it today developed at this point or any other. Essentially, there seem to be two different answers, both of which are equally important: physiology and function. Physiology refers to the fact that in the evolution of homo sapiens the species underwent a number of bodily changes which are today considered important or at least related to the development of certain cognitive skills, such as language. Some scholars believe, for example, that the development of bipedalism (the ability to walk on two legs), which came with the Australopithecus about 3.5 million years ago, led to changes in the skull and throat. As a consequence we find the L-shaped vocal tract. Much later, about 150.000 years ago we also find the so-called 'descended larynx' in adult humans, i.e. the larynx gradually moved from a rather high position to a position much lower in the (adult) throat, which not only facilitated the production of speech sounds but also brought with it the danger of suffocating on inhaled food. But we also need to keep in mind that the descended larynx is only facilitating and not necessarily a cause for language evolution. Other animals, like red deer and fallow deer, also have a descended larynx, but do not produce the same range of sounds as homo sapiens. And conversely, parrots do not have a descended larynx (in fact they have a syrinx), but are perfectly capable of producing most sounds of human language.

A second physiological factor which also seems to have played a role in the evolution of language is the development of brain lateralization (i.e. the development of two brain halves with different functions), which goes hand in hand (no pun intended) with handedness. Many mammals show **lateralization** (i.e. brain halves) and most mammals also show **handedness**. Thus, you can expect your cat or your dog to have 'a favorite paw' when performing tricks, just like humans are either right- or left-handed. The key difference, however, is that handedness in humans can be found on the population level. About 90% of the human population is right-handed. Mice, which also show handedness, have about a 50% chance of being left-handed, or rather left-pawed. This strong preference for being right-handed in humans goes back, we think, at least 1.5 million years. We only have very limited evidence here, but based on post-cranial asymmetries, tools, and works of art we believe that our ancestors were to a vast majority right-handed, and that left-handedness may have evolved some time between 1.5 million years ago and about 10,000 years ago, when we have evidence for left-handedness. Interestingly, we find some correlation between the development of handedness, proto-language, and tool-making about 2 million years ago. These developments seem to go together with certain developments in the brain, namely lateralization. This in turn may have been triggered by the development of some genetic mutation of the so-called $D*$ gene. Note, however, that after these first developments we witness a long period of stasis with no further innovations or developments. It all remained fairly primitive. It was only about 40,000 years ago that we see a massive evolutionary leap, concomitant with the rapid development of more complex linguistic structures, tool making, and art production. It has been claimed that this could have been the result of some further mutation of the $D*$ gene which eventually led to the development of the modern D allele which in turn led to development of the left brain hemisphere with its specific (language related) capacities. However, all these physiological developments in the evolution of the human species do not have any causal relationship with the development of language as a human capacity. They certainly were important facilitating steps, but as far as we can see, there is no reason to believe that some sort of language could have developed without these first physiological processes.

The second answer to the 'why question' raised above was function. We also need to ask ourselves what specific function(s) language has and in how far these may have contributed to its evolution. In other words, what sort of evolutionary advantage did we get by developing language? One of the more interesting proposals in this field looks at our ancestors and closest relatives who did not and do not use language the way we do. The claim is that a very important communication tool for primates is grooming and other bodily communication. Bonobos, for instance, use sexual intercourse as a central way to communicate and generate social cohesion in the group. But all this is only possible when you live in rather small groups. As soon as group size expands, it becomes increasingly more difficult to keep up "bodily" relationships with all the group members. The idea is that language developed to fulfill that particular function. Language is a very effective communication tool even for larger groups because of its vocal auditory nature. It also has the advantage that you can use it while you do other things, such as run, fight, work on something, eat and so on. One very important function of language, then and now, is gossiping. We also call this **phatic communication**, i.e. communication in order to establish and maintain social relations (the 'nice weather today' kind of conversation). Gossiping is also an exchange of 'goods' in the widest sense. I'll tell you a secret, you'll tell me a secret. Sharing gossip essentially is about social bonding, and thus it is also a good substitute for bodily grooming. Moreover, language can also be used to communicate real information, which can be helpful when looking for food, for example. And it can be used to create and share cultural artifacts, rites, and customs. Language is one of the most effective ways to remember events and facts, and to teach children about what happened before. This takes away the pressure to invent the wheel all over again. Language is also a very good way to organize even complex group relationships without having to fight it out. Verbal arguing then substitutes physical fights. So, in a word, having language comes in very handy in the evolutionary process. So we might want to say that the evolution of language may have been a symbiotic process of physiological developments together with the growing need to organize ever more complex social systems.

There is a vast amount of literature available dealing with language evolution from various perspectives. One of the most comprehensive overviews is offered by Finch (2010). Corballis (1991) is probably one of the most important scholars focusing on the physiological dimension, while Dunbar (1998) develops the idea of verbal grooming as driving force. Cavalli-Sforza (1997) takes a completely different perspective and uses genes and blood factors in present-day population to describe and analyze the spread of language from (southern) Africa to the rest of the world. There is also a great book series by Oxford University Press, *Studies in the Evolution of Language* (2001-today), edited by James Hurford & Frederik Newmeyer, with more than a dozen high quality volumes on various related aspects.

7.1.3.3 Grammaticalization

Our next topic connects nicely to language evolution. **Grammaticalization refers to the development of more grammatical items out of less grammatical items**. It is very likely that in language evolution the first linguistic items to emerge were lexical words, more specifically nouns and verbs. Speakers needed nouns in order to signify ideas and things, and verbs in order to signify actions. Something quite similar can also be observed in the language acquisition of children. Children usually begin their linguistic lives with concrete lexical items like nouns and verbs, and not with grammatical items such as prepositions or conjunctions. But this naturally leads to the question how we eventually arrive at something like grammar then. Grammaticalization is one approach that can help to explain this process. Let us look at a very simple textbook example. In English, we can refer to future events with the complex auxiliary *be going to* as in *John is going to buy a new car next week.* There is no doubt that *be going to* is an auxiliary, a part of the grammar. However, as such it is fairly new and only developed during the (late) Middle English period, i.e. after 1300. It goes back to a real lexical item with the meaning of *to go*, i.e. physical motion from A to B. Note that we still have and use this lexical verb: *Where is he? He is going to school.* In fact, the two verbs, lexical and auxiliary *go,* are related by a grammaticalization process. How did the lexical verb *go* turn into the auxiliary *go*? It all began with contexts in which the syntactic sequence "be going [to V NP]" – as in *I was going to visit Bill –* was somehow ambiguous and could be interpreted as either physical and directional 'I am physically moving from A to B' or as purposive 'I am going to A in order to V'. This led to a reinterpretation, or rather reanalysis of the syntactic sequence. Instead of seeing 'to V NP' as a syntactic unit, and 'be going' as the embedding VP structure, speakers began to regard 'be going to' as a unit, and 'V NP' as its complement. So, what we get is a new, reanalyzed sequence "[be going to] V NP". In a next step, this sequence is extended by a process called **analogy** to verbs which would usually not allow for purpose interpretations, such as *like* or even *go*: *I am going to go to London.* Finally, in present-day spoken English, the reanalyzed sequence 'be going to' is again reanalyzed 'be gonna' which can only be used with a future meaning. What this amounts to is that the lexical verb *to go* in the right kind of syntactic context was reinterpreted on the basis of pragmatic principles such as inference, as meaning having the purpose to do something. On that basis it spread into other contexts which were incompatible with physical motion and eventually even purpose until it eventually turned into a rather neutral futurity marker. As such, it even fused morphosyntactically with *to* into the monomorphemic *gonna.*

Grammaticalization may sound like a very complicated and rare process. In fact, however, it is extremely wide-spread and can be diagnosed as the source of a large variety of items, from tense, mood, and aspect markers, to prepositions and even articles. Grammaticalization research used to be one of the most productive lines of research in historical linguistics in the 1990s and the early twenty-first century. Today, much of it is standard textbook knowledge, while some technical questions still remain a matter of debate. Good summaries can be found in the classic textbooks by Hopper & Traugott (2003) and Diewald (1997), as well as the volumes edited by Fischer, Rosenbach & Stein (2000), and Traugott & Trousdale (2010).

7.1.3.4 Historical pragmatics

Historical pragmatics is a relatively new field of study. Essentially, it applies ideas and concepts from modern pragmatics to historical data. This is particularly noteworthy since most of modern pragmatics is based on language use in context – which is often spoken, informal language use. Needless to say, such data is rarely if ever available in historical contexts. Nevertheless, a number of studies have looked at historical materials which are relatively close to 'spoken' varieties. These include Shakespeare's plays, Chaucer's Canterbury Tales, or the Salem Witchcraft Trials. These are, of course, materially written, but it is also obvious that they are closer to actual language use than official, conceptually written documents such as treatises or contracts. Studies in historical pragmatics have investigated phenomena such as deixis, (im-)politeness, terms of address, pronoun use, curses, blessings, and swearing. A good introduction to historical pragmatics can be found in Jucker & Taavitsainen (2010) and the recently founded journal with the title *Historical Pragmatics* (1999-today), edited by Jucker & Taavitsainen.

7.1.3.5 Historical sociolinguistics

Historical sociolinguistics is also a relatively young field. It basically tries to use modern sociolinguistics in the analysis of historical language stages. In doing so, it applies correlational sociolinguistics, interactional sociolinguistics, and the sociology of language. Studies in correlational sociolinguistics today go back to about the late Middle English period (c. 1350-1500). The big problem these are facing is the availability of intra- and extra-linguistic data. For example, we have virtually no reliable data for female language use before about 1300 CE. This makes quantitative studies in gendered language use extremely difficult. Similarly, until about the seventeenth century we find a very limited range of data from the lower and possibly uneducated social classes, just as informal language use is often not recorded. Nevertheless, a number of studies are available today which still shed light on the sociolinguistic situation in the late Middle English and Early Modern English. Many of them are based on the Corpus of Early English Correspondence (CEEC), an electronic corpus developed at the University of Helsinki which mostly contains letters of various sorts (2.7 million words, formal and informal, by male and female authors from a variety or regions and social backgrounds), written between 1410-1681. Thus it became possible to investigate traditional sociolinguistic factors such as gender, age, social class and place of living, at least as far back as the Early Middle English period (c. 110-1350).

Other approaches in this domain rather opt for a more microscopic approach and focus on social networks and individual language use across time.

For studies in interactional sociolinguistics see section 7.1.3.4 on historical pragmatics. The sociology of language is also of particular interest to historical linguistics since it offers valuable insights in central topics such as standardization and the history of English, the development of colonial varieties of English, the impact of the printing and other media and of course the role of language contact.

There are a number of studies that can be used as introductions to historical sociolinguistics in the broadest sense. These include Nevalainen & Raumolin-Brunberg (2003) for work based on the CEEC, Bergs (2005), who uses a micro-sociolinguistic approach, Romaine (1982) and J. Milroy (1992), the two classic texts, Wright (1996), and Watts (2011), among many others, who discuss standardization and language contact.

7.1.4 Language Acquisition

Language acquisition is interested in how humans actually learn or acquire languages. Learning versus acquiring is already one of our first important keywords here. We usually distinguish between **language acquisition**, which is what happens naturally and without instruction, and **language learning**, i.e. 'instructed language acquisition'. Furthermore, scholars normally also distinguish between first and second language acquisition. Again, first language acquisition happens naturally and without instruction, second language acquisition is often, but not always, instructed.

7.1.4.1 First language acquisition

First language acquisition mostly happens between birth and the age of about five or six. During this time, speakers acquire the basic knowledge of their mother tongue(s) and become native speakers of their language(s). This means that they acquire a very intuitive feeling about what is permissible and what is not in their native language. Needless to say, however, first language acquisition does not stop at the age of five or six, but is a lifelong process. There is still a big deal of discussion, however, about whether the processes that can be observed after the age of about five or six are capable of influencing language competence or if they are only related to language use. So, are the changes that we see during adulthood real language changes in the individual, or only shifts in performance? This is still a matter of some debate in modern linguistics.

The history of modern studies in language acquisition probably begins with

Noam Chomsky's review of Skinner's book *Verbal Behavior* (1957), published
in 1959. Skinner is a representative of the school of **behaviorism**. Essentially,
he claimed that language behavior is acquired through a stimulus-response
model. Simplifying dramatically, one might say that a child wants some milk
and says "I want milk". In reaction to this, the caregiver says "Yes, of course"
and gives the child some milk. Thus, the verbal behavior of the child is
positively reinforced and therefore more likely to occur in the future.
Alternatively, if the child asks for "harfuntog" when it wants some milk it is
likely to get a negative reply or reinforcement like "What do you want?" and no
milk. This way, by a system of positive and negative reinforcement, the child
gradually acquires its native language, i.e. knowledge and competence about
what is linguistically acceptable and what is not.

Chomsky severely criticizes this model in his famous 1959 review of the
book. His basic objection is that the model fails to explain a number of facts
relating to the process of language acquisition. On the one hand, we have the so-
called **'poverty-of-stimulus'** problem. Obviously, children cannot have heard
all the linguistic material they are capable of producing at the age of about five.
In fact, it is likely that they will not have come across some constructions they
know in any sufficient frequency (note that the **stimulus-response model**
usually requires repetition for some items to be learnt eventually). So, the
stimulus or **input** is not big enough to explain the output. The second problem,
related to that, is the question of creativity. How do we explain the creation of
novel structures that children have not learned before? Learning in behaviorism
is very closely connected to **imitation**. But children obviously can do more than
just imitate. How does this extension of the system work? Third, this model does
not convincingly explain how and why the acquisition process can be so quick
and essentially flawless. Remember that children only need about five years
(two of which they are mostly silent!) to master their native language almost
flawlessly. This tremendous speed needs to be accounted for somehow.

But Chomsky not only criticized the behaviorist model, he suggested an
alternative theory within his framework of generative grammar. Chomsky's
model rests on two factors: a so-called **language acquisition device (LAD)** and
universal grammar (UG). The LAD is a hypothetical brain mechanism that
allows children to learn the structures of their native language automatically and
very rapidly from the poor data that is usually available (remember the poverty-
of-stimulus argument!). The LAD makes sure that language acquisition is an
automatic, unavoidable process (there are no known cases of healthy humans
not acquiring any language within the first years of their life!), and it helps
children to scan the data they find for any necessary cues that they need in their
process of building a language. UG is extremely important and helpful here
since it claims that all human languages share a number of basic features and
characteristics. These, then, do not have to be learned, but only activated the

right way. For example, all languages have different word classes. This is a fact that children do not have to learn. They intuitively "expect" different word classes in the data they hear and analyze their input accordingly. Similarly, all languages have ways of negating statements and of forming questions. All you need to know is how to do it. The LAD as a special device in the brain in combination with UG explains how children can learn their language so quickly and without fail.

It is probably fair to say that Chomsky's model of language acquisition in essence has been the most widely acknowledged one over the past fifty years or so. Recently, we have seen the development of some alternative models, though. One of the most prominent and promising alternatives goes back to the work of Michael Tomasello and the general framework of construction grammar. Tomasello (2005) suggests that acquiring a language does not necessarily require a specialized LAD or even UG. On the contrary, for Tomasello two very general principles of human cognition are sufficient for language acquisition: **intention reading** and **pattern recognition**. Children first need to understand the meaning, i.e. the intention behind certain verbal acts of communication. For example, they need to see that pointing towards a teddy-bear in combination with the sound-sequence [tɛdɪ] is the act of naming an object. So this "thing" is called [tɛdɪ]. The same applies, of course, to other and more complex acts of verbal communication. Pattern recognition is important because it helps us to segment utterances into individual units and to see the more abstract pattern behind single utterances. After hearing several hundred sentences like "Katie loves her teddy", "John wants cookies" and so on, we are led to believe that there is an underlying SVO pattern here. According to this model, children begin by learning (i.e. imitating) single words and unanalyzed sequences. Thus they might learn and say things like "wɑnkʊkɪ" even without knowing that the actual sequence is "(I) want (a) cookie". Learning begins with single, isolated elements. After a number of elements are learned like that, children begin to see that there is a pattern behind those isolated occurrences. Once they see the pattern, they can begin, by way of analogy, to use other material in the same way and thus use the pattern productively. In **construction grammar** (see Chapter 6), one might say that children do not acquire the items and rules of their language, as in **generativism**, but rather constructions, which they form into a constructional network. They begin with concrete, simple constructions, which are then gradually turned into abstract simple constructions and (abstract) complex constructions. Moreover, they acquire greater confidence in combining existing constructions in new ways (in other words, they learn what can be fused, and what can't). Needless to say, this whole model does indeed go back to early behaviorism. But in contrast to Skinner's model, it also includes more abstract patterns and the ability to combine constructions and use language creatively. Tomasello's work is based on extensive empirical studies with primates and children, and he was able to show that the data confirms that fast and efficient language acquisition is actually possible just with these two skills, intention reading and pattern recognition.

There is an extensive body of literature on first language acquisition. Some very good and accessible introductions include Clark (2009), Tomasello (2005) and Saxton (2010).

7.1.4.2 Second Language Acquisition

Second language acquisition can be very generally defined as the acquisition of one or more languages after first language acquisition took place. Of course, this definition is very vague and does not really take into account any cases of bilingualism in various degrees (i.e. the simultaneous acquisition of more than one mother tongue), but it is probably enough for present purposes. Second language acquisition, in contrast to first language acquisition, can happen either **spontaneously** (as real 'acquisition') or as **instructed language learning**. While in the European context the latter is more common, the former can be frequently found in many other parts of the world, for example in some post-colonial contexts. Here we will focus on instructed second language acquisition, though.

The first thing we notice is that, on average, second language acquisition (SLA) is much slower than first language acquisition. Acquiring a native language takes about five years, while acquiring a second language can easily take up ten or more years. Also, obviously, the results are quite different. Native speakers are, by definition, fluent in their mother tongue, while there is always a great deal of variability in the proficiency of second language learners. Some people know a language quite well after five or ten years, some others never go beyond elementary basic structures. The second important factor seems to be age. On average, speakers will find it easier to acquire a second language before the onset of puberty, the so-called critical period of language learning. The **critical period hypothesis** is still widely debated and suggestions for when this period actually is range from about the age of 10 to 21. While early studies pointed out that this may have to do with physiological factors of the human brain, more recent studies suggest that the decline in the capability of language learning goes hand in hand with the decline of learning capabilities in general and may thus not be specific to language.

Another problem that we are facing in studies on SLA is that language learning is a strongly individual, personal process and that a vast number of factors need to be considered. These include **motivation, personal, social and cultural attitudes, learner personality, and many more**. So in some cases it is very difficult to determine which factors actually led to the observable patterns. Nevertheless, studies in SLA have found that second language acquisition is a structured process that does not proceed randomly, but rather along fairly predictable pathways. These findings have led to influential models such as Stephen Krashen's **Input Hypothesis**. Krashen (1993) claimed that language acquisition is facilitated when the input for the language learner is structured in such a way that structures which the learner already knows are supplemented by bits and bits of new material. In other words, comprehensible input seems to facilitate language learning. This, of course, stands in contrast to so-called immersion models which would rather favor full, native-like input. But output was also at the center of attention. Numerous studies have investigated what we can learn about language acquisition from the data that language learners produce. In the early days of SLA research we find numerous studies in Error Analysis and Contrastive Analysis. We can distinguish between mistakes – these are simply based on performance – and errors in language learning. Errors are supposed to reflect competence (or lack of competence) on part of the language learner. On the basis of these errors Larry Selinker (1972) developed the important concept of **interlanguage**. This hypothesis claims that the language that learners produce is not a deficient copy of the target language, randomly or chaotically marred with various mistakes, but rather that it forms a dynamic system with structured heterogeneity. In other words, the language learner constantly constructs personal language systems on his way from source to target language. These dynamic language systems are then diagnostic of his progression or regression in the language learning process. Selinker identified three fundamental processes in the creation of interlanguage: 1) **language transfer** (positive and negative), in which structures from the source language are copied in the target language, 2) **overgeneralization**, in which rules of the target language are expanded into domains where they are not applicable and 3) **simplification**, in which learners simplify the rules of the target language. In how far these simplifications reflect language universals, for example, is still a matter of debate.

There are a number of highly recommendable introductions to second language acquisition research available. These include Ellis (1997, 2008), Gass & Selinker (2008) and Lightbown & Spada (2006).

7.1.5 Text linguistics and discourse analysis

Text linguistics and discourse analysis are two fields which look at linguistic elements and structures which are larger than just the single sentence. However, the jury is still out about a clear definition and distinction of the two fields. Text linguistics is more deeply rooted in a European tradition and tends towards the written text as its object of study. **Discourse analysis** is a more problematic term as it is used in slightly different senses in some frameworks. We can identify an American point of view here, which usually equates 'discourse' with spoken language or conversation. In that sense, discourse analysis also comes under the heading of conversation analysis. In a European and particularly English tradition discourse analysis is not restricted to either spoken or written language. In that sense, discourse is seen as any piece of language larger than the sentence. Thus discourse analysis comes close to what we have just described as **text linguistics**, at least when it deals with written language. A third approach, which goes back to German and French philosophy of the 1960s and 1970s (Habermas, Foucault, Lyotard, among others), defines discourse as the argumentative communication or action which critically analyzes and evaluates the claims to validity which are explicitly and implicitly built into communicative actions, with the aim of arriving ultimately at an intersubjective understanding and agreement. It is fairly obvious that the latter definition of discourse is somehow commensurable with the former definitions, but it is also clear that it goes beyond the rather technical, linguistic approaches and entails a variety of issues, including politics and ethics. Note that one particular strand in linguistics, so-called **Critical Discourse Analysis (CDA)**, is particularly associated with the philosophical understanding of the term 'discourse'. CDA seeks to describe and analyze power relations in discourse and social practices, for example in order to uncover in which ways certain political rhetorical devices are employed to influence or even shape the understanding of political issues in the public sphere.

For present purposes we will use a somewhat simplified understanding of the terms 'discourse' and 'text', and will restrict our discussion to 'text' as written forms of communication and 'discourse' as spoken forms.

7.1.5.1 Text linguistics

Text linguistics is a very wide and hardly unified field of study. It can be said to comprise studies in the **typology of texts (genres, registers, text types)**, in the so-called **'grammar'** of texts, and even in rhetoric. The basic assumption is that there are definable rules (like in traditional grammar) that apply to the production and understanding of texts. But the big problem is that we only have a fairly limited understanding of what a 'text' really is. To be sure, most speakers have very good intuitions about that, and can easily distinguish texts from non-texts. But when it comes to waterproof definitions, things are much less clear. How long does a text have to be? Does it have to have one single meaning, or several? Does it have to be produced by a single speaker?

So far, we believe that texts are usually characterized by two important factors: cohesion and coherence. **Cohesion** refers to the glue that keeps a text together, **coherence** is the meaningful situatedness of a text in a given context. Cohesion in a text can be created by **phoric elements** of various sorts (anaphora, cataphora), but also **ellipsis** and **substitution**. Non-cohesive texts would look like a list of unrelated sentences. Coherence, in contrast, is about the meaning of the text as a whole. Readers of texts are usually provided with a certain amount of contextual background that helps them to interpret the meaning of the text. Taken out of context, texts can become ambiguous, opaque, even meaningless.

Other features of texts have rather something to do with how the information in the text is structured. As we have discussed in Chapter 4 (Syntax), we need to consider factors such as theme and rheme, given and new information, focus, contrastiveness, and many more. These need to be aligned with the principles of English syntax. We have shown that English offers a variety of choices when it comes to syntactic alternatives to the unmarked SVO order (passives, clefting, fronting etc). Text linguistics uses all these factors in order to describe how a text is actually build and how things like thematic progression (the dynamics of a story, for example) can be explained on the basis of syntactic and pragmatic phenomena. Moreover, a number of studies also investigate how texts can be designed so that they can achieve certain effects: advertisements should make us want to buy the product, manuals need to be easily understandable, contracts need to be unambiguous, and so on. Some of these aspects have some serious consequences in real life, for example if a patient can show that the patient information leaflet was hard to understand, or maybe ambiguous, and that he therefore overdosed his medication. This automatically leads to a neighboring field, forensic linguistics, which will be discussed in Section 7.1.6 below.

Another important field in text linguistics is concerned with text typology. Again, most speakers have a very good feeling for what distinguishes different types of text, and literary theory since antiquity has dealt with poetry, drama, narration and similar labels in order to arrive at a classification of texts. However, many discussions in this domain oscillate between **descriptive** and **prescriptive** viewpoints. So, for example, it is not always clear whether 'poetry' is typically characterized by the conscious use of rhyme and meter, or if theorists require a piece of writing to have rhyme and meter in order to be classified as 'poetry'...

In any case, with the advent of modern digital corpus linguistics a whole new strand of research began to focus on the features and the empirical classification of texts. One of the most prominent approaches here was offered by the corpus linguist Douglas Biber in the late 1980s and 1990s. In a nutshell, Biber took a large number of texts and automatically searched for any clustering of any kind of (grammatical) feature. The results were quite astonishing. Biber (1995) discovered that indeed many texts show similar statistical clustering and that these texts indeed can be grouped into individual categories. So, for example, a number of texts showed a significantly higher frequency of past tense verb forms, third person pronouns and so-called 'public verbs' (like *say, ask, tell, question...*). Unsurprisingly, perhaps, these features typically clustered in narrative texts, such as novels. Other texts showed a clustering of first and second person pronouns, hedges (*I think, I guess...*), private verbs (like *think, believe, know, feel*), emphasis marker, *that*-deletion (*I think (THAT) he's stupid*), contracted forms (*I am > I'm*), demonstratives, sentence final prepositions, *wh*-questions and *be* as main verb. These feature clusters were typical for informal, personal spoken texts, such as face-to-face conversations, and also personal letters. The same analysis can be performed for a number of other texts and registers. They all seem to show specific feature clusters, which in turn can be classified along two major textual dimensions: involved versus informative (i.e. does the speaker's perspective and opinion play a role or not), and narrative versus non-narrative (i.e. does the temporal sequence in the text play a role). What is particularly interesting and valuable in this kind of approach is the fact that it works bottom-up. Instead of working with pre-fabricated patterns and classifications, it tries to uncover in how far certain features in real texts co-occur and whether these texts can be meaningfully grouped together. Similar analysis have also been used in historical text linguistics in the attempt to describe and analyze the style within certain traditional genres (such as novels or newspaper reports), or even the development of certain genres as such.

One of the very few up-to-date general introductions to text linguistics is Esser (2009). Most other discussions stem from the 1970s and are fairly outdated. Other readable texts that discuss particular aspects of the field include Halliday & Hasan (1977) on coherence and cohesion, Renkema (2009) on textuality and information structure, Biber (1995) on dimensions of register variation, and Fairclough (2001) on Critical Discourse Analysis.

7.1.5.2 Discourse analysis

We pointed out in section 7.1.5 above that, for present purposes, we regard discourse analysis simply as conversation analysis, i.e. the study of spoken interaction. Here we are dealing with questions such as "How does a speaker know when to start and stop with his contributions in a given conversation?", "How do we begin conversations, how do we end them?", "How do we signal (implicitly) that we agree or disagree with what is being said?", "What are all those funny noises like *hm* and *aha* and *uh* doing in our conversations?". The idea, just like with text linguistics, is that even conversations, i.e. interaction between two or more participants, can have structure and are organized according to identifiable patterns and rules.

Needless, there is also a great deal of overlap between this field, interactional sociolinguistics, and pragmatics, among others.

In order to be able to discuss these issues in any detail, discourse analysis had to develop some new technical vocabulary, since so far this level of interaction has been mostly ignored in systematic studies. Two of the most important concepts here are "(conversational) floor" and "turn". The **conversational floor** can be regarded as something like the "what's happening now" in psychological terms. It usually correlates with speaking time and the power to control what the conversation is about and how it proceeds. So, if speaker A "has the floor", speaker A controls what is being talked about by whom and when. Note that the floor in this sense must be jointly construed by the participants in the conversation. Participants have to agree that one speaker has the floor at a given point in time. If they do not agree, they have to challenge this. As you can again imagine, floor management, i.e. tacitly agreeing on who has the right to talk, is one of the most complex tasks in human verbal interaction. Nevertheless, very early on in our life, probably from about six or seven years of age onwards, we are fairly good at intuitively managing these issues. The conversational floor is managed in so-called turns. A **turn** can be defined, simplifying a bit, as the time a given participant speaks before somebody else takes over. There are a number of so-called turn-taking signals that help us to show people that we are willing to give the turn to somebody else, or that we want the turn from the present speaker. Signals that can tell the hearer to take over include full, grammatical sentences, a falling intonation with a statement, and a rising intonation with a question, tag questions and other discourse markers such as *uh?* or *ey?*. Nonverbal cues such as changing the direction of gaze or gestures are also helpful. Getting the floor is slightly more complicated, partly because it is usually considered to be rude to "interrupt" speakers in such a way. Again, we have some verbal cues such as *hm, ahh, errr* but also non-verbal cues such as coughing and gesturing.

Similarly, we have developed various ways of introducing certain terms. For example, if we are replying to something mentioned before and we expect our reply to be negative and dispreferred for our interlocutor, we often like to begin with hesitation or warning signals before we breach the news ("Can you help me?" – "ahh, well, mmm, you know, I am sorry but I am kind of busy right now"). Here we find a typical pattern which begins with hesitation markers, continues with an excuse and finishes with "reasons why" – without ever explicitly mentioning the negative reply ("no") as such. In a similar fashion we also tend to "hedge" utterances with hesitation markers and phrases such "I dunno", "I guess", "maybe" etc. if we are not sure about their truth value or if we expect unfavorable answers.

Interestingly, different cultures (even within one linguistic community such as "English speakers") can also have very different ideas about the general rules of conversation management. Most English speaking cultures (England, United States, Canada, Australia) have very little tolerance for pause and silence during conversations. Participants in a given interaction usually find it hard to bear longer periods of silence or pauses. 'Longer' in this case can be as little as one second. In other words, silent periods in conversation of one second or more are often regarded as uncomfortable or problematic. But this is not universally the case. There have been reports that some English speaking communities (e.g., Belfast) can have very long periods of silence without any problem at all (see L. Milroy 1987).

Just like the floor and turns are the **micro-level structure** of interaction, our conversations also have a **macro-level structure**. We have a number of ways in which we begin our conversations and how we can end them. These are, of course, highly context and culture dependent. While there are very formal ways of beginning a conversation ("How do you do?") there are also quite informal, personal ones ("Hello", "Hi,", "Good morning", "How are you?", "Howdie" etc.). The choice here clearly depends on the interlocutors, their relationship, and the occasion. Note that some of these structures also exemplify the sometimes highly formulaic structure of interaction. "How do you do?" requires as an answer "How do you do?"; "How are you?" does not expect a full-fledged answer about one's well-being, but rather "I am fine, how are you?". Ending a conversation is a little bit more difficult, of course, since all interlocutors have to agree – tacitly! – that it is time to come to an end (note that we rarely ever explicitly discuss these matters, except for formal occasions such as business meetings). What we usually find when a conversation comes to a close are so-called pre-closing sequences such as "ah, well, it was nice to see you again", "Well, I think I must be going", "Yeah, well, I just wanted to call and tell you about Myrtle", "Sorry to keep you away from work for so long..." which signal to the interlocutors that the speaker wants to come to an end and if there is anything left to be discussed this is the time to bring it up. Conversations then finally close with parting expressions such as "bye" or "see you, then".

The applications of our findings from discourse and conversation analysis are obvious and ubiquitous. They can help to enhance classroom discourse and doctor-patient interaction, they have been used by law enforcement agencies to improve interrogation techniques, and they are in use in psychology, psychotherapy, and business communication, to name but a few areas where discourse analysis is important.

However, as discourse and conversation analysis establish a new framework with new terminology and new concepts, there is not enough room here to discuss these in greater detail.

Recommendable introductions to the topic are Schiffrin (1993), Johnstone (2007) and Renkema (2004). Very helpful recent overviews are Schiffrin, Tannen, Hamilton (2007) and Renkema (2007).

7.1.6 Forensic Linguistics

Forensic linguistics investigates issues relating to language in the domain of law, i.e. in trials, criminal investigations, and judicial and legal procedures of all kinds. The most prominent application is perhaps the use of linguistics in the identification of telephone callers and letter writers. Linguists have developed numerous very sophisticated techniques that help us to identify the voice of speakers on the phone, or the authors of (anonymous) letters. One famous example includes the trial of O.J. Simpson in 1995, when the relationship of voice quality and race was a matter of serious debate. The FBI keeps an "anonymous letter database" at Quantico, in which it stores kidnapping and extortion notes, bank robbery demand notes and similar documents as a linguistic corpus that can help to identify the authors of documents like these. Needless to say, the identification of speakers and authors rests on an enormous amount of factors, ranging from detailed phonetic analysis, graphematics, through syntactic style analyses to pragmatics, sociolinguistics, and lexical choices. Detailed competence in linguistic structure is thus of greatest importance here.

But linguists are also called as expert witnesses to testify in other legal claims. For example, they can analyze whether a verbal insult should actually count as one, i.e. whether the illocutionary force could have been clear to the hearer. In other cases, they have to establish whether utterances and texts were clear and understandable. There have been a number of lawsuits in the United States in which arrestees have claimed they did not understand the Miranda warning ("You have the right to remain silent...") that was read to them. If they did not understand, and have not been able to understand, whatever they said cannot be used against them. If you do not understand the instructions of doctors or pharmacists (in speaking or in writing) this may be reason for a lawsuit if you overdose your medication, for example. The same applies to manuals of any kind. You may have a right to return that fancy lawnmower if you can't figure out how to assemble it because the manual is strongly deficient.

Equally important, using the tools of discourse analysis, linguists sometimes also have to evaluate the structure of interrogations by the police or in court. Needless to say, it is not allowed to threaten or intimidate suspects either physically or verbally. But what constitutes verbal intimidation, what doesn't? How do law enforcement agents know they are being understood by the people they talk to? Relating to the sociology of language discussed before we may also have to ask in how far a state is required to provide legal documents and assistance in several languages.

Another area which is of growing importance is plagiarism of various kinds. When are two documents or verbal products sufficiently similar so that they can be treated as copies? This is essentially a linguistic question. A related issue concerns trademark disputes. Did Quality Inns International, Inc. infringe on the McDonald's Corporation's trademark when they started calling their chain of basic hotels *McSleep* (cf. Shuy 2002: 95-109)? Or could the prefix *Mc-* be said to be a morpheme that means something like 'basic, convenient, inexpensive, standardized products and services' as in *McPaper, McClean,* or *McPrisons* – none of which had anything to do with fast food? Those are issues for which linguists are often asked to provide their expert opinion.

Finally, linguists are also deeply involved in contract law and law making, of course. Since both laws and contracts are essentially linguistic products, linguists are called in to evaluate whether laws and contracts contain any 'weak spots' or ambiguities, and whether a certain interpretation can be linguistically justified.

There are several introductions to forensic linguistics available. These include Coulthard & Johnson (2011), Olsson (2010), Gibbons (2003) and Shuy (2008).

7.2 Summary

The present chapter was not intended as an introduction to language in use. It was meant as a quick, rough, dirty roller-coaster ride through something which could broadly be entitled "What can you do with linguistics?". The aim was to show that what you have learned about linguistic structures, from phonology to semantics and pragmatics, does not only exist in isolation and as self-sufficient theory. Linguistic theory has a number of important practical applications, many of which are not well-known in the general public, but nevertheless central to our daily lives. This is not to say that language in use and applied linguistics should be the ultimate goal of all linguistics. Just like in physics we can have pure, basic research (phonology as string theory – how cool is that!), and applied aspects. Both can and should happily co-exist, possibly even feed into each other. We did not have enough room to go through all different aspects of applied linguistics. There was no mention of psycholinguistics, contact linguistics, language and business, anthropological linguistics, and so many more. But from what you have read so far, I am sure you have grown into an independent and critical linguistic thinker by now, so that you can discover the rest of the world of linguistics on your own. Have fun!

8. Solutions

8.1 Introduction

1. All languages have consonants and vowels, nouns and verbs, means of expressing negatives and interrogatives.

2. 1. Scientific study of human language
   2. Language structure, language use and language in context

3. b and c

4. Icon: picture-like representation
   Index: causal relationship to what it stands for, but does not resemble the entity it stands for
   Symbol: does not resemble what it stands for.

5. The signified/the signifier, coined by Ferdinand de Saussure, founding father of 20th-century linguistics.

6. Go to the webpage <http://corpus.byu.edu>. Make use of the British National Corpus (BNC) and the Corpus of Contemporary American English (COCA) and compare the results.
   - *Petrol*: 2287 (BNC) vs. 294 (COCA)
   - *Gas*: 7259 (BNC) vs. 38566 (COCA)

7. e.g. COCA: *Stealer* 68 vs. *thief* 2847

8.2 Phonetics and phonology

1. Phonemes are abstract units representing the smallest meaning distinguishing units in a given language. Phonemes are put in slanted brackets, e.g. /t/. The concrete realization of a phoneme is a phone. When there are different possible realizations of one phoneme (depending, e.g., on the phonological environment) these are called allophones. Phones and allophones are put in square brackets, e.g. [t], [d], [ʔ].

2. To show that two sounds are phonemes of a given language you can use the minimal pair test. The words *pat* [pæt] and *bat* [bæt] differ only in one sound. Since there is a difference in meaning if one is exchanged for the other /p/ and /b/ must be phonemes of English.

3. [m]   bilabial, voiced, nasal   [ɔ] mid, back, rounded
   [k]   velar, voiceless, stop   [ə] mid, central, unrounded
   [ʤ]   alveolar, voiced, affricate   [ɪ] high, front, unrounded

4. (see p. 13 (2.3 Phonology))

5. de.rive, young.ster, dream, stum.ble, hug.ging[1], sun, pho.no.lo.gy

   [1]In hugging [hʌgiŋ] the medial consonant can be treated as ambisyllabic since it is hard to ascribe it to one of the syllables alone (neither hugg.ing nor hu.gging seems satisfying). With hug.ging the [g] belongs to the coda of the first and the onset of the second syllable simultaneously.

6. *Elephant* could either be syllabified as e.le.phant following the 'Maximize Onset'-principle by assigning [l] to the onset of the second syllable or as el.e.phant arguing that [l] is the coda of the first syllable, due to the influence to the reduced medial vowel [ə].

7. In the given data the aspirated stops [pʰ], [tʰ], [kʰ] always occur word initially, as in [kʰat], or in the onset of a syllable, as in [ɪm.pʰə.laɪt]. The unaspirated stop sounds occur elsewhere, i.e in the middle or the end of a word or syllable, as in [skɪn] and [ɪn.stənt]. According to this data set the distribution of the unaspirated and aspirated voiceless stops depends on the phonetic context in which /p/, /t/ and /k/ are used. Thus, [p], [t], [k] and [pʰ], [tʰ], [kʰ] are in complementary distribution and are therefore allophones of English.

8.3 Morphology

1. The allomorphs of the English past tense suffix {ed} are [t], [d] and [əd] or [ɪd]. The usage of the different allomorphs depends on the preceding sounds. Verbs ending in the alveolar stops [t] or [d] take [əd] or [id] as the past tense suffix, such as *haunted* [hɔ:ntəd]. If a verb ends in a voiceless sound (other than [t]) the allomorph [t] is used, as in *kissed* [kɪst]. Verbs ending in voiced sounds (other than [d]) take the suffix [d], as in *planned* [plænd]. Further

allomorphs of the English past tense are the ø-affix, as in *cut*, and the various irregular past forms.

2.

Noun	Plural	Plural Morpheme
apple	apples	suffix [s]
sheep	sheep	Ø-affixation
tooth	teeth	vowel change [u] > [iː]
child	children	suffix [rən]
louse	lice	vowel change [aʊ] > [aɪ]
peach	peaches	suffix [ɪs]
man	men	vowel change [æ] > [e]

3. {im}{possible}, {de}{generate}, {cat}{s}, {character}{ize}{s}, {play}{ed}, {il}{legal}{ize}, {mis}{treat}{ment}

4. free lexical morphemes: few, thing, are, hard, put, annoyance, good
                              example, Pudd'nhead Wilson, Calendar
   free grammatical morphemes: to, up, with, than, the, of, a
   bound lexical morphemes: /
   bound grammatical morphemes: -s, -er, -'s

5. Inflectional morphemes: girl-**s**; sing-**ing**; boy-**s**; watch-**ed**; envious-**ly**
   Derivational morphemes: **un**-happy (some scholars would include envious-**ly** here – see 3.4.2)

6. Clipping: exam (examination), flu (influenza), phone (telephone)
   Blending: edutainment (education+entertainment),
               brunch (breakfast+lunch),
               smog (smoke+fog)
   Conversion: to butter, to google, to bottle
   Acronyms: NASA, laser, Aids

7. In oxen {en} is the plural suffix attached to *ox*, it is an inflectional suffix. In wooden the {en} is attached to the noun *wood* and turns it into the adjective *wooden*, it is therefore a derivational suffix.

8. *Downright* is created by compounding. Go check the OED on www.oed.com
    what word classes *down* and *right* belong to. According to the OED, *down*
    and *right* belong either to the word class of adjectives or adverbs. In *it was a
    down trip* or *it is a down word* (in a crossword puzzle) *down* is certainly
    used as an adjective. In combination with verbs, as in *to look down* or *to
    break down,* or when indicating the direction/location, as in *down in the
    valley, down* is an adverb. With the predicative use of *down,* however, the
    word class is debatable. The OED argues that *down* in *the computer's down
    again* is an adverb. This is not the only possible interpretation, comparing
    that phrase to *the computer is expensive* one could argue that down is a
    predicative adjective just like *expensive, big* etc. The example of *he is down,*
    in which *down* can be substituted by *depressed,* supports this argument
    because *depressed* is used as an adjective. Equally, *right* is classified as an
    adjective in e.g. *the right way* or *a right man.* In *run right home* or *stand
    right up, right* is clearly an adverb. Again, with respect to predicative uses
    one could ask why the OED sees *right* as an adjective in *be morally right* if
    it counts *down* in the example above as an adverb. *Right* is also listed as an
    interjection as in *yeah, right* but it is most likely that interjectional *right* is
    none of the word classes involved in the formation of *downright.* With the
    other word classes the answer is not that easy. Perhaps the word classes
    taken for the formation of *downright* depend on the meaning of the
    compound. The OED states three possibilities: *downright* as an adverb, as an
    adjective and as a noun. In *to sink downright* (indicating the direction) or *I
    was downright scared,* meaning *I was totally scared,* the adverb *downright* is
    most likely the result of combining the adverb *down* with the adverb *right.*
    In *he had a certain downright honesty* the adjective *downright* results from
    the combination of adjectival *down* and *right. Downright* as a noun involves
    two word formation processes, first compounding then conversion.

8.4 Syntax

1. Nouns: months, Oliver, victim, course, treachery, deception
    Verbs: was
    Determiners: the, the, a
    Adjectives: next, eight, ten, systematic
    Conjunctions: or, and
    Prepositions: for, of, of

2. [[The [naughty]$_{AP}$ boy]$_{NP}$ [threw [a ball]$_{NP}$ [through [the window pane]$_{NP}$ $_{PP}$]
    $_{VP}$]

3. The present is in the box behind the sofa.

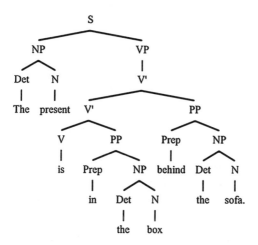

4. In this sentence the NP "a very good cook" is a subject complement.

5. In this sentence the PP "in the kitchen" is an adverbial.

8.5 Meaning in language

1. *fast:* rapid, quick, swift...
   (Note that these are only propositionally synonymous. They are differentiated by style, genre, collocation etc..)

2. large – small; *love –* hate*; dead –* alive*; easy –* hard*; evil –* good*;*
   gradable: *hot –* cold*; dark –* light*; large –* small, short; *short –* tall, large.

3. co-hyponyms of *flower:* tulip, rose, violet, sunflower, lily, forget-me-not....

4. meronyms of *house:* window, roof, door, room, cellar, bell, kitchen....

5. Possible prototype analysis of *chair:*

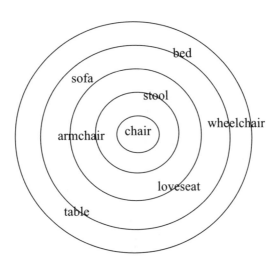

6. Personal deixis: I, they, I, that (you may also include *that,* though it does not
   point to a person, but a thing. On the other hand *that* is usually accompanied
   by a hand gesture, and so it might also belong to manner deixis)
   Spatial deixis: over there
   Temporal deixis: tomorrow, at ten, now

7. a) Maxim of Relevance
   b) Maxim of Quantity

8. The teacher here tries to motivate the students to talk about punctuation by
   using an indirect speech act. James (deliberately) misinterprets the indirect
   speech act as an information question asking *who* wants to talk about,
   answering that no one actually wants to talk about it.

9. a) Declarative
   b) Directive
   c) Expressive
   d) Representative

10. a) I (agent) gave Peter (recipient) a cookie (theme).
    b) Timothy (agent) sliced the bread (patient or theme) with a knife
       (instrument) in the kitchen (location).
    c) Fran (experiencer or patient) was bitten by the dog (agent).

Note that the assignment of thematic roles is largely debateable and depends
to a great deal on the approach that you are following. Some require 'agents'
to be human beings carrying out intentional actions, others don't. So, in *Fran
loves John*, *Fran* could be classified as either 'agent' or 'experiencer'.

11. B1. A2. D3. C4.

8.6 On doing things differently:
a construction grammar approach to language

1. Form-function pairing with a high frequency or a holistic meaning.

2. Form side:
   information about syntactic/morphological/phonological properties

   Function side (or meaning side):
   information about semantics/pragmatic properties and discourse-functional
   aspects of the construction

3. The meaning of the constructions is not derivable from the individual parts
   of the construction. Knowing the individual meanings of the words *kick, the*
   and *bucket* will not give you the meaning of the idiomatic expression *to kick
   the bucket*.

4. A construct.

5. Form: take X's hair down [teɪk ɛksəs hɛə(r) daʊn]
            X = pronoun
   Meaning: to throw off reserve; to become confidential

References

Abney, S. (1987): *The English Noun Phrase in its Sentential Aspect.* Massachusetts: Massachusetts Institute of Technology.

Adams, D. (2005): *The Ultimate Hitchhiker's Guide. Five Complete Novels and One Story.* New York: Gramercy Books.

Alexiadou, A., L. Haegeman & M. Stavrou (2007): *Noun phrase in the generative perspective.* Berlin/New York: Mouton de Gruyter.

Andersen, H. (1973): "Abductive and Deductive Change". *Language* 49(4): 765-793.

Bergen, B.K. & N. Chang (2005): "Embodied Construction Grammar in simulation-based language understanding". In: *Construction Grammar(s): Cognitive and Cross-Language Dimensions*, ed. by J.-O. Östman & M. Fried. Amsterdam/Philadelphia: John Benjamins, 147-190.

Bergs, A. (2005): *Social Networks and Historical Sociolinguistics. Studies in Morphosyntactic Variation in the Paston Letters (1421-1503).* Berlin/New York: Mouton de Gruyter.

Bergs, A. (2009): "The linguistics of text messaging". In: *Language and new media: linguistic, cultural, and technological evolutions*, ed. by C. Rowe & E. L. Wyss. Cresskill, NJ: Hampton Press, 55-75.

Bergs, A., Pfaff, M. & Th. Hoffmann (2012): "I was just reading this article – On the expression of Recentness and the English Past Progressive". In: *The English Verb Phrase: Corpus Methodology and Current Change*, ed. by B. Aarts, J. Close, G. Leech & S. Wallis. Cambridge: Cambridge University Press.

Biber, D. (1995): *Dimensions of Register Variation: a cross-linguistic Comparison.* Cambridge: Cambridge University Press.

Bierwisch, M. (1969): "Strukturelle Semantik". *Deutsch als Fremdsprache* 6(2): 67-74.

Birner, B. & G. Ward (2002): "Information packaging". In: *The Cambridge Grammar of the English Language*, ed. by R. Huddleston & G.K. Pullum. Cambridge: Cambridge University Press, 1363-1447.

BNC: *British National Corpus.* Available at <http://www.natcorp.ox.ac.uk/> and <http://corpus.byu.edu/bnc/>, accessed 18 April, 2012.

Boas, H. & I.A. Sag (2011): *Sign-Based Construction Grammar.* Stanford: CSLI Publications.

Bolinger, D.L. (1977): *Meaning and form.* London: Longman.

Bresnan, J. (2001): *Lexical Functional Syntax.* Oxford: Blackwell.

Brinton, L. & E. Closs Traugott (2005): *Lexicalization and language change.* Cambridge: Cambridge University Press.

Brizendine, L. (2006): *The Female Brain*. New York: Morgan Road Books.

Cavalli-Sforza, L.L. (1997): "Genes, peoples and languages". *PNAS* 94(15): 7719-7724.

Chambers, J. (2003²): *Sociolinguistic Theory*. Oxford: Blackwell.

Chen, M. (1970): "Vowel length variation as function of the voicing of the consonant environment". *Phonetica* 22: 129-159.

Cheshire, J. (1982): *Variation in an English dialect: a sociolinguistic study*. Cambridge: Cambridge University Press.

Chomsky, N. (1959): "A Review of B.F. Skinner's *Verbal Behavior* (New York: Appleton-Century-Crofts, 1957)". *Language* 35(1): 26-58.

Clark, E.V. (2009): *First Language Acquisition*. Cambridge: Cambridge University Press.

Coene, M. & Y. D'Hulst (2003): *From NP to DP. Vol.1: The syntax and semantics of noun phrases*. Amsterdam/Philadelphia: John Benjamins.

Corballis, M.C. (1991): *The Lopsided Ape: Evolution of the Generative Mind*. Oxford: Oxford University Press.

Coulthard, M. & A. Johnson (2010): *The Routledge Handbook of Forensic Linguistics*. London: Taylor & Francis/Routledge.

Croft, W. (2002): *Radical Construction Grammar*. Oxford: Oxford University Press.

Croft, W. (2005): "Logical and typological arguments for Radical Construction Grammar". In: *Construction Grammars*, ed. by J.-O. Östman & M. Fried. Amsterdam/Philadelphia: John Benjamins, 273-314.

Croft, W. & D.A. Cruse (2004): *Cognitive Linguistics*. Cambridge: Cambridge University Press.

Cruttenden, A. (1997): *Intonation*. Cambride: Cambridge University Press.

de Saussure, F. (1995 [1916]): *Cours de linguistique générale*. Paris: Grande Bibliothèque Payot.

Deutscher, G. (2005): *The Unfolding of Language*. New York: Metropolitan Books.

Dickens, C. (1838): *Oliver Twist*. London: Richard Bentley. Available at *Project Gutenberg* <www.gutenberg.org/etext/730>

Diewald, G. (1997): *Grammatikalisierung. Eine Einführung in Sein und Werden grammatischer Formen*. Tübingen: Niemeyer.

Dryer, M. (2005): "Order of Subject, Object and Verb". In: *The World Atlas of Language Structures,* ed. by M. Haspelmath, M. Dryer, D. Gil, B. Comrie. Oxford: Oxford University Press, 354-357.

Dunbar, R. (1998): *Grooming, Gossip, and the Evolution of Language*. Cambridge MA/London: Harvard University Press.

Eckert, P. (2000): *Linguistic Variation as Social Practice*. Oxford: Blackwell.

Ellis, N.C. & P. Robinson (2008): *Handbook of Cognitive Linguistics and Second Language Acquisition*. New York/Abingdon: Routledge.

Ellis, R. (1997): *Second Language Acquisition*. Oxford: Oxford University Press.

Esser, J. (2009): *Introduction to Text-Linguistics*. Frankfurt am Main: Peter Lang.

Fairclough, N. (2001): *Language and Power*. Harlow: Pearson Education Ltd.

Fillmore, C.J. (1968): "The Case for Case". In: *Universals in Linguistic Theory*, eds. E. Bach & R.T. Harms. New York: Holt, Rinehart and Winston, 1-88.

Fillmore, C.J., P. Kay & M.C. O'Connor (1988): "Regularity and idiomaticity in grammatical constructions: the case of *let alone*". *Language* 64: 501-538.

Finch, G., K. Allan, G. Heydon, J. Bradshaw & K. Burridge (2010): *The English Language and Linguistics Companion*. New York: Palgrave Macmillan.

Fischer, O., A. Rosenbach & D. Stein (eds.) (2000): *Pathways of change: Grammaticalization in English*. Amsterdam/Philadelphia: John Benjamins.

FrameNet. *The Berkeley FrameNet Project*. Available at <http://framenet.icsi. berkeley.edu>, accessed 6 June, 2011.

Freidin, R. (2007): *Generative Grammar. Theory and its History*. London: Routledge.

Fried, M. & J.-O. Östman (2004): *Construction Grammar in a Cross-Language perspective*. Amsterdam/Philadelphia: John Benjamins.

Gass, S.M. & L. Selinker (2008): *Second Language Acquisition: An Introductory Course*. New York/Abingdon: Routledge.

Gibbons, J. (2003): *Forensic Linguistics: An Introduction to Language in the Justice System*. Malden: Blackwell.

Givón, T. (1995): *Functionalism and Grammar*. Amsterdam/Philadelphia. John Benjamins.

Goldberg, A. (1995): *Constructions. A Construction Grammar approach to argument structure*. Chicago: University of Chicago Press.

Goldberg, A. (2006): *Constructions at Work. The Nature of Generalizations in Language*. Oxford: Oxford University Press.

Goldberg, A. & J. van der Auwera (in press): "This is to count as a Construction". *Folia Linguistica* 46(1).

Goldberg, A. & R. Jackendoff (2004): "The English Resultative as a Family of Constructions". *Language* 80: 532-568.

Grice, P. (1975): "Logic and conversation". In: *Syntax and Semantics Vol. 3, Speech Acts*, ed. by P. Cole & J.L. Morgan. New York: Academic Press, 41-58.

Gries, St. Th. (2008): *Statistik für Sprachwissenschaftler*. Göttingen: Vandenhoek & Ruprecht.

Gries, St. Th. (2010): *Statistics for Linguistics with R*. Berlin/New York: Mouton de Gruyter.

Gries, St. Th. & A. Stefanowitsch (2003): "Collostructions: Investigating the interaction between words and constructions", *International Journal of Corpus Linguistics* 8(2): 209-243.

Gries, St. Th. & A. Stefanowitsch (2004): "Extending collostructional analysis: a corpus-based perspective on 'alternations'". *International Journal of Corpus Linguistics* 9(1): 97-129.

Gut, U. (2009): *Introduction to English Phonetics and Phonology*. Frankfurt am Main: Peter Lang.

Halliday, M.A.K. & R. Hasan (1977): *Cohesion in English*. London: Longman.

Han, C. & A. Kroch (2000): "The rise of the do support in English: implications for clause structure", *Proceedings of the 30th Meeting of the North East Linguistics Society*, ed. by M. Hirotani, A. Coetzee, N. Hall & J.-Y. Kim. Amherst, MA: GLSA. 311-325.

Haspelmath, M., M.S. Dryer, D. Gil & B. Comrie (2005): *The World Atlas of Language Structures*. Oxford: Oxford University Press. See also <http:///wals.info>, accessed 18 April, 2012.

Hockett, C.F. (1960): "The Origin of Speech", *Scientific American* 203(3): 89-96.

Hoffman, Th. (forthc.) *Construction Grammar: The Structure of English*. Cambridge: Cambridge University Press.

Hoffmann, Th. & G. Trousdale (forthc.): *The Oxford Handbook of Construction Grammar*. Oxford: Oxford University Press.

Hogan, J. & A. Rozsypal (1980): "Evaluation of vowel duration a cue for the voicing distinction in the following word-final consonants". *Journal of the Acoustical Society of America* 67: 1764 - 1771.

Hopper, P. & E. Closs Traugott (2003²): *Grammaticalization*. Cambridge: Cambridge University Press.

Huddleston, R. & G. Pullum (2006): *The Cambridge Grammar of the English Language*. Cambridge: Cambridge University Press.

Hudson, R. (2007): *Language Networks. The new Word Grammar*. Oxford: Oxford University Press.

Hudson, R.A. (1996²): *Sociolinguistics*. Cambridge: Cambridge University Press.

Hudson, R.A. (2007): *Language Networks. The new Word Grammar*. Oxford: Oxford University Press.

Hurford, J.R. & F.J. Newmeyer (2001): *Studies in the evolution of Language*. Oxford: Oxford University Press.

International Phonetic Association (2005). Available at <http://www.langsci.ucl.ac.uk/ipa/index.html>, accessed 6 June 2011.

Johnstone, B. & C. Eisenhardt (2008): *Rhetoric in Detail. Discourse Analyses of Rhetoric Talk and Texts*. Amsterdam/Philadelphia: John Benjamins.

Jones, D. (1917): *An English Pronouncing Dictionary*. London: Dent.

Jucker, A.H. & I. Taavitsainen (eds.) (2010): *Historical Pragmatics*. Berlin/New York: Mouton de Gruyter.

Kay, P. & C.J. Fillmore (1999): "Grammatical constructions and linguistic generalizations: The What's X doing Y? construction". *Language* 75: 1-33.

Kemeny, S., J. Xu, G. Park, L. Hosey & A.R. Braun (2006): "Temporal Dissociation of Early Lexical Access and Articulation Using a Delayed Naming Task – An fMRI Study". *Cereb Cortex* 16(4): 587-595.

Kluender, K.R., R.L. Diehl & B.A. Wright (1988): "Vowel-length differences before voiced and voiceless consonants: An auditory explanation". *Journal of Phonetics* 16(2): 153-169.

Krashen, St. (1993): *The Input Hypothesis: Issues and Implications*. Beverly Hills, CA: Laredo Publishing Company.

Kreyer, R. (2010): *Introduction to English Syntax*. Frankfurt am Main: Peter Lang.

Labov, W. (1972): *Sociolinguistic Patterns*. Philadelphia: University of Pennsylvania Press.

Labov, W. (1973): "The boundaries of words and their meanings". In: *New Ways of Analyzing Variation in English,* ed. by C.-J. Bailey & R.W. Shuy. Washington, DC: Georgetown University Press, 340-373.

Labov, W., S. Ash & C. Boberg (2006): *Atlas of North American English: Phonology and Phonetics*. Berlin/New York: Mouton de Gruyter.

Levinson, S. (1983): *Pragmatics*. Cambridge: Cambridge University Press.

Lightbown, P. & N.M. Spada (2006): *How Languages are Learned*. Oxford: Oxford University Press.

Llyod, S. (1983): *Roget's Thesaurus of English Words and Phrases*. Harlow: Longman.

Lyons, J. (1977): *Semantics*. Cambridge: Cambridge University Press.

Lyons, J. (1995): *Linguistic Semantics. An introduction*. Cambridge: Cambridge University Press.

Mehl, M.R., S. Vazire, N. Ramirez-Esparza, R.B. Slatcher & J.W. Pennebaker (2007): "Are women really more talkative than men?". *Science* 317: 82.

Mey, J.L. (2001[2]): *Pragmatics: an introduction*. Malden, MA: Blackwell.

Michaelis, L. (2005): "Entity and Event Coercion in a Symbolic Theory of Syntax". In: *Construction Grammars*, ed. by J.-O. Östman & M. Fried. Amsterdam: John Benjamins, 45-87.

Miller, J. (2006): "Spoken and written English". In: *The Handbook of English Linguistics*, ed. by B. Aarts & A. MacMahon. Malden: Blackwell, 670-691.

Miller, J. & R. Weinert (1998): *Spontaneous Spoken Language: Syntax and Discourse*. Oxford: Clarendon Press.

Milroy, J. (1992): *Language Variation and Change*. Oxford. Blackwell.

Milroy, L. (1987): *Language and Social Networks*. London: Blackwell.

Milroy, L. & M. Gordon (2003): *Sociolinguistics: Method and Interpretation*. Oxford/Malden, MA: Blackwell.

Moravcsik, E. (2006a): *An Introduction to Syntactic Theory*. London: Continuum.

Moravcsik, E. (2006b): *An Introduction to Syntax: Fundamentals of Syntactic Analysis*. London: Continuum.

Mukherjee, J. (2009): *Anglistische Korpuslinguistik. Eine Einführung*. Berlin: Erich Schmidt.

Müller, S. (2010): *Grammatiktheorie*. Tübingen: Stauffenburg.

Muysken, P. (2005): *Bilingual Speech: A Typology of Code-mixing*. Cambridge: Cambridge University Press.

Olsson, J. (2010): *Wordcrime: Solving Crime through Forensic Linguistics*. London/New York: Continuum.

Pollard, C. & I.A. Sag (1994): *Head-Driven Phrase Structure Grammar*. Chicago: University of Chicago Press and Stanford: CSLI Publications.

Preston, D.R. (1989): *Perceptual Dialectology*. Dordrecht: Foris.

Pullum, G. (2008) "Noun noun noun noun noun verb". *Language Log*.

Quirk, R., S. Greenbaum, G. Leech & J. Svartvik (1985): *A Comprehensive Grammar of the English Language*. London: Longman.

Radford, A. (2004): *Minimalist Syntax: Exploring the Structure of English*. Cambridge: Cambridge University Press.

Raumolin Brunberg, H. & T. Nevalainen (2003): *Historical Sociolinguistics: Language Change in Tudor and Stuart England*. London: Longman.

Rayson, P., G. Leech & M. Hodges (1997): "Social differentiation in the use of English vocabulary: some analyses of the conversational component of the British National Corpus", *International Journal of Corpus Linguistics* 2(1): 133-152.

Renkema, J. (2004): *Introduction to Discourse Studies*. Amsterdam/Philadelphia: John Benjamins.

Renkema, J. (ed.) (2009): *Discourse, of course: An Overview of Research in Discourse Studies*. Amsterdam/Philadelphia. John Benjamins.

Rietveld, T. & R. Vanhout (2005): *Statistics in Language Research: Analysis of Variance*. Berlin/New York: Mouton de Gruyter.

Romaine, S. (1982): *Socio-historical Linguistics: its Status and Methodology*. Cambridge: Cambridge University Press.

Sag, I.A. (in press): "Sign-Based Construction Grammar: An Informal Synopsis". In: *Sign-Based Construction Grammar*, ed. by H. Boas & I.A. Sag. Stanford: CSLI Publications. Available at <http://lingo.stanford.edu/sag/papers/theo-syno.pdf>, accessed 18 April, 2012.

Saxton, M. (2010): *Child Language: Acquisition and Development*. London: Sage Publications.

Schiffrin, D. (1993): *Approaches to Discourse*. Malden, Mass: Blackwell.

Schiffrin, D., D. Tannen & H.E. Hamilton (2007): *The Handbook of Discourse Analysis*. Malden, Mass: Blackwell.

Searle, J.R. (1969): *Speech Acts, An Essay in the Philosophy of Language*. Cambridge: Cambridge University Press.

Selinker, L. (1972): "Interlanguage". In: *International Review of Applied Linguistics* 10, 209-231.

Sells, P. (1985): Lectures on Contemporary Syntactic Theories. Stanford, CA: CSLI Publishers.

Shank, R. & R. Abelson (1977): *Scripts, Plans, Goals and Understanding*. Hillsdale, NJ: Erlbaum.

Shuy, R. (2002): *Linguistic Battles in Trademark Disputes*. Basingstoke: Palgrave Macmillan.

Stein, D. (1992): *The semantics of syntactic change: aspects of the evolution of to in English*. Berlin/New York: Mouton de Gruyter.

The Oxford English Dictionary (2010). Oxford: Oxford University Press. Available at <http://www.oed.com/>, accessed 18 April, 2012.

Tomasello, M. (2005): *Constructing a Language: A Usage-based Theory of Language Acquisition*. London/Cambridge, MA: Harvard University Press.

Traugott, E. Closs & G. Trousdale (eds.) (2010): *Gradience, Gradualness and Grammaticalization*. Amsterdam/Philadelphia: John Benjamins.

Trudgill, P. (1983): *On Dialect: Social and Geographical Perspectives*. Oxford: Blackwell.

Trudgill, P. & J.K. Chambers (1998): *Dialectology*. Cambridge: Cambridge University Press.

Twain, M. (1894): *Pudd'nhead Wilson*. London: Chatto & Windus. Full text available at <http://www.cs.cofc.edu/~manaris/books/Mark-Twain-The-Tragedy-of-Puddnhead-Wilson.txt>, accessed 18 April, 2012.

Vendler, Z. (1967): *Linguistics in Philosophy*. Ithaca, NY: Cornell University Press.

Waite, M. (2004): *Oxford Thesaurus of English*. Oxford: Oxford University Press.

Watts, R.J. (2011): *Language Myths and the History of English*. Oxford/New York: Oxford University Press.

Whorf, B.L. (1956): *Language, Thought & Reality*. Cambridge, MA: MIT Press.

Wittgenstein, L. (1978 [1953]): *Philosophical Investigations*. Oxford: Blackwell.

Wright, L. (1996): "About the Evolution of Standard English". In: *Studies in English Language and Literature: 'Doubt Wisely' Papers in honour of E.G. Stanley*, ed. by E.M. Tyler & M.J. Toswell. London: Routledge, 99-115.

Wulff, S. (2006): "Go-V vs. go-and-V in English: A case of constructional synonymy?". In: *Corpora in Cognitive Linguistics*, ed. by St. Th. Gries & A. Stefanowitsch. Berlin/New York: Mouton de Gruyter, 101-125.

Yule, G. (1996): *Pragmatics*. Oxford: Oxford University Press.
Yule, G. (2010^4): *The Study of Language*. Cambridge: Cambridge University Press.

Index

Textbooks in English Language and Linguistics (TELL)

Edited by Magnus Huber and Joybrato Mukherjee

www.peterlang.de